Psychological Skill Training
(PGPS - 99)

Pergamon Titles of Related Interest

Cartledge/Milburn TEACHING SOCIAL SKILLS TO CHILDREN: Innovative
Approaches
Goldstein/Sorcher CHANGING SUPERVISOR BEHAVIOR
Goldstein/Sprafkin/Gershaw SKILL TRAINING FOR COMMUNITY LIVING:
Applying Structured Learning Therapy
Goldstein/Carr/Davidson/Wehr IN RESPONSE TO AGGRESSION: Methods
of Control and Prosocial Alternatives
Goldstein/Monti/Sardino/Green POLICE CRISIS INTERVENTION
Kanfer/Goldstein HELPING PEOPLE CHANGE: A Textbook of Methods,
Second Edition
Rathjen/Foreyt SOCIAL COMPETENCE: Interventions for Children and
Adults

Related Journals*

APPLIED RESEARCH IN MENTAL RETARDATION
CHILDREN & YOUTH SERVICES REVIEW
EVALUATION & PROGRAM PLANNING
JOURNAL OF PSYCHIATRIC TREATMENT & EVALUATION
SUBSTANCE AND ALCOHOL ACTIONS & MISUSE

*Free specimen copies available upon request.

Arnold P. Goldstein

Syracuse University

Psychological Skill Training

The Structured Learning Technique

PERGAMON PRESS

New York   Oxford   Toronto   Sydney   Paris   Frankfurt

Pergamon Press Offices:

U.S.A.	Pergamon Press Inc., Maxwell House, Fairview Park, Elmsford, New York 10523, U.S.A.
U.K.	Pergamon Press Ltd., Headington Hill Hall, Oxford OX3 0BW, England
CANADA	Pergamon Press Canada Ltd., Suite 104, 150 Consumers Road, Willowdale, Ontario M2J 1P9, Canada
AUSTRALIA	Pergamon Press (Aust.) Pty. Ltd., P.O. Box 544, Potts Point, NSW 2011, Australia
FRANCE	Pergamon Press SARL, 24 rue des Ecoles, 75240 Paris, Cedex 05, France
FEDERAL REPUBLIC OF GERMANY	Pergamon Press GmbH, Hammerweg 6, Postfach 1305, 6242 Kronberg/Taunus, Federal Republic of Germany

Copyright © 1981 Pergamon Press Inc.

Library of Congress Cataloging in Publication Data

Goldstein, Arnold P.
    Psychological skill training.

    (Pergamon general psychology series ; 99)
    Includes index.
    1. Mentally ill--Rehabilitation. 2. Life skills--
Study and teaching. I. Title. II. Series. [DNLM:
1. Behavior therapy--Education. 2. Behavior
therapy--Methods. LM 425 G624p]
RC439.5.G64   1981   362.2'0425   81-5861
ISBN 0-08-026321-6   AACR2

Printed in the United States of America

TO LENORE
FOR FILLING MY LIFE WITH LOVE, JOY, AND MEANING

Contents

Preface

In the early 1970s, several trends coalesced to give birth to the psychological skills training movement. Research on modeling, role playing, and social reinforcement—three of the major components of Structured Learning—was appearing with considerable frequency in the psychological literature. The inadequacy of prompting, shaping, and related operant procedures for adding *new* behaviors to individuals' behavioral repertoires was increasingly apparent. The widespread reliance upon deinstitutionalization which lay at the heart of the community mental health movement resulted in the discharge from America's public mental hospitals of approximately 400,000 persons, the majority of whom were substantially deficient in important daily functioning skills. And it had grown particularly clear, especially to this investigator, that what the American mental health movement had available to offer lower social class clients was grossly inadequate in meeting their psychotherapeutic needs. These factors—relevant supportive research, the incompleteness of operant approaches, large populations of grossly skill-deficient individuals, and the paucity of useful interventions for a large segment of American society—came together in the thinking of the present writer and others as demanding a new intervention, something prescriptively responsive to these several needs. Psychological skill training was the answer, and a movement was launched.

Our involvement in this movement, a psychological skills training approach we have called Structured Learning, began in 1970. At that time, and for several years thereafter, our studies were conducted in public mental hospitals with long-term, highly skill-deficient, chronic patients. It was while conducting research with these trainees that three investigative themes emerged, themes we have continued to pursue as our research shifted over the years to other settings and to other types of trainee populations. These central study concerns may be expressed by indicating that the overall goal of Structured Learning is to effectively lead trainees to high levels of (1) skill acquisition, and (2) skill transfer, and to do so (3) in a prescriptive manner. Investigative concern with acquisition, transfer, and prescriptiveness will be visited and revisited in a number of the investigations reported in the following chapters.

Structured Learning research with adult residents of mental hospitals, aggressive and other adolescents, children, change agents of diverse types, parents, teachers, industrial managers, police, and other populations will be examined. As these several studies were conceptualized, conducted, reported, and disseminated over the past decade, a number of creative and productive people joined our efforts. Early in this research program, and of special import for its eventual conduct and outcome, I was joined by two Veterans Administration psychologists who had become independently involved in applied psychological skills training, N. Jane Gershaw and Robert P. Sprafkin. The three of us have, over this ten-year span, conducted hundreds of Structured Learning trainee sessions, trainer preparation workshops, and, of special relevance to the present book, meetings about the nature of skills training in general and Structured Learning in particular—how to operationalize it and how to optimize it. Structured Learning as an entity is every bit as much theirs as it is mine. Their energetic and insightful collaboration in these several ways is very much appreciated.

A number of other persons have contributed in important ways to this research program, bringing their special perspectives and special expertise. In particular, I gratefully wish to acknowledge the substantial aid of Arnold Goedhardt of the Free University, Amsterdam, Holland; Martin Gutride, Nevada Department of Mental Hygiene; William Hoyer of Syracuse University; Martita Lopez of Rush-Presbyterian Hospital, Chicago; Paul Klein, Syracuse Public School system; Phillip Monti of the Syracuse Police Department; and especially, the large number of graduate students who enthusiastically and innovatively became part of our investigative team. We have indicated who they are throughout the text, as individual studies are considered.

We have been fortunate during the life of this research program to have had the sustained and substantial support of Syracuse University—collegially, environmentally, and, through a series of institutional grants, also financially. Financial support for this research program was also forthcoming from the National Institute of Mental Health (PHS Grants MH16426 and MH13669), and the State of New York (Health Research Council No. 1733). Their aid is gratefully acknowledged.

Chapter 1
Introduction

Until the early 1970s, there existed three major psychological approaches designed to alter the behavior of unhappy, ineffective, or disturbed individuals—psychodynamic/psychoanalytic, humanistic/nondirective, and behavior modification. Though each differs from the others in several major respects, one of their significant commonalities was the shared assumption that the patient had somewhere within himself, as yet unexpressed, the effective, satisfying, or healthy behaviors whose expression was among the goals of the therapy. Such latent potentials, in all three approaches, would be realized by the patient if the therapist were sufficiently skilled in reducing or removing obstacles to such realization. The psychoanalyst sought to do so by calling forth and interpreting unconscious material-blocking, progress-relevant awareness. The nondirectivist, who believes that the potential for change resides within the patient, sought to free this potential by providing a warm, empathic, maximally accepting therapeutic environment. And the behavior modifier, by means of one or more contingency management procedures, attempted to see to it that when the latent desirable behaviors or approximations thereto did occur, the patient received contingent reinforcement, thus increasing the probability that these behaviors would recur. Therefore, whether sought by means of therapeutic interpretation and working through, provision of a benevolent therapeutic climate, or by dint of offering contingent reward, all three approaches assumed that somewhere within the individual's repertoire resided the desired, effective, sought-after goal behaviors.

In the early 1970s, an important new intervention approach began to emerge—psychological skills training, an approach resting upon rather different assumptions. Viewing the helpee more in educational, pedagogic terms rather than as a patient in need of therapy, the psychological skills trainer assumed he was dealing with an individual lacking, deficient, or at best weak in the skills necessary for effective and satisfying daily living. The task of the skills trainer became, therefore, not interpretation, reflection, or reinforcement but the active and deliberate *teaching* of desirable behaviors. Rather than an intervention called psychotherapy, between a patient and psychotherapist, what emerged was training, between a trainee and a psychological skills trainer.

The roots of the psychological skills training movement lay within both education and psychology. The notion of literally seeking to teach desirable behaviors has often, if sporadically, been a significant goal of the American

1

educational establishment. The Character Education Movement of the 1920s, and more contemporary Moral Education and Values Clarification programs are but a few of several possible examples. Add to this institutionalized educational interest in skills training, the hundreds of interpersonal and planning skills courses taught in America's over 2,000 community colleges, and the hundreds of self-help books oriented toward similar skill-enhancement goals which are available to the American public, and it becomes clear that the formal and informal educational establishment in America provided fertile soil and explicit stimulation within which the psychological skills training movement could grow.

Much the same can be said for American psychology, as it too laid the groundwork in its prevailing philosophy and concrete interests for the development of this new movement. The learning process has above all else been the central theoretical and investigative concern of American psychology since the late nineteenth century. This focal interest also assumed major therapeutic form in the 1950s, as psychotherapy practitioners and researchers alike came to view psychotherapeutic treatment more and more in learning terms. The very healthy and still expanding field of behavior modification grew from this joint learning-clinical focus, and may be appropriately viewed as the immediately preceding context in which psychological skills training came to be developed. In companion with the growth of behavior modification, psychological thinking increasingly shifted from a strict emphasis on remediation to one that was equally concerned with prevention, and the bases for this shift included movement away from a medical model conceptualization toward what may most aptly be called a psychoeducational theoretical stance. Both of these thrusts—heightened concern with prevention and a psychoeducational perspective—gave strong added impetus to the viability of the psychological skills training movement.

Psychology's final and perhaps most direct contribution to psychological skills training came from social learning theory, and in particular from the work conducted by and stimulated by Albert Bandura. Based upon the same broad array of modeling, behavioral rehearsal, and social reinforcement investigations which helped stimulate and direct the development of the Structured Learning skill training approach, Bandura (1973) comments:

> The method that has yielded the most impressive results with diverse problems contains three major components. First, alternative modes of response are repeatedly modeled, preferably by several people who demonstrate how the new style of behavior can be used in dealing with a variety of . . . situations. Second, learners are provided with necessary guidance and ample opportunities to practice the modeled behavior under favorable conditions until they perform it skillfully and spontaneously. The latter procedures are ideally suited for developing new social skills, but they are unlikely to be adopted unless they

produce rewarding consequences. Arrangement of success experiences particularly for initial efforts at behaving differently, constitute the third component in this powerful composite method. . . . Given adequate demonstration, guided practice, and success experiences, this method is almost certain to produce favorable results. [P. 253.]

A FUNCTIONAL DEFINITION

It is hoped that the foregoing brief overview of the historical roots of psychological skills training provides a contextual perspective on both its development and intended thrust. To offer a more concrete statement of its content and operations, we now wish to define psychological skills training formally. *Psychological skills training is the planned, systematic teaching of the specific behaviors needed and consciously desired by the individual in order to function in an effective and satisfying manner, over an extended period of time, in a broad array of positive, negative, and neutral interpersonal contexts. The specific teaching methods which constitute social skills training directly and jointly reflect psychology's modern social learning theory and education's contemporary pedagogic principles and procedures.*

In this definition, we have described psychological skills training as *planned and systematic* in order to emphasize the organized, premeditated, and stepwise quality of such training, in contrast to the much more typically haphazard, unplanned, and unsystematic way in which most individuals are "taught" social skills, that is, by naturalistic reliance upon parents, friends, church, school, and other people, institutions, and events which may or may not cross one's path and which may or may not exert positive skill development influence on the individual.

Psychological skills training seeks to teach *specific behaviors*, and not—at least not directly—values, attitudes, or insight. It is a behavioral approach, designed to enhance the overt actions of the trainee, in contrast to those psychotherapeutic and educational interventions which seek to alter the individual's beliefs about himself, or his self-understanding, in the (typically vain) hope that behavior change will somehow follow.

In our definition, it is important that the behavior changes toward which the training is oriented be *needed and consciously desired* by the trainee. Overt behavior change in the form of higher levels of skill competence, especially on an enduring basis, will not result, however good the psychological skills training, if the trainee's motivational level is not adequate. The training may be recommended by a spouse, boss, friend, doctor, or other interested party in the trainee's life, but a definition of successful training must include a perceived skill deficiency, a felt need, a desire for improvement on the part of the trainee. If training is to succeed, there must be adequate levels of what we term trainee "competency motivation."

The goals of psychological skills training, optimally, are *both effectiveness and satisfaction.* Effectiveness, we feel, pertains to the impact on others deriving from one's newly enhanced skill level. Effectiveness pertains to the question, "Does it work?," "Did I succeed?," "Was I competent?" Satisfaction, in our view, is where behavior and feelings meet. Satisfaction is the inner consequence of overtly effective skill behavior. We have included both effectiveness and satisfaction in this definition of social skills training because we are aware of skill training programs in industrial, law enforcement, and other settings in which trainee "productivity," or on-the-job skill competence, is the *sole* training program goal. We are also aware of therapies and educational commitments initiated at the urging, and for the satisfaction of a spouse, parent, boss, teacher, or other figure, and not for the satisfaction of the patient, student, or trainee himself. We strongly feel this to be insufficient and short-sighted, and we urge that the pleasure, gratification, or personal satisfaction of the trainee be accepted as a regular, companion goal of equal importance to effectiveness in all such programs.

In order for a psychological skills training program to be satisfactory, in our view, it must energetically aspire to lead to trainee effectiveness and satisfaction *over an extended period of time and in a variety of positive, negative, and neutral contexts.* This part of our definition speaks to the issue of maintenance and transfer. Far too many psychotherapeutic and educational interventions succeed in changing trainee behaviors in the training setting, but fail to yield sustained change where it counts—in the real-world contexts in which the trainee works, plays, and exists. Thus, a satisfactory psychological skills training program will actively seek to incorporate specific procedures which help the trainee perform the skills he acquired in the training context when he is in both a variety of other contexts (i.e., setting generalization) and over a sustained period of time (i.e., response maintenance).

The skill training targets which constitute the actual content of a psychological skills training program are optimally both diverse and numerous, and should include both *interpersonal and personal skills.* Interpersonal skills are the competencies that individuals must bring to bear in their interactions with other individuals or groups of individuals. Communication skills, leadership skills, relationship skills, and conflict management skills are but a few examples. Personal skills are emotional, cognitive, observational, or skills that relate to practical aspects of daily living in work, school, or home environments. They include self-control, decision making, goal setting, preparing for stressful conversations, and setting problem priorities.

Finally, a comprehensive definition of psychological skills training must address not only matters of skill content, as we have done above, but also teaching procedure. Psychological skills training should consist of *procedures derived from psychology's social learning theory* (e.g., modeling, behavioral rehearsal, performance feedback) *and education's contemporary peda-gogic principles and procedures* (e.g., instructional texts, simulation and gaming, structured discussion).

These, then, are the definitional characteristics of psychological skills training. As best as we can discern, approximately 30 programs reflecting most or all of these characteristics currently exist. Table 1.1 provides an overview of these programs.

While all of the programs represented in Table 1.1 meet most or all of the criteria we have included in our formal definition of psychological skills training, nevertheless, considerable diversity is also represented. Some programs are broadly comprehensive in the interpersonal and personal skill competencies they seek to enhance. Others have a more narrow focus, on anxiety or assertiveness, for example. Yet others are especially concerned with particular interpersonal domains (dating, marriage, parent-adolescent conflict) or particular settings (school, work). Across programs, the range of potential trainees is especially broad, varying from early elementary school children through all stages of adolescence and adulthood and into old age. The trainees represented are also quite diverse in their pretraining levels of overall skill competence, varying from significantly unskilled retarded individuals and chronic, long-term psychiatric patients to essentially "average" individuals whose general skill competence level is adequate, but who are seeking to enhance a few "weak spots."

Consistent with what has occurred with psychotherapists in psychotherapy and, to a lesser extent, with teachers in education, the range of persons successfully utilized as trainers in these psychological skills training programs is not only broad and quite diverse, but also includes a substantial number of different types of paraprofessionals. That is, in addition to credentialed teachers or psychologists, we find that teacher aides, mental hospital attendants, college undergraduates, group home parents, and others can and do serve successfully in these programs as, to use Carkhuff's (1974) apt term, "functional professionals."

Somewhat in contrast to the apparent diversity across programs in skills, trainers, and trainees, the training methods involved seem to consist largely of one of two possible procedural combinations. The first, a series of procedures derived from social learning theory principles and research, typically consists of instruction, modeling, role playing, and feedback. The skills training approach which is the focus of this book is of this type, and thus the nature and utilization of these procedures will be elaborated in depth later. The second subgroup of programs—those growing more from strictly educational contexts—usually rely upon a combination of instructional texts, gaming and simulation exercises, structured discussion, and related didactic procedures. Perhaps most striking about both the social-learning-based and education-based procedural combinations is the degree to which they initial-

Table 1.1 Psychological Skills Training Programs.

Developer	Program	Trainers	Trainees	Training Methods	Skills
Adkins (1970, 1974)	Life Skills Education	Professional and paraprofessional	Disadvantaged adolescents and adults	Instruction, audio-visual demonstration, discussion	• Developing oneself and relating to others • Managing home and family responsibilities • Managing leisure time • Exercising community rights
Argyle et al. (1974); Trower et al. (1978)	Social skill training	Hospital and clinic	Psychiatric patients	Modeling, role playing, feedback	• Introductory skills • Observation skills • Listening skills • Speaking skills • Meshing skills • Expression of Attitudes • Social Routines • Tactics and Strategies
Bash & Camp (1980)	Think Aloud	Teachers	Elementary school children	Modeling, self-instruction, scripts, games, role playing	• Problem solving • Interpersonal skills • Self-control • Emotional awareness
Burka, Hubbel, Preble, Spinelli, & Winter (1972)	Communication Skills Workshop	Professional counselors	University undergraduates	Sensitivity group procedures, exercises, relaxation training, role playing, feedback	• Self-disclosure skills • Feedback skills • Intimacy skills • Other interpersonal skills
Carkhuff & Berenson (1967)	Facilitative interpersonal functioning	Professional and paraprofessional	Psychiatric patients, university undergraduates, disturbed children, parents	Didactic-experiential	• Empathy • Positive regard • Genuineness • Concreteness • Immediacy • Confrontation

Table 1.1 (Continued).

Developer	Program	Trainers	Trainees	Training Methods	Skills
Cox & Gunn (1980)	Interpersonal skills in the schools	Teachers	Elementary school children	Modeling, didactic instruction, performance feedback	• Interpersonal conflict-reduction skills
Curran (1977)	Dating and social skills	Professional, graduate student	University students	Instruction, modeling role play, coaching, video and group feedback, *in vivo* assignments	• Giving and receiving compliments • Nonverbal communication • Assertiveness • Feeling talk • Handling silence • Planning dates • Requesting dates • Handling intimacy problems
Egan (1976)	Interpersonal	Diverse (including trainees)	Unspecified (presumably non-"patient"); in-group format	T-group procedures, contracting, exercises, Modeling	• Self-presentation skills • Listening/responding skills • Challenging skills • Group participation skills
Elardo & Cooper (1977)	AWARE: Activities for social development	Teachers	Elementary school children	Structured discussion, exercises, games, role playing	• Getting acquainted skills • Recognizing feelings skills • Understanding individuals • Social living skills
Galassi & Galassi (1977)	Assertion training	Educators, human development specialists, mental health professionals	Unassertive individuals	Programmed text, relaxation, role playing, feedback	• Expressing positive feelings skills • Expressing negative feelings skills • Self-assertion skills
Goldstein, Sprafkin, & Gershaw (1973, 1976)	Structured Learning	Hospital and clinic staff, teachers	Hospital patients, adolescents	Modeling, role playing, feedback, transfer training	• Conversational skills • Expressive skills • Responsive skills • Dealing with feelings skills • Dealing with stress skills • Alternative to aggression skills • Planning skills

Table 1.1 (Continued).

Developer	Program	Trainers	Trainees	Training Methods	Skills
Gottman et al. (1977)	Couples communication	None	Couples	Instructional text, exercises, *in vivo* practice	• Listening and validation • Leveling • Editing • Negotiating agreements • Dealing with hidden agendas
Guerney (1977)	Relationship enhancement	Various professional and para-professionals	Couples, families	Instructions, modeling, role playing, social reinforcement	• Expressive skills • Empathic skills • Mode switching skills • Facilitator skills
Hanson (1971, 1972)	Basic Social Communication Skills	Hospital staff	Chronic psychiatric patients	Instruction, modeling, role playing, feedback	• Eye contact • Facial expression • Affective quality of speech • Introducing oneself • Listening • Asking questions • Responding to embarrassing questions • Speaking in front of a group
Hare (1976)	Teaching Conflict Resolutions	Teachers	High school students	Exercises, simulation, role play	• Developing awareness of conflict-management styles • Building trust • Alternatives to conflict
Hawley & Hawley (1975)	Developing Human Potential	Teachers	Elementary school children	Exercises, simulation, structured discussion	• Self-awareness skills • Communication skills • Relationship skills • Creativity skills
Heiman (1973)	Interpersonal Communication	Teachers	High school students	Lecture, exercises, role play	• Trust building • Sharing of self • Communication • Listening

Table 1.1 (Continued).

Developer	Program	Trainers	Trainees	Training Methods	Skills
Hersen & Eisler (1976)	Social Skill Training	Professional, graduate student	Psychiatric patients	Instruction, modeling, role play, feedback	• Assertiveness
Johnson (1978)	Interpersonal Career Skills	Self	Diverse	Instructional text, group discussion,	• Cooperating and leading skills • Communication skills • Relationship skills • Conflict-management skills
Liberman et al. (1975)	Personal Effectiveness	Hospital and clinic staff	Psychiatric patients	Modeling, behavioral rehearsal, prompting, shaping, feedback	• Language skills • Emotional expressiveness skills • Social interaction skills • Employment skills
McFall, (1976), McFall & Twentyman, 1973.	Interpersonal Skill Training	Professional, graduate student	Psychiatric patients, university undergraduates	Instruction, modeling, role playing, feedback	• Initiating and terminating conversations • Dealing with rejection • Self-disclosure • Assertiveness • Other interpersonal skills
Miller, Nunnally, & Wackman (1975)	Alive and Aware	None	Couples	Instructional text, in vivo practice	• Self-awareness skills • Awareness of others skills • Communication style skills • Communiation patterns skills
Patterson, Hops, & Weiss (1975)	Interpersonal Skill Training	Authors	Married couples	Instruction, role play, feedback	• Pinpointing problem behaviors • Negotiation • Reinforcement delivery • Problem solving
Rhode, Rasmussen, & Heaps (1971)	Effective Communication	Teachers	College Students	Role play, discussions feedback	• Communication skills
Robin (1980)	Problem-solving communication training	Family therapists	Parents and adolescents	Modeling, didactic instruction, behavioral rehearsal, performance feedback	• Interpersonal conflict-reduction skills

Table 1.1 (Continued).

Developer	Program	Trainers	Trainees	Training Methods	Skills
Rotherman (1980)	Cognitive Behavioral Assertion	Paraprofessionals	Elementary school	Simulation, coaching, shaping, behavioral rehearsal	• Interpersonal problem-solving skills
Stephens (1976, 1978)	Directive Teaching	Teachers	Children, aged 7-12	Modeling, rehearsal, social reinforcement, contingency contracting	• Environmental behaviors • Interpersonal behaviors • Self-related behaviors • Task-related behaviors
Terkelson (1976)	Parent-Child Communication Skill	Counselors	Parents, children, Grades 4-6	Exercises, role playing, review	• Listening • Sending "I" messages
Thiel (1977)	Habilitation Programs for mentally handicapped adults	Counselors, teachers, group home	Physically and mentally handicapped	Modeling, role playing, feedback, *in vivo* practice	• Social behavior skills • Practical living skills • Socialization skills • Job skills
Wehman & Schleien (1980)	Leisure Skills Programming	Teachers	Severely disturbed children & adolescents	Games, coaching, modeling, feedback	• Social, cognitive gross/fine motor skills

ly grew from and continue to receive careful and extensive experimental scrutiny. This reliance upon a substantial research foundation is clearly one of the strongest qualities of the psychological skills training movement (Authier, Gustafson, Guerney, & Kasdorf, 1975; Cartledge & Milburn, 1980; Goldstein, 1973; Hersen & Eisler, 1976; L'Abate, 1980; McFall, 1976; Nietzel, Winnet, McDonald, & Davidson, 1977; Rathjen & Foreyt, 1980; and Twentyman & Zimering, 1979).

We have now introduced psychological skills training, defined it, and provided an overview of the major psychological skills programs currently available. We now turn to the major concern of this book, an in-depth consideration of one such program, Structured Learning. Our focus is upon its rationale and development, its methods and materials, its utilization with a wide variety of trainee populations, and especially its supporting research.

Chapter 2
Origins of Structured Learning

Our initial interest in psychological skills training began with a concern seemingly very distant from enhancement of skills, namely the apparent inadequacy of existing helping interventions, particularly psychotherapy, for low-income patient populations. In the United States and elsewhere, the implications of a patient's social class for his psychotherapeutic treatment destiny are numerous, pervasive, and enduring. If the patient is from a lower social class, such implications are decidedly and uniformly negative. It has been consistently demonstrated that, in comparison with patients at higher social class levels, the lower-class patient-candidate seeking psychotherapeutic assistance in an outpatient setting is significantly more likely to:

1. be found unacceptable for treatment;
2. receive a socially less desirable formal diagnosis;
3. drop out (or be dropped out) after initial screening;
4. spend considerable time on the clinic's waiting list;
5. be assigned to the least experienced staff members;
6. hold expectations incongruent with those held by his therapist;
7. form a poor relationship with his psychotherapist;
8. terminate or be terminated earlier; and
9. improve significantly less from either his own or his therapist's perspective.

Analogous dimensions relevant to mental hospital settings yield an even grimmer pattern for the lower-class inpatient. As but one example, as a result of the deinstitutionalization philosophy, this has been a decade during which the rate of mental hospital discharges has increased significantly in the United States. But the proportion of lower-class inpatients still hospitalized has *increased*. In a ten-year followup of Hollingshead and Redlich's (1958) research, Meyers and Bean (1965) discovered that significantly more middle- and upper-class patients had left the hospital, as compared to those of lower social class standing. Furthermore, the likelihood of rehospitalization was significantly greater for those lower-class patients who had been discharged.

At the broadest level of generalization, we would assert that the lower social class patient has fared so poorly in psychotherapy because the type of psychotherapy we are most prone to offer—traditional, verbal, insight-oriented psychotherapy—is almost singularly a middle-class enterprise. It is middle class in its underlying philosophies of man, in its theoretical rationales, and in its specific therapeutic techniques. Schofield (1964) has taken an analogous position by suggesting that most psychotherapists prefer to work with what he describes as the YAVIS patient—Young, Attractive, Verbal, Intelligent, and Successful, and most typically middle or upper social class. Mr. YAVIS seeks psychotherapy voluntarily; he does not wish drug or physical therapy, but, as his therapist prefers, he expects to explore his inner world and to participate actively in seeking insight. He tends to form a favorable therapeutic relationship, to remain in treatment for an extended period, and in about two-thirds of such therapist-patient pairings, Mr. YAVIS indeed apparently derives psychotherapeutic benefit.

Our own clinical and research interest lies more with a contrasting type of patient, whom we might term Mr. *non*-YAVIS. He is typically lower or working class, often middle-aged, physically ordinary or unattractive, verbally reticent, intellectually unexceptional or dull, and vocationally unsuccessful or marginal. In our mental hospital studies, Mr. *non*-YAVIS has usually been diagnosed schizophrenic, psychoneurotic, inadequate personality, drug addict, or alcoholic, though it is his social class level and its associated learning style which we consider of greater consequence than his diagnosis per se. How else might we describe the *non*-YAVIS patient? He seeks psychotherapy often not with full volition. He anticipates not introspective behavior on his own part, but advice and active guidance from his psychotherapist. Since Mr. *non*-YAVIS often views his problems as physical in nature, physical or drug therapies are also consistent with his expectations and even preferences. As noted earlier, he tends to remain in treatment very briefly, to form a poor therapeutic relationship, and to derive minimal benefit from psychotherapy. In the United States, 50 percent of the psychotherapies involving *non*-YAVIS patients at community mental health centers last only one or two sessions—clearly less successful an effort than therapy with middle-class clients.

ALTERNATIVE INTERVENTIONS

Increased Directiveness

How are we to help the lower-class patient more effectively? Four approaches can be identified. The first consists of simple exhortations in the psychiatric, social work, and psychological literatures urging therapists to "be more directive, concrete, specific, advice giving," and the like. While this is indeed good prescriptive advice, like most advice, it is rarely followed. Perhaps this is in part because the training analyst, psychology professor, or psychiatrist writing these articles rarely see such patients in their own private therapy practices. Instead, while they write of Mr. *non*-YAVIS, and urge us on in his direction, they themselves treat Mr. Yavis. They ask us to do as they say, not as they do. Young therapists respond to their model's behavior, not to their words. Thus, this approach—consisting of admonitions and beseeching in the literature—has essentially failed. The gap between the typically middle-class therapist and the lower-class patient—a gap in values, language, beliefs about psychopathology and its remediation—is simply too great to close in this manner.

Paraprofessional Psychotherapists

If this is the case, many have held that a second and viable solution to the psychotherapeutic needs of low-income patients is to employ therapists who share values, language, and therapy beliefs with the low-income, *non*-YAVIS patient. That is, the lower social class or working-class psychotherapist. If such therapists could be found, this position held, then congruent therapist-patient expectancies, a positive relationship, and a favorable outcome all might well ensue. It was in large measure this set of assumptions and hopes which, in the United States, led to the so-called "paraprofessional therapist" movement. This was a period in the late 1960s and early 1970s in which individuals of lower- and working-class status were identified and (briefly) trained to function as what were termed paraprofessional, nonprofessional, indigenous, neighborhood, or community therapists. And in fact a great many indeed proved of therapeutic value. In fact, as a recent review of existing comparative studies indicates, such persons rather often proved to be more helpful to low-income clients than were professional, credentialed psychotherapists (Durlak, 1979). Unfortunately, a series of economic and political events (Vietnam War, recession) have combined to keep this an underfunded movement, one that is yet to reach its full therapeutic potential.

The Conformity Prescription

If admonitions are not enough, and paraprofessionals are too scarce, what solutions remain? There are two, and both are what we have termed pre-scriptive. The first seeks to "make the patient fit the therapy." It is a con-formity prescription which seeks to alter the patient, his expectancies, relat-ability, or similar therapy-readiness characteristics in order that he more adequately fit the patient role appropriate to whatever (unchanged) psycho-therapy is offered.

Our own earlier research program is one example of such a conformity prescription for the lower-class patient (Goldstein, 1971). Our broad goal was to implement and evaluate procedures designed to enhance the favorableness of the psychotherapeutic relationship. Social psychologists have focused a great deal of research attention upon procedures predicted to increase what they term interpersonal attraction, i.e., the degree to which one member of a dyad likes or is attracted to the other. Working in laboratory settings, usually with college students for subjects, researchers have developed several different procedures for reliably enhancing interpersonal attraction. These are the procedures we extrapolated from laboratory to clinic as a means of seeking to increase the attraction of patients to their psychotherapists. Concretely, the procedures included:

1. Direct structuring, in which the patient is directly led to believe he will like his therapist;
2. Trait structuring, in which the patient is provided with information about his therapist, such as his "warmth" or "experience";
3. Status, in which both verbal and physical information is used to lead the patient to believe his therapist is of high status;
4. Effort, in which the therapeutic interaction itself is deliberately made more effortful for the patient;
5. Modeling, in which the patient is provided with the opportunity to view a model who is highly attracted to his psychotherapist;
6. Matching, in which therapist and patient are paired based upon test results concerning their interpersonal needs or therapy-relevant attitudes; and
7. Conformity pressure, in which both an attracted model and cohorts rating him as attractive are utilized.

In a series of investigations (Goldstein, 1971), we examined each of these procedures with separate middle-class and lower-class patient samples. Almost every one of our procedures worked successfully with the middle-class patient samples. Almost every procedure failed to do so with our lower-class samples. This failure is not an uncommon outcome. Although there exist some notable exceptions (Hoehn-Saric, Frank, Imber, Nash, Stone, & Battle, 1964; Lerner, 1972), most efforts to teach low-income patients "good patient" skills, to socialize them into traditional, verbal, insight-oriented therapy, to have them play the therapeutic game as it is usually structured, have not been successful.

The Reformity Prescription

In response to both these findings and the literature summarized earlier, an alternative approach to the lower-class patient seemed appropriate. Rather than make the patient fit the therapy, that is, rather than implement a conformity prescription, we opted to try to develop a therapy to fit the lower-class patient, to try to alter or reformulate our psychotherapeutic offering to correspond more adequately to or be consistent with patient needs and therapy-relevant characteristics. In other words, we sought what might be termed a reformity prescription. To determine the nature of such an approach, we turned this time primarily to developmental psychology research on child rearing and sociological writing on social class and life styles. These bodies of literature consistently reveal that middle-class child rearing and life style—with their emphasis upon intentions, motivation, inner states, self-regulation, and the like—are excellent "basic training" for participation in traditional, verbal psychotherapies, should such persons become emotionally disturbed in later life. Lower-class child rearing and life style, with their emphasis upon action, motor behavior, consequences rather than intentions, and their reliance upon external example and authority and a restricted verbal code, ill prepare such persons for successful involvement in traditional psychotherapy, but, we speculated (Goldstein, 1973), might prepare them very well for a treatment which *was* responsive to such life-style characteristics. This would be a treatment which was brief, concrete, behavioral, actional, authoritatively administered, and which required imitation of specific overt examples, taught role-taking skills, and provided early, continuing, and frequent reinforcement for enactment of seldom-used but adaptive skill behaviors. These are the defining characteristics of Structured Learning.[1] Its major procedures are modeling, role playing, performance feedback, and transfer training. That is, the patient (i.e., trainee) is provided with specific, detailed, frequent, and vivid displays of adaptive behavior or of specific skills in which he is deficient (i.e., modeling); he is given considerable opportunity and encouragement to rehearse or practice such modeled behavior (i.e., role playing); he is provided with positive feedback, approval, or reward for successful enactments (i.e., performance feedback); and is required to engage in a number of behaviors which enhance the likelihood that the behaviors we teach him in the therapy room will be used reliably in the community and other application settings (i.e., transfer training).

Deinstitutionalization and Skill Deficiency

At the very time that we were formulating the Structured Learning reformity prescription, a major movement was developing in the United States—the

---

1. As we noted in conjunction with Table 1.1, very similar teaching methods—instructions, modeling, role playing, performance feedback—are with great frequency also the core teaching methods of many other psychological skills training programs. It is of interest that most of these programs appear to have initially arrived at essentially the same selection of methods as we, but from a rather different route, i.e., clinical practice and experimental research in behavior modification and applied social learning theory. These social class-related origins of Structured Learning are examined in greater breadth in *Structured Learning Therapy: Toward a Psychotherapy for the Poor* (Goldstein, 1973).

deinstitutionalization movement. This is the movement from public mental hospital to community of chronic adult mental patients—85 percent of whom are socioeconomically lower or working class. In the United States, in the last 15 years, the public mental hospital patient census has decreased from approximately 550,000 to 150,000. In terms of the movement of people out of institutions, the deinstitutionalization movement seems a marked success. For many of the people thus moved, however, very major problems have ensued. Many newly discharged individuals came into the community ill prepared to meet even the routine minor demands of daily living. Many were, after all, persons who in adolescence and early adulthood were too schizoid, incompetent, or unskilled to succeed in effective community functioning. They entered mental hospitals and remained there for 10, or 20, or even more years. Their "training" during hospitalization involved socialization into the "good patient" role or what others have described as a colonization effect; they were not taught what one needs in order to function adequately outside the hospital in the real and often demanding world. These years and years of hospitalization, of an unskilled, chronic, ward existence, of an existence far removed in its demands from the requirements of adequate community functioning left thousands of these expatients ill prepared for what was to confront them. As they moved from hospital to group home, welfare hotel or halfway house, many proved too deficient in daily living skills to remain out of the hospital. They too often had moved from "back ward" to "back alley" and couldn't make it. Thousands became part of the revolving-door, discharge-readmission cycle. Frequent short stays in the hospital proved necessary; frequent long stays in the community proved impossible. It was this challenge to which we sought to respond in our initial implementations of Structured Learning.

STRUCTURED LEARNING PROCEDURES[2]

Modeling

Structured Learning requires first that trainees be exposed to expertly portrayed examples of the specific skilled behaviors we wish them to learn. To accomplish this, we developed a library of audiocassette modeling displays.

---

2. The description of Structured Learning procedures provided here is presented at this point to give the reader a sense of Structured Learning in operation. But this presentation is a summary overview. A detailed and complete presentation of the procedures which constitute this approach appears in the Structured Learning Trainer's Manual, which is included as Appendix A of this book, and in the text *Skill Training for Community Living* (Goldstein, Sprafkin & Gershaw, 1976).

Each of the 59 tape displays listed below depicts a different daily living skill or skill combination.[3] Each skill is broken down into four to six different behavioral steps. The steps constitute or are the operational definition of the given skills. Each tape depicts one skill, and consists of ten vignettes in each of which actors expertly portray the steps of that skill in a variety of community, hospital, and transitional settings. The six to twelve trainees constituting the Structured Learning group are selected based upon their shared skill deficiencies, essentially independent of their formal diagnoses. Trainers describe the first skill to be taught and hand out skill cards to all trainees on which the name of the skill and behavioral steps are printed. The first modeling tape is then played. Trainees are told to listen closely to the way the actors in each vignette on the tape follow the behavioral steps.

The 59 Structured Learning skills include:

A. Single Skills
  Series I.   Conversations: Beginning Skills
              Skill   1. Starting a conversation
              Skill   2. Carrying on a conversation
              Skill   3. Ending a conversation
              Skill   4. Listening
  Series II. Conversations: Expressing Oneself
              Skill   5. Expressing a compliment
              Skill   6. Expressing appreciation
              Skill   7. Expressing encouragement
              Skill   8. Asking for help
              Skill   9. Giving instructions
              Skill 10. Expressing affection
              Skill 11. Expressing a complaint
              Skill 12. Persuading others
              Skill 13. Expressing anger
  Series III. Conversations: Responding to Others
              Skill 14. Responding to praise
              Skill 15. Responding to the feelings of others (empathy)
              Skill 16. Apologizing
              Skill 17. Following instructions
              Skill 18. Responding to persuasion
              Skill 19. Responding to failure
              Skill 20. Responding to contradictory messages
              Skill 21. Responding to a complaint
              Skill 22. Responding to anger
  Series IV. Planning Skills
              Skill 23. Setting a goal

---

3. Basic Skill and Application Skill Tapes for Skill Training for Community Living (Goldstein, Sprafkin & Gershaw, 1976).

Skill 24. Gathering information

Skill 25. Concentrating on a task

Skill 26. Evaluating your abilities

Skill 27. Preparing for a stressful conversation

Skill 28. Setting problem priorities

Skill 29. Decision making

Series V. Alternatives to Aggression

Skill 30. Identifying and labeling your emotions

Skill 31. Determining responsibility

Skill 32. Making requests

Skill 33. Relaxation

Skill 34. Self-control

Skill 35. Negotiation

Skill 36. Helping others

Skill 37. Assertiveness

B. Skill Combinations

Application Skills*

Skill 38. Finding a place to live (through formal channels)

Skill 39. Moving in (typical)

Skill 40. Moving in (difficult)

Skill 41. Managing money

Skill 42. Neighboring (apartment house)

Skill 43. Job seeking (typical)

Skill 44. Job seeking (difficult)

Skill 45. Job keeping (average day's work)

Skill 46. Job keeping (strict boss)

Skill 47. Receiving telephone calls (difficult)

Skill 48. Restaurant eating (typical)

Skill 49. Organizing time (typical)

Skill 50. Using leisure time (learning something new)

Skill 51. Using leisure time (interpersonal activity)

Skill 52. Social (party)

Skill 53. Social (church supper)

Skill 54. Marital (positive interaction)

Skill 55. Marital (negative interaction)

Skill 56. Using community resources (seeking money)

Skill 57. Using community resources (avoiding red tape)

Skill 58. Dealing with crises (inpatient to nonpatient transition)

Skill 59. Dealing with crises (loss)

*Each application tape portrays a model enacting three to eight Basic Skills, in a sequence and combination chosen to deal completely with a real-life problem.

Role Playing

A brief, spontaneous discussion almost invariably follows the playing of a modeling tape. Trainees comment on the steps, the actors, and very often on how the situation or skill problem portrayed occurs in their own lives. Since the primary goal of role playing in Structured Learning is to encourage realistic behavioral rehearsal, a trainee's statements about his individual difficulties using the skill being taught can often develop into material for his or her first role play. To enhance the realism of the portrayal, the Structured Learning trainer should have the trainee (now the main actor) choose a second trainee (coactor) to play the role of the significant other person in his life who is relevant to the skill problem. One of the group's two trainers should be responsible for keeping a record of who has role-played, which role, and for which skill, to be sure that all participate about equally. The main procedure of the role playing is that the main actor seek to enact the steps he has just heard modeled.

The main actor is asked to describe briefly the real skill problem situation and the real person(s) involved in it, with whom he could try the skill's behavioral steps in real life. The coactor should be called by the name of the main actor's significant other during the role play. One trainer instructs the role players to begin. It is the trainers' main responsibility, at this point, to be sure that the main actor keeps role playing and that he attempts to follow the behavioral steps while doing so. If he "breaks role" and begins making comments or explaining background events, the trainers should firmly instruct him to resume his role. One trainer should position himself near the chalkboard and point to each step, in turn, as the role play unfolds, being sure none is either missed or enacted out of order. If the trainers or actors feel the role play is not progressing well and wish to start it over, this is appropriate. Observers should be instructed to hold their comments until the role play is completed.

The role playing should be continued until all trainees have had an opportunity to participate, even if all the same steps must be carried over to a second or third session. Note that while the framework (behavioral steps) of each role play in the series remains the same, the actual content can and should change from role play to role play. It is the problem as it actually occurs, or could occur, in each trainee's real-life environment that should be the content of the given role play. When completed, each trainee should be better armed to act appropriately in the given reality situation.

Performance Feedback

Upon completion of each role play, a brief feedback period should ensue. The goals of this activity are to let the main actor know how well he followed the skill's steps or in what ways he departed from them, to explore the psychological impact of his enactment on his coactor, and to provide him encouragement to try out his role-play in real life.

In these critiques, it is crucial that the behavioral focus of Structured Learning be maintained. Comments must point to the presence or absence of specific, concrete behaviors, and should not take the form of general evaluative comments or broad generalities.

Transfer Training

Several aspects of the training sessions described above had, as their primary purpose, augmentation of the likelihood that learning in the therapy setting will transfer to the trainee's actual real-life environment.

Provision of general principles. It has been demonstrated that transfer of training is facilitated by providing trainees with general mediating principles governing successful or competent performance on the training and criterion tasks. This procedure has typically been operationalized in laboratory contexts by providing subjects with the organizing concepts, principles, strategies, or rationales that explain or account for the stimulus-response relationships operative in both the training and application settings. The provision of general principles to Structured Learning trainees is operationalized by the presentation in verbal, pictorial, and written form of appropriate information governing skill instigation, selection, and implementation principles.

Overlearning. Overlearning is a procedure by which learning is extended over more trials than are necessary merely to produce initial changes in the trainee's behavior. The overlearning, or repetition of *successful* skill enactment, in the typical Structured Learning session is quite substantial, with the given skill taught and its behavioral steps (1) modeled several times; (2) role-played one or more times by the trainee; (3) observed live by the trainee as every other group member role-plays it; (4) read by the trainee from a chalkboard and on his skill card; (5) written by the trainee in his trainee's notebook; (6) practiced *in vivo* one or more times by the trainee as part of his formal homework assignment; (7) practiced *in vivo* one or more times by the trainee in response to adult and/or peer leader coaching; and (8) practiced *in vivo* one or more times by the trainee in response to skill-oriented, intrinsically interesting stimuli introduced into his real-life environment.

Identical elements. In perhaps the earliest experimental concern with transfer enhancement, Thorndike and Woodworth (1901) concluded that when there was a facilitative effect of one habit on another, it was to the extent that and because they shared identical elements. More recently, Ellis (1965) and Osgood (1953) have emphasized the importance for transfer of similarity between stimulus aspects of the training and application tasks. The greater the similarity of physical and interpersonal stimuli in the Structured Learning setting and the homework, community, or other setting in which the skill is to be applied, the greater the likely transfer.

The "real-lifeness" of Structured Learning is operationalized in a number of ways. These operational expressions of identical elements include: (1) the representative, relevant, and realistic content and portrayal of the models, protagonists, and situations on the modeling tapes, all designed to be highly similar to what low-income trainees face in their daily lives; (2) the physical props used in, and the arrangement of, the role-playing setting to be similar to real-life settings; (3) the choice, coaching, and enactment of the coactors or protagonists to be similar to real-life figures; (4) the manner in which the role plays themselves are conducted to be as responsive as possible to the real-life interpersonal stimuli to which the trainee must actually respond with the given skill; (5) role-play implementation which provides behavioral rehearsal of each skill as the trainee actually plans to employ it; (6) the *in vivo* homework assignments, coached and practiced during training; and (7) the training of living units (e.g., all the members of a given ward) as a unit.

Stimulus variability. Callantine and Warren (1955), Duncan (1958), and Shore and Sechrest (1961) have each demonstrated that positive transfer is greater when a variety of relevant training stimuli are employed. Stimulus variability is implemented in our Structured Learning sessions by use of: (1) rotation of group leaders across groups; (2) rotation of trainees across groups; (3) having trainees re-role-play a given skill with several coactors; (4) having trainees re-role-play a given skill across several relevant settings; and (5) use of multiple homework assignments for each given skill.

Real-life reinforcement. Given successful implementation of both appropriate Structured Learning procedures and the transfer enhancement procedures presented above, positive transfer may still fail to occur. As Agras (1967), Gruber (1971), Patterson and Anderson (1964), Tharp and Wetzel (1969), and dozens of other investigators have shown, stable and enduring performance in application settings of newly learned skills is very much at the mercy of real-life reinforcement contingencies.

We have found it useful to implement, outside the Structured Learning setting, several supplemental programs which can help to provide the rewards trainees need so that their new behaviors are maintained. These programs include provision for both external social reward (provided by people in the trainee's real-life environment) and self-reward (provided by the trainee himself).

In this chapter, we have described the origins of Structured Learning, sketched its application to low-income adult trainees, and introduced its specific procedures. It is the developmental course of many helping interventions that, though originally designed for one type of client, it is subsequently applied to numerous other types. Such is the case with Structured Learning. The following chapters describe these diverse applications, present the materials (e.g., skills, prescriptively modified training procedures, etc.) developed in each instance and, in particular, present and examine our evaluative studies of the skill-enhancement efficacy of this psychological skills training approach.

Chapter 3
Mental Hospital Patient Trainees

We seek to accomplish two goals in this chapter. First, we wish to present the major Structured Learning investigations which we and others have conducted over the past decade in an attempt to enhance the psychological skills level of individuals residing in or recently discharged from public mental hospitals. Our second purpose is to begin highlighting certain characteristics of our operating research philosophy, as well as a number of methodological considerations, which appear and reappear throughout not only these adult patient trainee studies, but also in the other investigations with different types of trainee samples examined in subsequent chapters. These philosophical and methodological themes include our behavioral perspective on programmatic evaluation research, the behavioral assessment outcome approach we have implemented, our companion focus upon skill acquisition and skill transfer, and our emphasis upon the prescriptive modification and implementation of Structured Learning in response to relevant characteristics of diverse trainees.

Thus, as will become concretely apparent as our studies are presented, with regard to experimental design and procedure, most of the investigations we have conducted include:

1. Acceptance into the study trainee sample based upon concurring assessment by the trainee himself and by a relevant other (e.g., ward nurse) regarding the presence of target skill deficiency.

2. Random assignment to Structured Learning, comparison treatment (often implemented by means of Structured Learning plus diverse transfer-enhancing procedures), and control experimental conditions, cast in a factorial design.

3. Application of experimental conditions, with Structured Learning implementation occurring in a manner prescriptively responsive to relevant trainee characteristics.

4. Multilevel, behavioral, posttreatment assessment for:
   a. Skill acquisition;
   b. Minimal skill transfer; and
   c. Extended skill transfer

5. Inclusion, when possible, of measures which are potential correlates of

Structured Learning-induced skill acquisition. Such information is obtained for utilization as guides to prescriptive modification of Structured Learning, as well as for covariate data analysis purposes.

6. Data analysis by means of analyses of variance and covariance.

Note that our design strategy also purposefully omits certain measurement targets. As is true for behavioral assessment in general, our skill-oriented approach does not concern itself with "personality," "psychodynamics," or related covert processes. We do believe that behavioral interventions are also ultimately self-concept interventions, but that the optimal route for enhancing the positiveness of an individual's self-concept is to enhance his self-perceived level of competency. "As I observe myself *acting* more effectively on my world, I will feel better about myself" would be our perspective, rather than the nonbehavioral view which seeks first to alter the person's view of himself by psychodynamic or existential means, in the hope that such enhancement of the self-concept will somehow lead to enhanced skill competence.

STUDY 1. SOCIAL INTERACTION I
(GUTRIDE, GOLDSTEIN, & HUNTER, 1973)

Withdrawal, apathy, and minimal social interaction have long been recognized as major descriptive features of chronic schizophrenic and other long-term mental hospital patients. Diverse explanations of such overt social skills deficiency in institutionalized mental patients have been offered, including: (1) deficiency in social motivation (Cameron, 1944); (2) inadequate role-taking ability (Bloom & Arkoff, 1961); (3) purposeful avoidance of stimuli which evoke complex responses in order to reestablish the capacity for stabilized thinking and perception (Broen, 1968); (4) as deriving from long-term familial and environmental patterns of social isolation (Faris & Dunham, 1960); and (5) as behavior literally taught and maintained by the prevailing patterns of reinforcement contingencies which tend to be provided in many staff-oriented, orderliness-oriented, colonization-enhancing mental hospitals (Paul, 1969; Zusman, 1966). Whatever its singular or multiple origin, it does indeed seem to be the case, as noted in the previous chapter, that psychological skill deficiencies associated with long-term institutionalization render the individual ill prepared and vulnerable for the myriad of skill-associated tasks which constitute independent community functioning following hospital discharge. It is the case that early evaluations of the efficacy of milieu therapy (Kasius, 1966; Sanders, Smith & Weinman, 1967) and the token economy (Atthowe & Krasner, 1968; Ayllon & Azrin, 1968) for skill-enhancement purposes have shown both to make a modest positive contribution in this regard. We felt, however, that the direct skills teaching focus of

Structured Learning might well yield more substantial skill-acquisition and skill-transfer outcomes. This, then, was the primary evaluation goal of our first investigation.

Procedure

Participants in this investigation were 87 patients in a state mental hospital who were invited to participate in the study after each had been identified by a selection panel—the experimenter and the psychiatrist and chief nurse from each of nine wards—as an individual consistently displaying major social interaction skill deficiencies. Diagnostically, 75 percent of these persons were schizophrenic, the remainder were diagnosed primarily psychotic depression, schizoid personality, or inadequate personality. In addition to this investigation's major comparisons involving the presence and absence of Structured Learning, our design was such as to permit two sets of exploratory questions to be addressed to our data. In response to Magaro's (1969) cogent arguments predicting differential treatment responsiveness to interventions such as ours as a function of acute versus chronic status, acute-chronic was used as our second experimental variable. Acute status was defined as less than one year of hospitalization and no more than two prior hospitalizations. Patients who had been in the hospital for longer than one year and had had more than two prior hospitalizations were defined as chronic for purposes of this investigation. The final study N consisted of 30 acute and 57 chronic patients. Fifteen acute and 30 chronic patients constituted the experimental group; 15 acute and 27 chronic patients made up the control group sample. Finally, to complete our $2 \times 2 \times 2$ design, we chose to inquire into the possible additivity of treatment interventions by utilizing presence versus absence of psychotherapy as our third variable—psychotherapy being defined for this investigation as participating in two or more sessions per week of individual or group psychotherapy.

We developed four modeling videotapes for use as this study's stimulus materials. Each depicted several variants on a single social interaction theme. Concretely, the first tape contained enactments indicating how one individual (the model) can interact with another individual who approaches him. The second, how an individual (the model) can initiate interaction with a second person. The third, how an individual (the model) can initiate interaction with a group of people. Finally, continuing this progression reflecting increasing complexity of social interaction, the fourth tape depicted how an individual (the model) can resume relationships with relatives, friends, and coworkers from outside the hospital. In several respects, in both the development and experimental usage of these modeling displays, we sought to be responsive to laboratory research findings that have identified characteristics of the observer, the model, and the modeling display that function to enhance the level of vicarious learning which occurs. This included our portrayal of several heterogeneous models; the introduction and summarization of each tape by a high status narrator (hospital superintendent and clinical director), who sought by his introduction to maximize observer attention and by his summary to reemphasize the nature of the specific, concrete social interaction behaviors which constituted each modeling display; portrayal of the model's characteristics as similar to that of most participating study patients (age, sex, patient status); and frequent and readily observable rewards provided the model contingent upon his social interaction behavior.

Prior to the commencement of the Structured Learning sessions, and for possible later covariance usage, each ward psychiatrist completed the Psychotic Inpatient Profile (Lorr & Vestre, 1968) on each study patient residing on his ward. We viewed the Seclusiveness and Disorientation subscales of this instrument as potential covariates, since each appeared on an a priori basis to be a likely influence upon patient social interaction. Also at this point in time, the Ward Atmosphere Scale (Moos, 1969) was completed by each patient, of which the Affiliation and Autonomy subscales were of potential interest to us for later covariance analysis.

Experimental group patients were constituted into eight subgroups of five to eight patients each and met with two group leaders three times per week for a four-week period. The group leaders were 20 undergraduate volunteers who underwent a 12-hour training program in the application of Structured Learning immediately prior to the beginning of the investigation. Each of the four modeling tapes served as stimulus materials for three consecutive group meetings. Each session began with the modeling tape display, during which the group leaders actively drew attention to the specific behavioral steps which constituted each display. These included the following effective social interaction behaviors:
1. Eye contact;
2. Forward leaning;
3. Physical contact;
4. Smiling;
5. Initiation of conversation;
6. Response to conversation; and
7. Talking for ten or more consecutive seconds.

Each tape was immediately followed by an "idiosyncratizing" group discussion in which the behaviors and circumstances depicted were related to each patient's personal experiences and environmental demands. The remainder of each session was devoted to role playing. Throughout all role playing, singular focus was devoted to enactment in the proper manner of the specific social interaction behavioral steps which had constituted each modeling display. The role-playing enactments were themselves videotaped and played back to the group for comment and corrective feedback. Both the group leaders and, frequently, other group members provided the role-play enactor with frequent social reinforcement as his depiction increasingly approximated that of the videotaped models.

Posttesting across experimental and control patients was conducted during the week following completion of the Structured Learning program. Since our main dependent variable concern was with overt social interaction behavior, certain behavioral observation criteria were developed and measured. The first may be termed "Standardized Observation" of patient social interaction behavior. Each patient was brought to a waiting room and requested to wait a brief period prior to taking certain psychometric measures administered for purposes ancillary to our behavioral focus. A second "patient" (an experimental accomplice) was already seated in this room, apparently also waiting to complete his posttesting. Their subsequent interaction, during which the accomplice sought to behave in a prearranged, standardized manner, was observed through a one-way mirror by a rater trained to rate, at 30-second intervals, the presence or absence of the seven behavioral steps enumerated above. During this 5-minute period of standardized observation, the accomplice sought to behave in a friendly and interested manner and, on a schedule set at 30 seconds, 60 seconds, 90 seconds, 2 minutes, 3 minutes, and 4 minutes, would ask one of the following questions if the patient were not talking at that given point in time:

1e.[1] Were you in the program?
1c.   Are you in the program?
2e.   How many people were in your group?
2c.   How many people are coming from your ward?
3e.   What did you think of the program?
3c.   What do you think of the program?
4e.   Would you go through this again?
4c.   Do you really want to go through this?
5e&c. What time is it? and
6e&c. What do you do when this is over?

Our second observational outcome criteria may be termed "Naturalistic Observation" of patient social interaction behavior. Eight raters were trained in the use of a social interaction checklist developed by us for this investigation, by means of which they could rate the following interactional patient behaviors:

1. Eye contact;
2. Forward leaning;
3. Physical contact;
4. Smiling;
5. Initiates conversation;

----

1. e = question asked to experimental patients; c = question asked to control patients.

6. Responds to conversation;
7. Talks ten or more consecutive seconds;
8. Seated alone; and
9. Seated with others.

Interrater reliability for these ratings, determined during three training sessions, yielded an overall percentage agreement (taking raters two at a time in all possible pairings) of 85 percent. Patients were observed by these raters during mealtimes for the two-week period immediately following the posttesting described above. Each rater was randomly assigned to rate 10 or 11 patients; each patient was observed for one ten-minute period.

Results and Discussion

Covariance check. As noted earlier, based upon scale descriptions and items as well as relevant research, we selected the Seclusiveness and Disorientation subscales of the Psychotic Inpatient Profile and the Affiliation and Autonomy subscales of the Ward Atmosphere Scale as potential covariates for our social interaction dependent measures. A correlational analysis comparing patient scores on these four subscales against each of the 16 scores reflecting overt social interaction behavior (Naturalistic and Standard Observation scores) revealed the appropriateness of this a priori covariate selection. Each subscale score correlated at .25 or greater with five or more social interaction scores. Based upon this outcome, a series of $2 \times 2 \times 2$ analyses of covariance was conducted across the study's data.

As Table 3.1 indicates, a number of significant effects emerged—singly and in interaction—for our three treatment factors on our behavioral dependent variable measures of social interaction.

Of particular interest to us, of course, were the Structured Learning results. Structured Learning yielded significant differences on four of the seven social interaction behaviors obtained under Standard Observation test and rating conditions. These differences held across both the acute and chronic samples. No Structured Learning main effects emerged under Naturalistic (mealtime) behavior observation test conditions, although a number of combined effects for Structured Learning and psychotherapy were obtained. On those significant results on the acute-chronic dimension, it was the case in each instance that the acute patients performed in a reliably more socially interactive manner.

What meanings and implications may be drawn from these findings, especially when viewed as the outcome of the initial investigation in our research series? The results for Structured Learning under Standard Observation conditions provide, in our view, an initial, and certainly tentative, demonstration of the skill *acquisition* potency of Structured Learning, for both acute and chronic patients. The absence of main effects for Structured Learn-

Table 3.1. Analyses of Covariance (F Values) for Social Interaction.

Measure	Source[a]
Standard Observation	
1. Forward leaning	SL (97.91***)
2. Smiling	SL (7.56***); PTX (4.47**)
3. Responds to conversation	SL (31.35***); SL × AC (3.12*)
4. Talks ten or more consecutive seconds	SL (5.51**)
Naturalistic Observation	
1. Eye contact	AC (7.47***); SL × PTX (4.90**); SL × AC (2.85*)
2. Forward leaning	PTX (4.11**)
3. Initiates conversation	AC (3.74*)
4. Responds to conversation	AC (4.21**); SL × PTX (5.48**)
5. Talks ten or more consecutive seconds	AC (9.61***)
6. Seated alone	SL × PTX (8.56***); SL × AC (3.54*)
7. Seated with others	SL × PTX (11.83***)

[a] Source key: SL—Structured Learning; PTX—Psychotherapy; AC—Acute-Chronic.
   *$p > .05 < .10$
  **$p < .05$
 ***$p < .01$

ing (alone) when social interaction behaviors were measured in actual mealtime contexts may appropriately be viewed as a failure of skill acquisition to transfer. This distinction between acquisition and transfer will be an especially salient one throughout this book. As is true for many psychotherapeutic, educational, and training interventions, obtaining trainee change in or near the training context, e.g., acquisition, is in a relative sense easy to accomplish. In most of the studies reported in this book, enhanced skill acquisition was a reliable outcome of our Structured Learning training intervention. Transfer of competent skill usage from the training setting to real-life context (i.e., transfer of training) or effective use of the acquired skills at later, postintervention points in time (i.e., response maintenance) are each much more difficult effects to obtain. In fact, we have elsewhere estimated that the average transfer/maintenance rate for all psychotherapies combined is but 14 percent! (Goldstein & Kanfer, 1979). We feel this essential failure of transfer/maintenance is a core weakness of psychological intervention in general and, thus, efforts to increase the likelihood experimentally that transfer of training and/or response maintenance will occur became a central feature of our research program. It is of interest in this regard that, in the present study, there did emerge a series of significant interaction effects on mealtime social interaction behaviors favoring trainees who participated in both Structured Learning and psychotherapy—a clue to transfer enhancement to which we had the opportunity to return in a later investigation.

STUDY 2. SOCIAL INTERACTION II
(GUTRIDE, GOLDSTEIN & HUNTER, 1974)

In this second investigation, our purpose was to begin examining more directly the possibility of incorporating additional procedures into Structured Learning that were specifically designed to enhance the level of trainee skill transfer and/or maintenance. It has by now been well established that real-life reinforcement contingencies serve as a major determinant of whether or not behaviors changed in a therapy or training context maintain and transfer to new real-life contexts (Goldstein & Kanfer, 1979; Kazdin, 1975; Marholin & Touchette, 1979; Nay, 1979). If the ward nurse, the spouse, the parent, the boss, or any other potential dispenser of rewards in the trainee's living or working environment in fact provide such rewards, newly acquired skills or other recently altered behaviors will be likely to persist and transfer. When such rewards are not forthcoming, when trainee transfer attempts are met with indifference or explicitly negative reactions, extinction and not transfer will occur. In the present investigation, we sought to determine whether the provision of such real-life reinforcement in fact enhanced the transfer of skills acquired by means of Structured Learning.

Procedure

Study selection and assignment-to-condition procedures rather closely paralleled those described for the preceding investigation. Participants were 106 psychiatric inpatients residing in a state mental hospital, each of whom agreed to be involved in the study after a recommendation to do so by a screening panel consisting of the experimenter and the psychiatrist and head nurse on each of the 12 participating wards. Most were diagnosed schizophrenic, all were overtly and substantially deficient in social interaction skills.

Five experimental conditions formed the investigation's experimental design, in a 1 × 5 format. Within certain hospital administrative restrictions, patients were randomly assigned to one of the following:
1. Structured Learning (5 weeks), plus transfer training (2 weeks);
2. Structured Learning (5 weeks), plus Structured Learning (2 weeks);
3. Structured Learning (5 weeks);
4. Companionship control (7 weeks);
5. No treatment control.

The Structured Learning for experimental conditions 1, 2, and 3 consisted (during the first five weeks) of meeting with two group leaders, in groups of six to ten patients each, three times per week for sessions lasting one hour each. Thus, Structured Learning during the first five weeks of the program consisted of a total of 15 meetings per group. Five modeling videotapes were developed for this investigation, all oriented toward displaying optimal social behavior in an eating and mealtime context. As in our other investigations, we sought to enhance the level of observer modeling by using several heterogeneous models; by including on each tape an introduction and summarization by a high status narrator who sought to increase attention and provide reinforcement to the model; by displaying several instances of each behavior we were seeking to teach; by utilizing models similar in age and dress to most observers; by scheduling the tapes in order from the least to the most complex; and by providing frequent and obvious social reinforcement to the model throughout all five tapes. In outline form, the content of these modeling displays was:

1. The most rudimentary social eating behavior, e.g., how to hold a knife and fork, use of napkin, posture at the table, etc.
2. Very simple social behaviors, e.g., what and how one might say something when joining an already occupied table, excusing onself when passing by someone in a tight space between tables, helping someone with a tray, etc.
3. Somewhat more lengthy, if still brief interactive behaviors, e.g., offering to get seconds for someone, greeting other patients or dietary personnel, asking for the salt, excusing oneself from the table, etc.
4. A series of longer, more complex conversations, all of which were positive in tone.
5. A series of negative social interactions, e.g., someone yelling at you to get out of his way, someone spilling something on or near you, etc.

Following tape presentation, in the three Structured Learning conditions, a brief "idiosyncratizing" discussion was held in which patients had the opportunity to relate the behaviors depicted to their own typical behavior and real-life environments. Role playing then ensued, during which the behaviors displayed were rehearsed. Group leaders, as part of the role playing, placed special emphasis on pointing out (on the modeling display), portraying (during live modeling), and eliciting (during role playing) various aspects of body language relevant to successful social interaction, e.g., smiling, eye contact, posture, gestures, and so forth. To maximize the opportunity to provide patients with social reinforcement contingent upon correct enactments, or to provide other performance feedback, all patient role playing was itself videotaped and immediately displayed. The foregoing describes the first five weeks of participation for patients in conditions 1, 2, and 3. At the completion of this series, study procedures were varied for each of these three groups.

1. Structured Learning plus Real-Life Reinforcement. This experimental condition operationalized our effort to seek or enhance transfer of skill acquisition by rewarding its occurrences in a significant real-life context. One of the Structured Learning group trainers and an experimenter joined

patients for every lunch and dinner meal for a period of two weeks following the initial (five weeks) training. During this period, patients who were observed to be enacting the target behaviors were immediately provided social reinforcement. Patients not doing so were provided further modeling or prompts *in situ*.

2. Structured Learning plus Structured Learning. In planning this experiment, we realized that patients receiving the initial training plus a two-week period of real-life reinforcement might later perform more adequately than those receiving only the initial training, not because the former received transfer training, but simply because the first group received more training relevant to the target skills. That is, the extra two weeks of training might have proven to be the responsible variation, not the fact that it occurred *in situ*. To control for this possibility, patients in this second condition received two additional weeks of Structured Learning in the training studio after their initial five weeks of training. One tape was represented and role-played each day, with the last day of additional training devoted to a general discussion and summary.

3. Structured Learning. Patients assigned to this condition participated in the initial five-week, fifteen-session program only.

4. Companionship Control. In behavior change research, it is important to control for effects which may be attributable to interpersonal attention from a change agent, rather than a function of our planned, independent variable intervention. In the present study, patients in the three Structured Learning conditions may change more than those who receive no treatment (Condition 5), not because of what we perceive as the active ingredients in Structured Learning, but because of the attention given patients by group leaders offering interest, concern, or involvement. Thus, the need for an appropriate experimental control. We operationalized this attention control condition by providing each patient with an undergraduate student companion for the same number of hours (15) involved in Structured Learning participation. The companion-patient pairs engaged in a wide variety of activities (walks, playing cards, etc.) and in a broad range of conversations. The companions sought to be warm, nonjudgmental, empathic friends. Such companionship has been tentatively demonstrated to yield a variety of positive effects, several of which are clearly describable as enhanced social behavior (Beck, Kanto, & Gelineau, 1963; Gruver, 1971; Holzberg, Knapp, & Turner, 1967; Umbarger, Dalsimer, Morrison, & Breggin, 1962).

Posttesting was conducted following completion of these several interventions. Two sets of systematic observations were made of patient social behavior. The first, Standard Observation, involved bringing each patient individually into the TV studio which, for postmeasurement purposes, had been furnished with tables, chairs, silverware, etc.—to simulate the hospital's dining hall. The patient was told he and a helper would "go through a make-believe meal," and that the patient "should do whatever he thought best in each situation which would occur." A series of simulated situations or tasks were then initiated by the investigator and the helper (accomplice), such as waiting on the food line, getting one's food, sitting at an already occupied table, the spilling of food, and so forth. The patient's responses to each situation were observed through a one-way mirror and rated for the presence and absence of both situation-specific appropriate responses (e.g., excusing oneself if appropriately passing someone on line; sitting at an unoccupied table; acknowledging others at table, etc.) and more generally appropriate social responses (e.g., eye contact, smiling, initiating and responding to conversation, etc.).

Each patient's mealtime social behavior was also observed in the hospital dining hall. Naturalistic Observations involved the observation of the first 15 minutes of one randomly chosen meal for each participating patient. Raters recorded, at 30-second intervals, the presence or absence of the following behaviors:

1. Talks on line;
2. Sits at occupied table;
3. Acknowledges others as he sits down;
4. Puts napkin in lap;
5. Initiates conversation at table;
6. Responds to conversation;
7. Talks ten consecutive seconds;
8. Smiles;
9. Gestures;
10. Eye contact;
11. Uses napkin correctly before leaving; and
12. Acknowledges others when leaving.

The final study measure was a global rating form, cast in Semantic Differential format, completed by all naturalistic observers on the dimensions: (1) general social skills, (2) interaction with others, and (3) social impact on others.

Results and Discussion

The major findings of this investigation are presented in Table 3.2. As this table indicates, several significant findings emerged between treatment conditions. As a group, they largely confirm the major results of our earlier attempt to enhance social interaction behaviors. Social behaviors specific to a mealtime context and more generally applicable social behaviors were both enhanced by Structured Learning participation. While the usefulness of Structured Learning for these purposes thus appears further supported, no consistent evidence is apparent in these results to suggest the relative superiority of any of the three implementations of Structured Learning. That is, as operationalized, transfer training seems to have added only relatively little to the impact of the five-week Structured Learning Program. It is also generally true of our findings that seven weeks of Structured Learning participation (5 + 2) yielded no greater skill enhancement than did participation for five weeks. All three Structured Learning conditions, however, yielded consistent and at times considerable increments in social interaction behaviors which were significantly greater than those following from companion control and no treatment control conditions. The effects of Structured Learning, therefore, appear to be attributable to factors beyond the interpersonal attention inherent in its procedures. Such interpersonal attention, in the form of the companion control condition, yielded essentially no effects on our criteria beyond no treatment participation.

Table 3.2. Analyses of Variance (F Values) and t Tests for Social Interaction.

Measure	Source[a]	
Standard Observation		
1. Excuses self on line (F = 4.51**)	SL+TT	> COMP
	SL+C	> COMP
	SL+N	> COMP
2. Sits at occupied table (F = 2.39*)	SL+TT	> COMP
	SL+N	> COMP
3. Acknowledges others when sitting down (F = 3.48*)	SL+TT	> COMP
4. Smiles (F = 2.78*)	SL+TT	> SL+N
5. Proper use of napkin (F = 2.96*)	SL+TT	> COMP
6. Acknowledges others when leaving (F = 2.78*)	SL+TT	> COMP
	SL+C	> COMP
Naturalistic Observation		
1. Talking to others on line (F = 2.70*)	SL+TT	> SL+N
	SL+C	> NTR
	SL+N	> COMP
	SL+N	> NTR
2. Sits at occupied table (F = 3.40*)	SL+TT	> COMP
3. Initiates conversation (F = 3.85**)	SL+TT	> SL+C
	SL+TT	> SL+N
	SL+C	> COMP
	SL+C	> NTR
	SL+N	> COMP
	SL+N	> NTR
4. Responds to conversation (F = 5.00**)	SL+TT	> NTR
	SL+C	> NTR
	SL+N	> NTR
	SL+N	> COMP
	COMPT	> NTR
5. Smiles (F = 2.42*)	SL+N	> NTR
	SL+N	> COMP
	SL+N	> NTR

(Continued on page 36)

Table 3.2. (Continued).

Measure	Source[a]	
6. Gestures (F = 2.35*)	SL+N	> COMP
	SL+N	> NTR
7. Acknowledges others when leaving (F = 2.89*)	SL+C	> COMP
	SL+C	> NTR
Social Behavior Ratings		
1. General social skills		
2. Interaction with others (F = 2.07*)	SL+TT	> NTR
	SL+C	> NTR
	SL+N	> NTR
	COMP	> NTR
3. Social impact upon others (F = 2.51*)	SL+TT	> NTR
	SL+C	> NTR
	SL+N	> NTR
	COMP	> NTR

[a] Source key: SL+TT—Structured Learning (5 weeks) + transfer training (2 weeks); SL+C—Structured Learning (5 weeks) + Structured Learning (2 weeks); SL+N—Structured Learning (5 weeks); COMP—Companion control (5 weeks); NTR—No treatment control.
*p < .05
**p < .01

STUDY 3. EFFECTS OF OVERLEARNING AND PRETRAINING STRUCTURING (LOPEZ, 1980)

Consistent with the overall goals of our research program, the present study also had transfer enhancement as a focal concern. As will be seen clearly in subsequent chapters, the several Structured Learning studies conducted with diverse trainees in the years between the Gutride et al. studies described above and those we report in the remainder of this chapter had firmly established two conclusions. The first was that skill *acquisition* was a reliable consequent of trainee participation in Structured Learning. The second was that skill *transfer* was a more elusive outcome, obtained at some times but not at others, seemingly in large part as a function of how well study procedures had incorporated tecniques explicitly designed to enhance transfer. In the present study, overlearning was the potential transfer enhancer examined.

Transfer of training has been shown in laboratory and real-life contexts to be enhanced by overlearning procedures, which function to maximize response availability. The likelihood that a response will be available is very clearly a function of its prior usage. We repeat and repeat foreign-language phrases we are trying to remember, we insist that our children practice playing the piano for an hour per day, and we devote considerable time practicing to make a golf swing smooth and "automatic." These are simply expressions of the overlearning notion, that is, the more we have practiced (especially correct) responses, the easier it will be to call them forth in later contexts or at later times. We need not rely solely here on everyday experience. It has been well established empirically that, other things being equal, the response that has been emitted most frequently in the past is quite likely to be emitted on subsequent occasions. This finding derives from studies of the frequency of evocation hypothesis (Underwood & Schulz, 1960), the spew hypothesis (Underwood & Schulz, 1960), preliminary response pre-training (Atwater, 1953; Cantor, 1955; Gagne & Foster, 1949) and overlearning (Mandler, 1954; Mandler & Heinemann, 1956). In all of these related research domains, real-life or laboratory-induced prior familiarization with given responses increased the likelihood of their occurrence on later trials. Mandler (1954) summarizes much of this research as it bears upon transfer by noting that "learning to make an old response to a new stimulus showed increasing positive transfer as degree of original training was increased" (p. 412). Mandler's own studies in this domain, that is, studies of overlearning, are especially relevant to our present theme, for it is not sheer practice of attempts at effective behaviors which we feel is of most benefit to the transfer needs of the skill training trainee. As will be seen, it is practice of successful attempts.

Overlearning is a procedure whereby learning is extended over more trials than are necessary merely to produce initial changes in the individual's behavior. In all too many instances of near-successful intervention, one or two successes at a given task are taken as evidence to move on to the next task, or the next level of the original task. To maximize maintenance and transfer via response availability, and in particular from the perspective of research on overlearning, moving on after a success or two is a training technique error. Mandler's (1954) subjects were trained on the study task until they were able to perform it without error either 0, 10, 30, 50, or 100 consecutive times. As noted earlier, transfer varied with the degree of original learning. To maximize transfer in skill training via this principle, the guiding rule should not be practice makes perfect (implying simply practice until one gets it right, and then move on), but practice *of* perfect (implying numerous overlearning trials of correct responses *after* the initial success).

Procedure

Participants in this investigation were 70 persons residing in a state mental hospital who volunteered to participate following their selection into a pool of potential trainees by an experimenter-staff panel screening for low levels of social interaction skills. The mean age of the trainees was 65.5 years, and the mean length of institutionalization was 20.7 years. There were 45 females and 25 males, most of whom were from lower socioeconomic levels. Ten trainees were randomly assigned to each of the six experimental conditions and to the control condition. The six experimental conditions included three groups who received pretraining training (described below) and either high, medium, or low overlearning, and three more groups who received either high, medium, or low overlearning without pretraining training.

Modeling vignettes. Six modeling vignettes on audiotape were developed. Since the skill to be taught was *Expressing appreciation*, each vignette concerned a situation in which one person performed a favor for another person who expressed his or her appreciation by following three behavioral steps:
1. Clearly describe to other people what they did for you that deserves appreciation.
2. Tell other people why you appreciate what they did.
3. Ask other people if there is anything you can do for them.

Dependent measures. The following dependent measures were developed and utilized:

1. Direct Test. This measure, given both before and after the Structured Learning training, consisted of the first parts of the six audiotaped modeling vignettes used during training. For each of the six items, a situation was briefly described, and the trainee was asked to say aloud what he or she would say in that situation. Trainees' responses were tape recorded. Responses on this measure and on the Minimal Transfer and the Role Play tests were rated by independent raters on a four-point scale for quality of skill performance. Interrater reliabilities were .86 and .90 for the two pairs of raters involved.

2. Minimal Generalization Test. New vignettes, similar to those presented during training but previously unfamiliar to the trainees, comprised this measure; they were given only as a posttest. As with the Direct test, trainees were asked to respond to six situations presented on audiotape as if they themselves were in the situations. All responses were tape recorded.

3. Extended Generalization Test. Each trainee was asked to interact individually with a psychiatric aide in a prestructured role-play situation as if it were really happening. This situation was similar to those on the Minimal Generalization test, except that it was more complex and involved face-to-face interaction with a person not associated with the training. The interaction was tape recorded.

4. Observation measure. A staff member was assigned to work closely with each resident at the institution. These staff members, blind to the purpose of the study, were asked to keep a five-day record of each trainee's number of "skill performances" on the unit during the week following the training. Skill performances for this measure were defined as any one or any combination of the three behavioral steps comprising the skill.

Pretesting. For possible covariance analysis usage, the following measures were administered to all trainees during the two weeks prior to the beginning of training: Cornell Medical Index Cardiovascular Scale, Mini-Mental State, STAI (A-State), and the Direct test.

Pretraining structuring. All trainees attended a session of their small training groups prior to the beginning of Structured Learning proper. Half of these subjects received pretraining structuring, whereas the other half did not. It was our exploratory suspicion that the additional structure provided by this pretraining procedure might enhance the subsequent level of trainee skill acquisition and transfer. For groups receiving pretraining structuring, this session included information on trainer and trainee roles, discussion of how the skills to be taught would help in the real world, and a detailed description of the Structured Learning procedure, emphasizing its essentially supportive atmosphere and the many ways risk was minimized. Trainees were encouraged to ask questions and to talk about other times they had spoken or otherwise participated in groups. For groups not receiving pretraining structuring, this session consisted of discussions of trainer and trainee schedules, plus announcements of the time and length of training sessions. The pretraining session was 40 minutes long for all groups.

Structured Learning and overlearning. Training involved 12 experimental groups consisting of two trainers and five trainees per group. Each experimental condition was composed of two of these groups and therefore included ten subjects and at least three different trainers. All groups followed basic Structural Learning procedures to learn the skill of expressing appreciation. (See Appendix A, Structured Learning Trainer's Manual for Adult Trainees.) Groups differed only in the amount of overlearning incorporated into the training, as may be seen in the following description of training.

After a brief introduction to Structured Learning, cards were handed out on which the three behavioral steps that comprised the skill were written. The first modeling vignette on audiotape was played, and the trainers focused group attention and discussion on each behavioral step and on the outcome of the vignette. All vignettes depicted correct portrayals of the skill with a positive outcome for the person using the skill. The second session began with a brief recapitulation of what had transpired during the previous session, and then another audiotaped modeling vignette was played. Again, discussion focused on the behavioral steps and their positive consequences.

After discussion of the second vignette, role playing was introduced. In all experimental groups, each trainee role-played the skill correctly at least once. Trainees were encouraged to devise their own situations and to furnish their own dialogue. Social reinforcement, positive feedback, and prompting were used liberally to encourage and to guide correct performance of the skill.

Between the role playing of various trainees, the remaining four modeling vignettes were played as good examples of the skill.

For the groups receiving high overlearning, Structured Learning ended when each trainee had correctly role-played three times. In the medium-overlearning groups, each trainee correctly role-played twice; for the low-overlearning groups, each trainee correctly role-played once. It should be noted that trainees had opportunity to overlearn not only during their own role playing but also while observing the role playing and reinforcement of others. The high-, medium-, and low-overlearning groups met for eight, six, and four sessions, respectively. These figures do not include the one pre-Structured Learning session for each group. All sessions lasted 40 minutes and were completed during the same three-week period.

Attention/brief instruction control group. As in each experimental condition, two groups of five trainees with two trainers comprised the control condition. These two groups each met for a total of nine 40-minute sessions during the three weeks that Structured Learning training was going on. This equaled the number of sessions of the longest experimental groups. Control group subjects and trainers discussed a variety of neutral topics, including the weather and the food at the institution. All pretests and posttests for these subjects were identical to those administered to experimental subjects, with one exception. Immediately prior to posttesting, control subjects were told both the skill being tested and the behavioral steps they needed to follow to enact the skill correctly, i.e., they were given brief instructions.

Posttesting. During the week following the completion of Structured Learning, all subjects were given the Direct Test, the Minimal Generalization Test, and the Extended Generalization Test. The observation measure was also completed during this week.

Results and Discussion

It was expected that trainees from each treatment condition would score higher on the dependent measures than would the attention/brief instruction control trainees. Dunnett's test (Kirk, 1968) for the comparison of control group means with treatment group means was used for all comparisons. On the Direct Test, as expected, the results of comparisons on pretest means indicated that differences between the presence or absence of pretraining structuring and the high, medium, or low levels of overlearning were not significantly different ($p < .05$) than the control group mean. For posttest comparisons, representing our measure of skill acquisition, Dunnett's statistic (t_D) was significant for the pretraining structuring analysis, $t_D = 3.45$, $p < .01$, and no pretraining structuring analysis, $t_D = 3.49$, $p < .01$, as predicted. Significant differences were also found in posttest comparisons on the Direct Test between the medium overlearning condition, $t_D = 4.06$, p $<$ .01, and the low-overlearning condition, $t_D = 3.77$, p $<$ .01, and the control condition. The comparison, however, for the high-overlearning group did not achieve significance.

For the Minimal Transfer Test, given on posttesting only, Dunnett's tests verified that comparisons between control trainees, trainees receiving pretraining structuring, $t_D(4,58) = 3.34$, p $<$ .01, and those not receiving pretraining structuring, $t_D(4,58) = 3.38$, p $<$ .01, were significantly different. Also as predicted, statistics computed for differences between controls and high overlearning trainees, $t_D(3,58) = 2.22$, p $<$ .05, medium overlearning trainees, $t_D(3,58) = 3.91$, p $<$ .01 and low overlearning trainees, $t_D(3,58) = 3.28$, p $<$ .01, were significant.

For the Extended Generalization Test, Dunnett's comparisons between control group trainees and those who received and did not receive pretraining structuring failed to achieve significance. Comparisons involving controls and high and low overlearning groups were also nonsignificant. A significant difference, however, was found between medium overlearning trainees and controls, $t_D(3,58) = 3.33$, p $<$ .01. Dunnett's comparisons for the observation measure revealed no significant differences between any treatment condition and the control condition.

In considering these several findings, we wish to revisit the two dependent variable themes which emerged in our consideration of the Gutride et al. (1973, 1974) investigations, namely skill acquisition and skill transfer. As in these earlier studies, when provided with the concrete, repetitive, structured, stepwise learning sequence which constitutes Structured Learning, trainees of diverse types acquire the skill being taught at levels which significantly exceed that demonstrated by control group trainees. When training procedures also incorporate explicit implementation of transfer enhancement techniques, significant increments in skill transfer indeed occur. On the Minimal Transfer Test, all overlearning conditions demonstrated significantly greater transfer than controls; on the (more real-life) Extended Generalization Test, only medium overlearning trainees did so, and on the (most real-life) Observation test, no overlearning conditions significantly exceeded controls. In combination, we view these findings as a partial, but clearly not unimportant demonstration of transfer enhancement. Overlearning procedures do in fact appear to increase the likelihood of subsequent skill transfer.

It is of interest to speculate about the bases for absence of significant transfer enhancement on the Extended Generalization Test for high overlearning trainees. If medium overlearning enhances transfer, shouldn't high overlearning enhance it even further? Craig, Sternthal, and Olshan (1972) and Hulicka and Weiss (1965) examined the effects of varying degrees of overlearning on retention, the former with young subjects and the latter with both young and old persons. The conclusions reached by the two sets of authors regarding overlearning were very similar. Craig et al. suggested that high overlearning generated hostility that detracted from performance. Medium levels of overlearning led to greater retention than did high or low amounts. Hulicka and Weiss wrote that overlearning appeared to function as a form of punishment for their elderly subjects. In light of this evidence, the results of the present study concerning the high overlearning group may be construed as being at least partially due to hostility or other negative affects induced by the repetitiveness of the training. Training interventions, it may be, must seek to incorporate optimal and not necessarily maximal levels of trainee overlearning.

Pretraining structuring, which is essentially an effort on our part to increase the comprehension of detail about Structured Learning and participation in it, as well as to reassure trainees about its low threat value, yielded a Minimal Transfer effect only. Hoehn-Saric, Frank, Imber, Nash, Stone, & Battle (1964) have shown analogous procedures to be useful when offered prior to traditional, insight-oriented psychotherapies, all of which are considerably less inherently structured than is Structured Learning. The high level of structure already incorporated into Structured Learning is our explanation for the modest dependent variable impact of the pretraining structuring procedures.

STUDY 4. PRESCRIPTIVE CORRELATES OF SKILL ACQUISITION AND TRANSFER (HOYER, LOPEZ, & GOLDSTEIN, 1981)

Researchers and change agents concerned with the effectiveness of their interventions must ultimately focus their attention not only upon questions of transfer and maintenance, but also on a different matter of equal significance in determining overall training outcome. We refer here to prescriptiveness. As we have argued at length elsewhere (Goldstein & Stein, 1976; Goldstein, 1978), training, treatment, and educational interventions are likely to be maximally effective to the degree that trainer × trainee × intervention characteristics are optimally matched. This matching, tailored, differential treatments or prescriptive intervention strategy is certainly not original with us. Hunt (1971), Kiesler (1969), Magaro (1969), Palmer (1978) and Klett & Mosley (1963) are among the several others who have articulated and, in at least a few instances, obtained evidence in support of this viewpoint. Though its potential payoff seems likely to be high, it is not an easy research strategy to implement fully. Potentially active ingredients, that is, those characteristics of the intervention process and its participants which may relate to effectiveness of outcome, must be identified. Various combinations of such ingredients, i.e., trainer × trainee × intervention matches must be constituted and, usually by means of fairly expensive (in time, effort, etc.) factorial designs, examined for their outcome efficacy. We have described this prescriptive research process in detail elsewhere (Goldstein & Stein, 1976) and have sought to reflect both its spirit and substance throughout the Structured Learning research program described in this book. The investigation we now wish to describe exemplifies the first facet of this approach, the effort to identify participant characteristics potentially relevant to intervention outcome.

Our intervention is Structured Learning, and our specific prescriptive goal in this investigation was to identify trainee characteristics predictive of positive skill acquisition and transfer outcomes. It was hypothesized that a trainee's capacity to learn and to remember would be an important predictor of that individual's degree of benefit from this skill-training program. Recently, Erickson and Scott (1977) suggested that three factors are important in the assessment of learning and memory in clinical populations. These writers indicated that tests which take into account neurophysiological status, the ability to learn new material (e.g., paired-associated acquisition), and the ability to use already acquired information (e.g., mental status) can be used together to provide a thorough clinical appraisal of memory. Such indices were included in the present study along with measures of depression, trait anxiety, and morale. Previous research has supported these personality variables as common hindrances to learning and memory by older persons (Botwinick, 1973) which, as will be seen, constituted the trainee sample in the present investigation.

Procedure

Trainees were 60 residents of a state mental hospital for elderly individuals. Their mean age was 66.8 years, their mean length of hospitalization was approxmately 20 years. Kahn et al's (1980) Mental Status Questionnaire indicated that trainees were generally low functioning and moderately confused (mean Kahn score + 11.12). There were 12 Structured Learning groups, each composed of two trainers and five trainees. All trainees were individually pre- and posttested. Pretest measures included the following: (a) Direct Test, consisting of six audiotaped vignettes describing situations in which the skill taught would be appropriate to which the trainee was asked to respond; (b) Kahn et al's Mental Status Questionnaire (1980); (c) a Digit Symbol Substitution task (Wechsler, 1958); (d) a Paired-Association task (Inglis, 1959); (e) Zung's Depression Self-Rating Scale (1965); (f) the Philadelphia Geriatric Center Morale Scale (Lawton, 1975); and (g) Spielberger's State-Trait Anxiety Inventory (A-trait only) (1970). Also prior to training, a staff member familiar with the patient completed the Geriatric Rating Scale

(Plutchik et al., 1970) which concerned each subject's ward behavior. All participants received Structured Learning for the skill, "Expressing a complaint." Groups met five times over a two-week period for 40 minutes per session. Posttests were administered within a week after the end of training and included: (a) Direct Test, given again; (b) Minimal Generalization Test, consisting of six audiotaped vignettes similar to those on the Direct Test, but never heard by the trainee before; and (c) Extended Generalization Test, an additional measure of transfer of training in which the subject acted out live with another person what he would do in a situation in which the appropriate response was to express a complaint.

Results and Discussion

Hierarchical multiple regression analyses were performed on the dependent measures of Direct Posttest, Minimal Generalization Test, and Extended Generalization Test. The initial predictors for the regression equations were the patients' scores on Paired Associates, Mental Status, Digit Symbol, Direct Pretest, Trait Anxiety, Geriatric Rating Scale, and Zung Depression Inventory. For the Direct Posttest measure, the best predictor was Mental Status which alone accounted for 23 percent of the variance in Direct Posttest scores. Furthermore, Mental Status alone was as good a predictor as the full model, including all predictors. The best predictive model for the Minimal Generalization Test consisted of the Mental Status, Trait Anxiety (inversely), and Direct Pretest measures, each of which accounted for 18, 15, and 7 percent of the unique variance, respectively. None of these accounted for a significant portion of the variance on the Extended Generalization measure.

It is a mere scratch-the-surface beginning to point to Mental Status and Trait Anxiety as prescriptively useful in selecting (at least elderly) trainees for participation in Structured Learning. But a beginning it is. It is with an accumulation of such findings that reliably effective prescriptive matching will become possible. The next investigation we report, conducted by colleagues not part of our research group, takes us a significant step further in this direction.

STUDY 5. PRESCRIPTIVE IMPLICATIONS OF TYPE AND LEVEL OF PSYCHOPATHOLOGY (MAGARO & WEST, 1981)

Each of the investigations we have examined thus far sought to evaluate the effectiveness for *single* skill acquisition and transfer of a brief sequence (one to three sessions) of Structured Learning. Yet, as we indicated earlier (see page 17, in 1976 we published a library of modeling audiotapes depicting the expert enactment of 59 separate skills (Goldstein, Sprafkin, & Gershaw, 1976). While research evaluations focusing upon a single skill are necessary preliminary studies, it is ultimately necessary to conduct research evaluating the efficacy of Structured Learning as a means of teaching a full array of skills, in order that we come closer to ascertaining its potential usefulness in preparing trainees for actual community functioning. In addition to their explicit concern with prescriptiveness, Magaro & West (1981) provide this efficacy test across the full skill series.

Procedure

In this investigation, 39 long-term patients in a state mental hospital were constituted into eight Structured Learning groups which met four times a week for a six-month period. Each group's planned curriculum during this period covered the first 20 skills listed in chapter 2 (see p. 18). A test battery was administered to each trainee before their Structured Learning participation began, and after three and six months. This battery consisted of the Structured Learning Skill Survey (Goldstein et al., 1976), the Psychiatric Inpatient Profile (Lorr & Vestre, 1968),[2] the Social Participation Scale (Sanders, Smith, & Weinman, 1967), and the FIRO-B (Schutz, 1957).[3]

Results and Discussion

Data analysis for this investigation proceeded by means of t test comparisons made between pretest and three-month and six-month test scores across all study measures. The Structured Learning Skill Survey showed significant increases in total skill competence between pretest and three-month ($t = 2.09$, df $= 38$, $p < .01$) and pretest and six-month ($t = 5.01$, df $= 38$, $p < .01$) levels. Analysis of Social Participation Scale scores (an on-the-ward behavioral measure of skill transfer) also yielded significant increases from pretest to three months ($t = 4.18$, df $= 38$, $p < .01$). No significant changes occurred on the FIRO-B. Significant change over the training period also occurred on all Psychiatric Inpatient Profile psychopathology scales except Seclusiveness, Care Needed, and Disorientation.

Of special prescriptive significance was the finding that the trainees who improved most across the Psychiatric Inpatient Profile scales as well as on both the Structured Learning Skill Survey and the Social Participation Scale

---

2. This instrument, based on a structured interview conducted with each patient, yields the scores: Excitement, Hostile Belligerence, Paranoid Projection, Anxious Depression, Retardation, Seclusiveness, Care Needed, Psychotic Disorganization, Grandiosity, Perceptual Disorganization, Depressive Mood, and Disorientation.

3. The latter two measures were administered at pretest and three-months only.

were those who were at least at a medium level on pretesting, and often high on the Psychiatric Inpatient Profile scales: (1) Paranoid Projection, (2) Psychotic Disorganization, and/or (3) Depressive Mood. It is not clear at this early stage of implementation of the prescriptive strategy why these particular psychopathology variables functioned so well as prescriptive markers, and their success in this regard certainly requires replication. But Magaro and West have taken at least a few important strides forward here in the realm of active ingredient identification, and it is hoped that their work will serve as a model of future investigative strategy and implementation.

The five investigations of Structured Learning we have examined in this chapter—each involving mostly long-term mental hospital patients as trainees—combine to offer a beginning picture of Structured Learning as an intervention which (1) reliably yields skill acquisition effects; (2) yields skill transfer effects in rough proportion to the incorporation into its techniques of explicit transfer enhancement procedures; and (3) is likely to be more effective on both types of outcome criteria when implemented prescriptively. We will pursue these acquisition, transfer, and prescriptiveness themes further, along with concerns we have not yet addressed, as we now turn to investigations of Structured Learning involving other types of trainee populations.

Chapter 4
Adolescent Trainees

In the late 1970s, our research and clinical interest expanded beyond the needs of adult mental hospital residents to include a rather different type of trainee population, the skill-deficient adolescent. Unchanged in this shift was our belief in and commitment to a behavior-deficit model underlying our intervention approach, and our desire to apply this model to trainee populations hitherto benefiting rather poorly from other available interventions.

How can skill-deficient youngsters best be described? A number of diverse attempts have been undertaken to develop classification systems which adequately describe children and adolescents exhibiting behavior disorders. Prior to 1966, 24 such systems had been proposed (Group for the Advancement of Psychiatry, 1966). Unfortunately, most of these systems essentially lacked evidence of sufficient reliability or evidence that they related meaningfully to decisions about the types of remedial treatment recommended. The Group for the Advancement of Psychiatry's (1966) own classification system made some beginning strides at dealing with these chronic deficiencies, but it was still inadequate. A truly useful system of classifying behavior disorders did not appear until multivariate statistical techniques and sophisticated computer technology were developed. With this new technology, recent investigators have been able to make use of very diverse types of information drawn from a broad range of behaviorally disordered adolescents. In this regard, Quay, Peterson, and their colleagues have used observational behavior ratings by teachers, parents, clinic staff, and correctional workers; case history materials; the responses of adolescents themselves to personality testing, and other types of information—all obtained from and about adolescents in public schools, child guidance clinics, institutions for delinquents, and mental hospitals. By using multivariate statistical techniques on these bodies of information, a three-category classification pattern emerged. These three categories are aggression, withdrawal, and immaturity, and they account for the vast majority of behaviors typically included under the term behavior disorders. Although the particular classification system proposed by Quay and his coworkers will be described in this chapter, it is important to note that the same patterns found by these researchers have emerged consistently in other equally sophisticated classification efforts (Achenbach, 1966; Achenbach & Edelbrock, 1978; Brady, 1970; Hewitt & Jenkins, 1946; Patterson & Anderson, 1964; Peterson, Quay, & Tiffany, 1961; Ross, Lacey, & Parton, 1965).

Aggression

Quay (1966) comments:

> Almost without exception multivariate statistical studies of problem behaviors
> . . . reveal the presence of a pattern involving aggressive behavior, both ver-
> bal and physical, associated with poor interpersonal relationships with both
> adults and peers. This pattern has received a variety of labels: e.g., unsocialized
> aggressive (Hewitt & Jenkins, 1946); conduct problem (Peterson et al., 1961;
> Quay & Quay, 1965); aggressive (Patterson & Anderson, 1964); unsocialized
> psychopath (Quay, 1964); psychopathic delinquency (Peterson, Quay, & Cam-
> eron, 1959); antisocial aggressiveness and sadistic aggressiveness (Dreger et
> al., 1964); and externalizing (Achenbach, 1966). [P. 9.]

This classification reflects such specific behaviors as fighting, disruptiveness, destructiveness, profanity, irritability, quarrelsomeness, defiance of authority, irresponsibility, high levels of attention-seeking behavior, and low
levels of guilt feelings. In Quay's research, youngsters in this category typically answer affirmatively to such questionnaire items as:

- I do what I want to whether anybody likes it or not.
- The only way to settle anything is to lick the guy.
- If you don't have enough to live on, it's OK to steal.
- It's dumb to trust other people.
- I'm too tough a guy to get along with most kids.

Quay (1966) observes that the essence of this pattern is an active antisocial
aggressiveness that inevitably results in conflict with parents, peers, and
social institutions. Children and adolescents whose behavior reflects this
pattern in the extreme are likely to be in such difficulty as to be involved in
the courts and institutions for delinquents.

Withdrawal

The behavior disorder pattern characterized by withdrawal has been variously labeled overinhibited (Hewitt & Jenkins, 1946), personality problem (Peterson et al., 1961), disturbed neurotic (Quay, 1964), internalizing (Achenbach, 1966), and withdrawn (Patterson & Anderson, 1964; Ross, Lacey, &
Parton, 1965). Quay (1966) describes this pattern further:

> These behaviors, attitudes, and feelings clearly involve a different pattern of
> social interaction than do those comprising conduct disorder; they generally
> imply withdrawal instead of attack. In marked contrast to the characteristics of
> conduct disorder are such traits as feelings of distress, fear, anxiety, physical

complaints, and open and expressed unhappiness. It is within this pattern that the child who is clinically labeled as an anxiety neurotic or as phobic will be found. [P. 11.]

The behavior disorder pattern characterized by withdrawal is also often marked by depression, feelings of inferiority, self-consciousness, shyness, anxiety, hypersensitivity, seclusiveness, and timidity.

Immaturity

Immaturity, the third prominent class of adolescent behavior disorders, has been identified in samples of adolescents studied in public schools, child guidance clinics, and institutions for delinquents. Behaviors included in the immaturity pattern include short attention span, clumsiness, preference for younger playmates, passivity, daydreaming, and incompetence. This pattern represents a persistence of behaviors that were largely age-appropriate earlier in the youngster's development, but which have become inappropriate in view of his current age and society's expectations of the adolescent.

Quay's (1966) reflections on the three patterns of behavior disorders are most relevant to our skill deficiency focus. He comments:

The characteristics of the three . . . patterns may all be said to be clearly maladaptive either from the social or individual viewpoint. Extremes of such behaviors are at variance with either the expectations of self, parents, or educational and other social institutions. . . . Each of the previous patterns also involves interpersonal alienation with peers, attack in the case of conduct disorders, withdrawal in the case of personality disorders, or lack of engagement in the case of immaturity. [Pp. 13–14.]

These descriptions of the aggressive, withdrawn, or immature adolescent focus on what each youngster does. But from a skill-deficiency viewpoint it is also profitable to examine what each youngster does not do. Thus, the aggressive adolescent often is not only proficient in fighting, disruptiveness, destructiveness, and similar antisocial skills, but may also be deficient in such prosocial skills as self-control, negotiation, asking permission, avoiding trouble with others, understanding the feelings of others, and dealing with someone else's anger. The withdrawn youngster, in an analogous manner, may lack proficiency in such prosocial skills as having a conversation, joining in, dealing with fear, decision making, dealing with being left out, responding to persuasion, and dealing with contradictory messages. This kind of youngster also lacks the skills relevant to expressing or receiving apologies, complaints, or instructions. The parallel skill deficiency pattern for the immature adolescent may typically involve a lack of competence in sharing, responding to teasing, responding to failure, dealing with group pressure, goal setting, and concentration. The prosocial skills listed here are a brief sampling of the target skills that form the major focus of our Structured Learning work with skill-deficient adolescents.

Developmental Hurdles

We have proposed that behaviorally disordered youngsters may be reliably categorized in terms of three major types. Each type may be described in terms of both the presence of a repertoire of dysfunctional and often antisocial behavior and of the absence of a repertoire of prosocial or developmentally appropriate behaviors. It is our belief that a training program oriented toward the explicit teaching of prosocial skills can remediate many of these skill deficits. Desirable, functional skills missing from an individual's behavior repertoire can be taught successfully. It is not, however, only the aggressive, withdrawn, or immature youngster who may benefit from such training. Many other adolescents who are less likely to come to the attention of school, clinic, or institution personnel can also benefit from skill training efforts. In *Adolescent Development and Life Tasks*, Manster (1977) describes the sequence of life tasks that all adolescents must master. In school, at work, in the community, with peers, family, and authority figures—in all of these settings the developing adolescent meets, must cope with, and master an increasingly complex series of personal and interpersonal life tasks. Love, sex, and peer relationships are likely to require social skills (e.g., having a conversation, listening, joining in), skills for dealing with feelings (e.g., dealing with fear, expressing affection, understanding the feelings of others), and skills useful for dealing with stress (e.g., dealing with embarrassment, preparing for a stressful conversation, responding to failure). School-related tasks demand proficiency at yet other skills, in particular, planning skills (e.g., goal setting, gathering information, decision making). School settings also require daily success at tasks involving both peers (e.g., dealing with group pressure) and authority figures (e.g., following instructions). Similarly, work settings are also multifaceted in their task demands and, hence, in their requisite skills, especially those requiring planning and stress management. For many youngsters, whether in school, at work, or elsewhere, the skill demands placed on them will frequently involve the ability to deal satisfactorily with aggression, either their own or someone else's. In these instances, skills to be mastered may include self-control, negotiation, and dealing with group pressure.

The developmental tasks we have described are not often easily mastered, and efforts to aid their progression appear to be worthwhile. It is in this sense that the "average" adolescent, experiencing the need for assistance over certain developmental hurdles, is also a potential target trainee for Structured Learning.

In a prescriptive sense, therefore, these four types of youngsters were viewed by us as particularly appropriate training targets for Structured Learning. The complete series of skills developed for these training purposes, is listed below and described in detail in our text, *Skillstreaming the Adolescent* (Goldstein, Sprafkin, Gershaw, & Klein, 1980).[1] In the present chapter, we wish to present and examine a series of Structured Learning investigations involving such trainees. As was the case for the adult trainee studies reported in the previous chapter, we sought here simultaneously to address concern with prescriptive implementation, skill acquisition, skill transfer, and other aspects of the skill enhancement process.

Series I.   Beginning Social Skills
           Skill   1. Listening
           Skill   2. Starting a conversation
           Skill   3. Having a conversation
           Skill   4. Asking a question
           Skill   5. Saying thank you
           Skill   6. Introducing yourself
           Skill   7. Introducing other people
           Skill   8. Giving a compliment
Series II. Advanced Social Skills
           Skill   9. Asking for help
           Skill 10. Joining in
           Skill 11. Giving instructions
           Skill 12. Following instructions
           Skill 13. Apologizing
           Skill 14. Convincing others
Series III. Skills for Dealing With Feelings
           Skill 15. Knowing your feelings
           Skill 16. Expressing your feelings
           Skill 17. Understanding the feelings of others
           Skill 18. Dealing with someone else's anger
           Skill 19. Expressing affection
           Skill 20. Dealing with fear
           Skill 21. Rewarding yourself
Series IV. Skill Alternatives to Aggression
           Skill 22. Asking permission
           Skill 23. Sharing something

---

1. In addition to these modeling display descriptions, this text provides a variety of other types of information of use in the prescriptive application of Structured Learning to adolescent trainees, e.g., trainer preparation, trainee selection and grouping, live modeling procedures, the behavioral steps for all adolescent skills, dealing with resistance, and a host of related utilization concerns.

Skill 24. Helping others
Skill 25. Negotiating
Skill 26. Using self-control
Skill 27. Standing up for your rights
Skill 28. Responding to teasing
Skill 29. Avoiding trouble with others
Skill 30. Keeping out of fights
Series V. Skills for Dealing With Stress
Skill 31. Making a complaint
Skill 32. Answering a complaint
Skill 33. Sportsmanship after the game
Skill 34. Dealing with embarrassment
Skill 35. Dealing with being left out
Skill 36. Standing up for a friend
Skill 37. Responding to persuasion
Skill 38. Responding to failure
Skill 39. Dealing with confusing messages
Skill 40. Dealing with an accusation
Skill 41. Getting ready for a difficult conversation
Skill 42. Dealing with group pressure
Series VI. Planning Skills
Skill 43. Deciding on something to do
Skill 44. Deciding what caused a problem
Skill 45. Setting a goal
Skill 46. Deciding on your abilities
Skill 47. Gathering information
Skill 48. Arranging problems by importance
Skill 49. Making a decision
Skill 50. Concentrating on a task

The long-term mental patient of concern to our earlier training and research efforts, while very often markedly deficient in psychological skills, was rarely viewed by us as blatantly resistive. He was deficient because he was untutored, unstimulated or, at worst, unmotivated. But the adolescents of concern to us here are a qualitatively different matter. In our view, their skill deficiencies are often a function of active (or passive) resistance, of intentional or less conscious desire to avoid. And beyond skill acquisition, the two populations diverge even more clearly. The newly trained adult mental patient discharged from hospital to family or friends is likely to find an interpersonal transfer environment which at best supports and encourages his newly learned skills; at worst it is indifferent to them. Rarely will he receive active *dis*couragement. But the adolescent, particularly the antisocial adolescent returning to his often antisocially oriented peer group, is likely to be met with active, nonsupportive, and even hostile responses to his attempted use of prosocial skills. It is our view, therefore, that both skill acquisition and, especially, skill transfer, will be particularly difficult to obtain among antisocial adolescent trainees, and thus our acquisition and transfer training efforts must be particularly energetic, creative, and prescriptive. It was in this spirit that the studies reported in this chapter were undertaken.

STUDY 6. SKILL ACQUISITION AND THE HELPER THERAPY PRINCIPLE (LITWACK, 1976)

In 1965, Riessman drew attention to what he termed the Helper Therapy Principle. Based upon his observations of such self-help groups as Alcoholics Anonymous, Synanon, and Recovery Incorporated, he sought to document the therapeutic-like effects upon individuals of serving in a helper role. In his view, transforming recipients of help into dispensers of help led to changes analogous to those experienced in successful counseling and psychotherapy. A large number of successful (and mostly anecdotal) demonstrations of Riessman's proposition appeared in the years which followed, including demonstrations with adolescent helper-helpees. Rosenbaum's (1973) Peer-Mediated Instruction and Vorrath and Brendtro's (1974) Positive Peer Culture are two prominent illustrations. Each involves the teaching by peers of both psychological and academic skills—in regular schools, residential treatment centers, juvenile detention centers, and like places—to the apparent skill enhancement advantage of the adolescent trainers involved. Other similar programs which have emerged include Cross-Age Helping, Each One Teach One, Learning With Partners, Tutorial Community, and Youth Tutoring Youth.

A number of other, largely anecdotal demonstrations of the Helper Therapy Principle have also focused upon the resistive, difficult to reach adolescent, i.e., those from a disadvantaged background, with behavior and academic problems (Thelen, 1969), "troublemakers who lack control" (Fleming, 1969), juvenile delinquents (Slack, 1960), and high school dropouts (Landrum and Martin, 1970). Improved overt behavior, attitude change, and enhanced academic performance are the typical purported outcomes of these interventions.

Why these apparent effects occur remains a matter of active speculation. Riessman (1965) speaks of self-persuasion through persuading others, as well as the enhanced attention and status of the helper role as the factors seemingly responsible for the changes indicated above. Skovholt (1974) suggests that the helper experience may lead to increased feelings of competence and a heightened sense of worth and self-esteem. Gartner, Kohler and Riessman (1971) point to decreased self-centeredness and a positive sense of accomplishment. Our view is somewhat less self-evaluative and rather more clearly functional. Serving as a helper or, as is of greater relevance to our own study, even anticipating that one will serve as a helper, is likely to have a motivational effect upon the individual. As Litwack (1976) suggests:

> There is an increased relevance of material. Students are learning the material, not because an outsider has determined it to be of value, but rather because there is a definite use for the skill. Students are provided with a more positive, meaningful, functional reason for participating and learning the skill. . . . The result is greater skill acquisition, and possibly more active participation and less therapeutic resistance. [Litwack, 1976, p. 62.]

In response to this motivation-enhancement reasoning, as well as a study by Fremouw and Harmatz (1975) in which "latent helpers" changed significantly more than control group students and nearly as much as actual helpers, the present study sought to test the effectiveness of what we termed "helper role structuring."

Helper role structuring, in general terms, was defined in this investigation as informing individuals that they would be given the opportunity to serve as helpers. Our study hypotheses were (1) that Structured Learning would be an effective means to skill acquisition and transfer in passive resistant adolescents, and (2) that such acquisition and transfer would be enhanced by the provision of helper role structuring. All skills are not equal in difficulty, personal relevance, and complexity, however, and we speculated on an exploratory basis that our procedures might function differentially such that a resistance-relevant skill (Following Instructions) might be learned at different levels than one not relevant to resistance (Expressing a Compliment). In the present study, both skills were taught via Structured Learning and their acquisition and transfer were compared.

Procedure

This investigation was conducted in a middle-sized (1,400), rural, public high school servicing a mostly lower-class to lower middle-class socioeconomic community. All ninth-grade teachers helped identify a pool of potential trainee participants in response to our request for a population of inactively or passively resistant students. Such students were further defined as those frequently failing to follow instructions, appearing inactive and even lethargic, slow to complete work or failing to do so, often seeming not to be paying attention, but one who is not belligerent or disruptive. We invited 78 such students nominated to participate, and 53 chose to do so. Parental permission to participate was then obtained for these 53 students.[2] The 37 males

---

2. This (1) nomination, (2) opportunity to volunteer, and (3) parental permission selection sequence was utilized in almost all of our adolescent and child Structured Learning investigations.

and 16 females thus included were randomly assigned to six experimental conditions, as depicted in Fig. 4.1.

Experimental conditions I, II, IV, and V each consisted of approximately nine students, trained within each condition in Structured Learning groups of four to five students each, i.e., two Structured Learning groups per condition. Training procedures followed those described in detail in the *Structured Learning Manual for Adolescents* (See Appendix B). Trainees in the Helper Role Structuring conditions (I and IV) were, in addition, told:

> You have all volunteered for this group. Other students have volunteered to be in other groups. This group is going to work on the skill of Following Instructions [Expressing a Compliment]. This is a valuable skill to know and be able to use. We all have trouble with Following Instructions [Expressing a Compliment], at times, and with certain people. In a few minutes, the other group leader will tell you how we are going to work on this skill. Another reason that we are teaching this skill is so that you can help us teach it to younger students. You will each be given the chance to volunteer to work with us and other students.

This helper role structuring induction was reiterated at various points throughout the Structured Learning procedures, e.g., the behavioral step breakdown of the skill was presented in part as "an easy way for you to teach this skill to other children," role playing was explained in part as "a good way to have the other children practice the skill," and feedback was in part described as a means to "help others improve and better learn the skill."

The behavioral steps for Following Instructions were:
1. Listen carefully while instructions are being given.
2. Give your reactions to the instructions.
3. Repeat the instructions to yourself.
4. Imagine yourself following the instructions, and then do it.

The modeling tape utilized in this investigation to depict this skill consisted of expert portrayal of these steps in the context of ten in-school situations in which a teacher or principal asks a student (the model) to follow given

	Structured Learning plus Helper Role Structuring	Structured Learning	Brief Instruction Control
Skill Relevant to Resistance	I	II	III
Skill Not Relevant to Resistance	IV	V	VI

Fig. 4.1. Experimental design for helper role structuring study.

instructions. An analogous modeling tape was utilized for Expressing a Compliment, a skill whose behavioral steps were:
1. Decide what it is about the other person that you want to compliment.
2. Decide whether the other person would like to hear this compliment.
3. Choose the right time and place to express the compliment.
4. Express the compliment in a sincere and friendly manner.

Students assigned to experimental conditions III and VI constituted Brief Instructions control groups for the two study skills. We implemented Brief Instructions controls in this and several other of our investigations in response to the possibility that what appears to be Structured Learning-induced skill acquisition in skill-deficient trainees may in fact be instructions and attention-induced skill performance in persons who already (pretraining) have the given skill(s) in their behavioral repertoires but who simply are not displaying the skills for lack of motivation. In such an event, Structured Learning would, in a sense, be taking credit for teaching something the person already knew, but wasn't motivated to enact. If experimental results should in fact indicate that persons receiving brief instructions perform as well on posttesting as those receiving Structured Learning, we must conclude that with that skill and those trainees, Structured Learning was not prescriptively appropriate. Brief Instructions trainees participated in the study's pretesting, received no Structured Learning, and then participated in the relevant posttesting—as part of which they were provided brief instructions detailing the skill's behavioral steps and the desirability of seeking to express these steps on the posttest they were about to take.

The testing sequence for all study participants included:
1. Direct Test (Pre). Participants met individually with the experimenter and were presented with a series of ten taped, in-school situations in which the skill relevant to their experimental condition would be an appropriate response, and asked to state in detail exactly what they would say and do if they were in that situation.[3] The following are examples of the stimulus situations employed in the dependent variable examination of the two study skills.
A. Following Instructions:
   (1) When you arrive late to class, your math teacher says, "Do the problems."
   (2) While waiting for the bus in your homeroom, the teacher asks you to straighten out the room.
   (3) During study hall, you are told to go to the library to look up some information.

---

3. These or the second set of ten situations, plus a model's expert portrayal of the behavioral steps of either Following Instructions or Expressing a Compliment, constituted the study's two modeling tapes.

B. Expressing a Compliment:
   (1) You are sitting near the end zone. A friend makes a good move and runs for a touchdown.
   (2) As you are on the way to class, you pass the bulletin board. You notice that a friend has gotten the lead part in the school play.
   (3) A friend drives by in a new car which you hadn't seen before. You really like the color and style.

2. Direct Test (Post). Following either Helper Role Structuring plus Structured Learning (I and IV), Structured Learning alone (II and V), or Brief Instructions (III and VI), the same ten stimulus situations used on the trainee's pretest and on his or her modeling tape were represented. Since the situations on the Direct Test (pre), the modeling tape, and the Direct Test (post) were the same for each skill, posttest scores controlled for pretest level are this (and other) study's measure of skill acquisition. It is a measure which seeks to learn whether the trainee can, at minimum, reproduce or closely match the skilled behavior he has just heard or seen modelled.

3. Minimal Generalization Test. This measure seeks to go beyond the matching response demands of the Direct Test and asks whether the trainee can generate skilled responses to new skill-relevant situations, ones he has never heard, seen, or been asked to respond to before. It is this quality of newness, or previous nonexposure which makes this a transfer measure; its portrayal of situations (like the Direct Test) on tape and not in a live, face-to-face format leads us to term this a *minimal* generalization measure.

4. Overt Passive Resistance. All training sessions were tape recorded and independently rated by two judges to discern the number of times in which Structured Learning group leaders presented actual situations in which trainees were expected to respond, e.g., questions, pregnant pauses, etc. Trainee reactions to these situations were also rated. Nonresponse, long pauses, or other behaviors causing the leader to requestion were classified as passive resistance.

Results and Discussion

A one-way analysis of variance on Direct Test (pre) scores across both skills and all experimental conditions revealed no significant differences prior to training (F (2,25) = 1.190 and F (2,22) = .120), respectively, for Following Instructions and Expressing a Compliment. Trainee Direct Test (post) minus Direct Test (pre) mean change scores were then determined, as indicated in Table 4.1.

One-way analyses of variance were conducted across these data, as indicated in Table 4.2.

Minimal Generalization Test results are presented in Tables 4.3. and 4.4. Table 4.3 reports mean scores by condition; Table 4.4 shows analysis of variance results across these scores.

Table 4.1. Mean Change in Skill Behavioral Steps.*

Source	Mean Change	S.D.
Following Instructions:		
Helper Role Structuring plus Structured Learning	28.89	2.16
Structured Learning alone	20.67	2.91
Brief Instructions	−.20	2.25
Expressing a Compliment:		
Helper Role Structuring plus Structured Learning	27.50	2.42
Structured Learning alone	19.13	2.81
Brief Instructions	−.22	2.05

* Trainee scores are a rating by independent judges of the presence of the skills behavioral steps in the trainees' responses to the stimulus situations. Since the Direct Test for each skill in this study consists of ten situations, and each skill consists of four behavioral steps, the maximum score possible for each skill is 40 and, for example, the mean change score of 28.89 in Condition I indicates that, on the average, trainees undergoing the procedures defining this experimental condition provide an average of 28.89 more correct behavioral steps on Direct Test (post) than they had on Direct Test (pre).

In response to these significant F tests, a series of orthogonal comparisons was conducted utilizing Dunn's procedure for multiple comparisons. The two Following Instructions training groups (I and II) gained significantly more through training than did the corresponding Brief Instructions group (III), i.e., $t(25) = -9.74$, $p < .05$. Similarly, for Expressing a Compliment, IV and V gained significantly more than VI, $t(22) = -10.49$, $p < .05$. Planned comparisons on the Minimal Generalization Test data also yielded significant findings. For both Following Instructions and Expressing a Compliment, Structured Learning with or without Helper Role Structuring each led to significantly more behavioral steps than did Brief Instructions, $t(25) = -8.23$, $p < .05$; $t(22) = -7.25$, $p < .05$ respectively. Thus, for this investigation, skill acquisition and (minimal) transfer results are straightforward. With passive resistive adolescents, Structured Learning induces significant

Table 4.2. Analyses of Variance on Pre-Post Change Scores.

Source	df	MS	F
Following Instructions:			
Treatments (between)	2	2157.47	51.052*
Error (within)	25	42.26	
Expressing a Compliment:			
Treatments (between)	2	1675.78	60.002*
Error (within)	22	27.93	

*$p < .01$

Table 4.3. Mean Scores on Minimal Generalization Test.

Source	Mean Change	S.D.
Following Instructions:		
Helper Role Structuring plus Structured Learning	13.11	1.85
Structured Learning alone	10.55	5.01
Brief Instructions	1.10	1.30
Expressing a Compliment:		
Helper Role Structuring plus Structured Learning	16.25	4.34
Structured Learning alone	9.87	3.33
Brief Instructions	3.78	1.62

gains in skill proficiency—in terms of both acquisition and (minimal) transfer—across both a resistance-relevant and a resistance-irrelevant skill.

Beyond this initial test of the skill training potency of Structured Learning with adolescents, it will be recalled that this investigation also sought to learn whether anticipation of functioning as a helper will further enhance this skill acquisition and transfer effect. Our results essentially demonstrate an affirmative answer to this question.

On Direct Test mean change scores, both Following Instructions (t (25) = -2.68, p $<$ .05) and Expressing a Compliment (t (22) = -3.17, p $<$ .05) show significantly greater skill acquisition for those Structured Learning trainees who anticipate serving as a helper than do those who do not. On our transfer measure, the Following Instructions (t (25) = -4.15, p $<$ .05), but not the Expressing a Compliment (t (22) = -1.63, p $>$ .05) trainees anticipating the helper role significantly exceed those who do not.

The potency of Helper Role Structuring as a means of potentiating skill transfer is shown further by our final study result. Analysis of trainee overt passive resistance during training indicated that those groups receiving Structured Learning alone (II and V) exhibited significantly more overt passive resistance than did trainees receiving both Structured Learning and Helper Role Structuring.

Table 4.4. Analyses of Variance on Minimal Generalization Test Scores.

Source	df	MS	F
Following Instructions:			
Treatments (between)	2	384.99	35.12*
Error (within)	25	10.96	
Expressing a Compliment:			
Treatment (between)	2	329.55	34.87*
Error (within)	22	9.45	

*p $<$ .01

Litwack's study has shown that the skill acquisition potency of Structured Learning prescriptively developed originally for certain adult populations also holds for a specified type of skill-deficient adolescent. Beyond acquisition, a modest transfer effect also emerged. In addition, not only does *receiving* Structured Learning matter; when the adolescent also expects to *dispense* it, to function himself as a Structured Learning trainer, even higher levels of skill acquisition and transfer result. In all, Litwack's study is an impressive initial demonstration of the impact of Structured Learning with a chronically difficult-to-reach trainee population. Our subsequent adolescent studies aimed at further progress in these directions.

STUDY 7. ENHANCEMENT OF PERSPECTIVE-TAKING SKILLS IN EGOCENTRIC ADOLESCENTS (TRIEF, 1977)

Piaget (1956) defined egocentrism as a perceptual "embeddedness in one's own point-of-view," the overcoming of which was a major developmental task of childhood. With age and certain developmental experiences, he held, certain perspective-taking skills largely supplanted egocentricity. Flavell and his coworkers (Flavell, Botkin, Fry, Wright, & Jarvis, 1968) and Feffer (1970) broadened the Piagetian construct in their focus upon social interaction and perspective taking in an interpersonal, rather than a perceptual realm. Their efforts were responsive to research demonstrating that poorly socialized youngsters are developmentally delayed in this process of egocentrism reduction and growth in interpersonal perspective taking. Trief (1977) speculated that this process might appropriately be construed as a skill deficiency–skill proficiency shift, a shift which might be responsive to a skill training intervention such as Structured Learning.

Enhancement in interpersonal perspective taking looms as a particularly worthwhile prescriptive goal for the types of skill-deficient youngsters described at the beginning of this chapter. Neale (1966) demonstrated that highly aggressive, poorly socialized youngsters evidence significantly more egocentric perception than do nonaggressive youngsters. Similarly, Simeonson (1973) found that three different samples of emotionally disturbed children were each significantly more egocentric than a comparison sample of nondisturbed youngsters. On yet different egocentricity measures, Chandler (1973) reported the same result for juvenile delinquents as compared with nondelinquent adolescent samples. Relevant to the present investigation, Chandler distinguished between two components of interpersonal perspective taking, namely (1) cognitive perspective taking—defined as the ability to anticipate how someone else understands and views a situation when that viewpoint is different from one's own, and (2) affective perspective taking—the ability to anticipate how someone else might feel in a situation when those feelings are different from one's own. The present investigation sought to examine the effectiveness of Structured Learning as a means of teaching cognitive and affective perspective taking, singly and in combination, to highly egocentric adolescents. Furthermore, in response to the work of Johnson (1967, 1971) dealing with the relationship between egocentrism and cooperation, we also sought to discern if heightened skill in taking the (cognitive and affective) perspective of others, would lead to increased levels of overtly cooperative behavior.

Procedure

Participants in this investigation were 58 adolescents living in a residential treatment center in the Northeastern United States. Their mean age was 16 years, 4 months; their age range 14.2 to 18.2. Fifty-two were males, six females. The 58 participants were those who accepted our invitation to participate from a larger pool of 82 youngsters screened by us, on a measure drawn from Chandler (1974), as highly egocentric. These youngsters were randomly assigned to the study's five experimental conditions, conditions arranged in a factorial design depicted in Fig. 4.2.

All study participants began their study involvement by taking the Direct Test (pre) developed for this investigation, for cognitive and affective perspective taking. As was true for the Direct Tests constructed for our other investigations, this one consisted of a series of stimulus situations relevant to the circumstances of study participants, presented via audiotape, to which an optimal response would be the study skill being taught—in this instance cognitive or affective perspective-taking. Examples of these stimulus situations included:

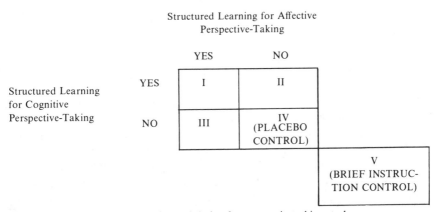

Fig. 4.2. Experimental design for perspective taking study.

A. Affective Direct Test:
  (1) *Narrator:* Your house mother has been doing a lot of things to help the citizens in your cottage before she's been able to relax and sit down. You want to ask her for help on your homework, but before you ask her you hear her say:
    Actor: Boy, I'm really tired. Everybody keeps asking me to do things for them. (*tired, annoyed*)
    Narrator: Look at her. What would you say?
  (2) *Narrator:* You're really happy about some good news that you got today. You want to tell your house parent about it so you just walk into his apartment, forgetting to knock. He says:
    Actor: What's the matter with you? Haven't you learned anything since you've been here? (*anger*)
    Narrator: Look at him. What would you say?
B. Cognitive Direct Test:
  (1) *Narrator:* At your house meeting, you've just heard that your house parents have asked another citizen to be the Big Brother (or Big Sister) for the new person in the cottage. You're angry, because you really wanted to be picked. Your house mother says:
    Actor: I'm sorry, but I've gotten bad reports from your employer, and you've been doing things around the house that you know you're not supposed to.
    Narrator: Look at her. What would you say?
  (2) *Narrator:* You and another citizen have been arguing and yelling at each other, and have started shoving each other around. Just then, your house parent comes in, and says:
    Actor: I'm going to have to write a case against you two for disorderly conduct. You know there's no fighting allowed around here.
    Narrator: Look at your house parent. What would you say?

Structured Learning groups of four to six trainees each were then constituted. The Cognitive Perspective Taking groups (II), The Affective Perspective-Taking groups (III), and the Placebo control groups (IV) each met for five 50-minute sessions. The groups receiving both cognitive and affective training (I) met for eight such sessions. As in our other studies, the specific procedures which constituted the Structured Learning sessions are those described in detail in the *Structured Learning Manual for Adolescents* (see Appendix B). The behavioral steps which comprised the two study skills were:

Cognitive Perspective-Taking[4]
1. Figure out what the other person thinks has happened by:
    a. Deciding what he saw.
    b. Deciding what he heard.
2. Decide if there is something he doesn't know about what happened.
3. Tell him you understand what he is thinking.
4. Tell him the new information.
Affective Perspective-Taking[5]
5. Figure out what the other person may be feeling by:
    a. Listening to what he has said, his words.
    b. Listening to his tone of voice.
    c. Looking at the expression on his face.
    d. Looking at his posture.
2. Tell him what you think he is feeling.

Since the several procedures which constitute Structured Learning combine in action to yield a high level of within-group, i.e., peer, interaction, it may be that such interaction per se, rather than the vicarious exposure of modeling, the behavior rehearsal of role playing, and the skill-relevant information provided by performance feedback is the source of trainee development of perspective-taking skill. To control for this possibility, the Placebo control condition (Condition IV) was implemented. Here, participants listened to modeling displays, role-played, and engaged in all other Structured Learning procedures, but focused on skills *not* likely to increase perspective taking. The Placebo control condition, therefore, provided interaction opportunity equivalent to that provided in the Structured Learning groups, but no direct perspective-taking skill training. The skills taught in this condition were those developed for Litwack's (1976) investigation, i.e., Following Instructions and Expressing a Compliment.

Experimental condition V, The Brief Instruction control condition, was constituted and implemented, as described in connection with its utilization in our earlier studies, to control for the possibility that the study skills were already a part of trainees' behavioral repertoires before the study commenced and were being elicited by motivational enhancement growing from participation in the training groups.

Following participation in training or control procedures each trainee was given (1) The Direct Test (post), (2) a Minimal Generalization Test, consisting of new taped stimulus situations to which the trainee had not been exposed in the Direct Tests or on the modeling displays, and (3) a behavioral measure of overt cooperation (and related behaviors described later), The

---

4. In structuring and conducting the Structured Learning groups, this skill was termed "Understanding Another Person's Point of View."
5. Labeled "Understanding Another Person's Feelings."

Interpersonal Situations Simulation Test, developed by us earlier for use in a related investigation (Berlin, 1976).

Results and Discussion

One-way analyses of variance across Direct Test (pre) scores revealed no significant between-group differences. Since IQ has been shown to be significantly negatively correlated with egocentrism (Chandler, 1973), and perspective taking has been theoretically conceived of as a developmentally based ability, IQ and age were employed as covariates in our data analyses. When significant effects emerged from these analyses of covariance, additional *a posteriori* comparisons of means were conducted using the Newman-Keuls method for unequal size samples (Winer, 1962).

Affective perspective taking. Analysis of covariance on the Direct Test (post) of affective perspective taking revealed a significant between-groups difference ($F = 8.78$, $p < .001$). Simple main effects analyses showed that the two training groups receiving Structured Learning for affective perspective taking (I and III) differed significantly from the two study control groups (IV and V). The two Structured Learning groups did not differ significantly from each other, and the same was true for the two control groups.

Although it may at first appear to duplicate the analysis we have just reported, ANCOVA across Direct Test (post) less Direct Test (pre) difference scores is not largely redundant in that it also reflects preintervention individual differences in target skill proficiency. Thus, this difference score analysis—employed in almost all of our investigations—permits comparison of trainees not only to other trainees, but also to themselves. This analysis yielded a significant overall effect ($F = 11.13$, $p < .001$). Newman-Keuls comparisons revealed that the two training groups (I and III) learned affective perspective taking to a significantly higher level than did the two control groups (IV and V), while neither the two training groups nor the two control groups differed from one another.

ANCOVA results for the Minimal Generalization Test of affective perspective taking also yielded a significant between-groups difference ($F = 6.156$, $p < .002$). Subsequent Newman-Keuls comparisons revealed that Condition I, in which trainees were taught both affective and cognitive perspective taking, achieved significantly higher affective perspective-taking levels on this transfer measure than did both control groups. This training versus control difference was not obtained for the comparison involving Condition III, in which trainees were taught affective perspective taking only.

Cognitive perspective taking. Skill acquisition results for this skill directly paralleled those just described for the affective dimension. On Direct Test (post), the relevant training groups (I and II) significantly exceeded the posttraining cognitive perspective-taking level of the control groups (IV and V) (F = 11.84, p < .001). Comparisons within training groups and within control groups yielded no signficant differences. Direct Test (post) minus Direct Test (pre) difference scores yielded comparable training versus control significant effects (F = 13.12, p < .001) and, again, no significant within training groups or within control groups effects. On the ANCOVA for Minimal Generalization Test of cognitive perspective taking, group II (taught only cognitive perspective taking—but not group I, taught both skills—significantly exceeded control group levels (F = 3.23, p < .03).

Cooperation. The Interpersonal Situations Simulation Test, our face-to-face, role-play transfer measure, yields scores on four cooperation-related dimensions: (1) competitive-aggressiveness, (2) avoidance, (3) accommodation, and (4) collaboration. A comparison of the three training conditions combined (I, II, III) against this study's two control conditions combined (IV and V) revealed the former to be significantly less competitive-aggressive (F = 4.716, p < .03), less avoidant (F = 4.753, p < .03) and more collaborative (F = 4.707, p < .03) than the combined control groups. Berlin (1976) and Trief (1977) have suggested that the four scores yielded by this measure essentially reflect diverse positions on two dimensions, assertiveness and cooperativeness, and as such enable us to derive two more basic scores from each participant's Interpersonal Situations Simulation Test performance. This may be done as follows:
1. Competitive-aggressive = assertive + uncooperative
2. Avoidant = unassertive + uncooperative
3. Accommodative = unassertive + cooperative
4. Collaborative = assertive + cooperative
In this scheme, therefore, assertiveness = (1 + 4) − (2 + 3) and cooperativeness = (3 + 4) − (1 + 2). Our ANCOVA for assertiveness failed to yield a significant result. For cooperativeness, however, ANCOVA results revealed that experimental conditions did differ significantly (F = 2.52, p < .04). Subsequent Newman-Keuls analyses indicated that both the Cognitive Perspective-Taking condition (II) and the Affective Perspective-Taking condition (III) were significantly more cooperative on this transfer measure than were Brief Instructions controls (V). When, as in the separate score analysis, we pooled all training conditions (I, II and III) and compared them to both control conditions (IV and V), a significant ANCOVA difference favoring trained participants emerged (F = 8.589, p < .005) on cooperativeness, but not on assertiveness.

The results of this investigation add to our picture of Structured Learning as a set of procedures which yields reliable skill acquisition and, to a large extent, skill transfer. Perspective-taking skills, as we elaborated earlier, are central to the reduction of egocentricity—a developmental hurdle which is often of considerable difficulty for behavior-disordered adolescents. Participants in a brief sequence of Structured Learning not only learned and (minimally) transferred such skills, but also typically performed at higher levels on an important behavioral consequent of enhanced perspective taking, namely cooperation.

STUDY 8. THE USE OF PEERS AS SKILL TRANSFER PROGRAMMERS (GREENLEAF, 1978)

In Chapter 2, we identified a number of procedures used successfully to enhance transfer of training in laboratory contexts, and we illustrated our operationalization of these procedures within the context of Structured Learning. As an integral part of our implementation of modeling, role playing, and performance feedback, trainees are exposed to potential transfer enhancement by means of (1) provision of general principles, (2) overlearning, (3) identical elements, (4) stimulus variability, and (5) performance feedback. The central importance of transfer in the behavior change venture, and the great difficulty experienced by all types of interventions in seeking to attain it regularly, meant that the continuous study, refinement, and expanded implementation of both these and other transfer enhancers is a research and practice concern of the first magnitude. In the studies described thus far, we have already begun to focus on a number of these potential transfer enhancers, namely, *in vivo* training (Gutride et al., 1974), overlearning (Lopez, 1980) and helper role structuring (Litwack, 1976). We wish here to continue in this quest by examining Greenleaf's (1978) effort to study skill transfer by means of the procedures he termed Transfer Programming.

It is a common observation among those interested in adolescent development that the typical teenager is immensely responsive to peer group influences. Unfortunately, this influence often takes form in the provision of reinforcement for negative behaviors. Buehler, Patterson, and Furniss (1966) found that the delinquent peer group in an institutional setting provided exceedingly high levels of positive reinforcement for deviant behavior and withdrawal of such reinforcement for socially conforming behavior. Meichenbaum et al. (1968) report similar findings, as do Solomon and Wahler (1973), who worked with disruptive youngsters in regular school settings. Can this powerful influence be reversed? Can the power of the peer group be harnessed or captured, as it were, so that a peer group norm emerges in which an individual youngster's prosocial behavior is attended to, praised, or otherwise reinforced, and peers respond with indifference or social punishment to the antisocial? Patterson and Anderson (1964) used peers as social reinforcement dispensers in a study in which certain simple motor responses of seven- to ten-year olds were successfully conditioned.

Axelrod, Hall, and Maxwell (1972) used peer reinforcement successfully to alter the study behavior of a disruptive youngster. Bailey, Timbers, Phillips, and Wolf (1971) made similar use of peer reinforcement to alter speech behavior, and other investigators report similar peer effectiveness in modifications of various interpersonal or school-related behaviors (Freeman, 1970; Nelson, Worell, & Polsgrove, 1973; Noonan & Thibeault, 1974; Walker & Buckley, 1972). The present investigation sought to extend this finding to the transfer domain, by examining whether the transfer of a newly acquired skill can be enhanced by peer reinforcement.

Procedure

This investigation was conducted at an urban junior high school with approximately 800 students. Potential participants were, as our first screening hurdle, male students identified by teachers or school guidance counselors as continually disruptive and aggressive. The main teacher for the 75 candidates thus identified was asked to complete the Classroom Adjustment Rating Scale (CARS) (Lorian, Cowen, & Caldwell, 1975) for each student. To provide a further sense of the type of youngster involved in this investigation, the following items reflecting the CARS factor Acting-Out were used for deciding which candidates would actually be invited into the study sample:
1. Disruptive in class.
2. Fidgety, hyperactive, can't stay in seat.
3. Talks out of turn, disturbs others while they are working.
4. Constantly seeks attention, "clowns around."
5. Overly aggressive to peers (fights, is overbearing, belligerent).
6. Defiant, obstinate, stubborn.
7. Impulsive, is unable to delay.
8. Does not trust others.
9. Poor work habits.

The final study sample consisted of 43 youngsters with the highest scores on this measure who, in addition, agreed to participate and from whose parents we obtained permission for inclusion. The racial composition of this sample was 24 white, 18 black, and one native American.

With regard to our selection of a target skill for this investigation, Greenleaf (1978) comments:

> The thrust of Structured Learning is to teach prosocial skills which will provide alternative behaviors which will be effective in securing desirable consequences. . . . Learning the skill of Helping Others will perhaps provide a behavioral option for adolescents to accomplish such desired consequences as social attention, approval from others, avoiding trouble from teachers, and dealing with boredom. [Pp. 33–34.]

The behavioral steps which constitute Helping Others are:
1. Decide if the other person could use help.
2. Decide if you should help him and how.
3. Ask the person if he needs and wants your help.
4. Help the other person.

The design employed in this investigation implemented the presence and absence of Structured Learning, the presence and absence of transfer programming, and both brief instructions and attention control conditions. This design is depicted schematically in Fig. 4.3.

As in most of our other investigations, our experimental procedures involved the following measurement and training sequence:
A. Pretesting:
   Direct Test (pre)
B. Training:
   Structured Learning and/or transfer programming or control
C. Posttesting:
   Direct Test (post)
   Minimal Generalization Test
   Extended Generalization Test

The Minimal Generalization Test, as in our other studies, consisted of skill-relevant, taped stimulus situations to which participants had not been previously exposed on either the Direct Tests or modeling tapes. Examples of the stimulus situations used included:

1. You are sitting in class and your friend is at the desk next to you. The teacher has just given the class an assignment. You notice that your friend is looking at his book and getting very upset. He is having some kind of trouble with the assignment. What would you say to him?

Transfer Programming

		Present	Absent	
Structured Learning	Present	I	II	
	Absent	III	IV (Brief Instr. Control)	
				V (Attention Control)

Fig. 4.3. Experimental design for transfer programming study.

2. You had to stay after school to take a make-up exam. There are not many people left in the school when you finish. As you walk past the gym, you notice one of the teachers is alone in the gym pushing large tables around to get ready for the Disco Dance. What would you say? What would you do?

3. It is between classes. You notice a student whose foot is in a cast walking with crutches up the stairs. He has several books under his arm. You also notice that he is carrying his lock so you figure that he is on his way to Mr. Klein's room. He's making it up the stairs all right, but he's moving very slowly and with difficulty. What would you do? What would you say?

4. It is the end of the day, and as usual, everyone is trying to get out of the building without delay. You notice a student, whom you know pretty well, hanging around the hallways. He comes up to you and tells you that he thinks some guys are going to hassle him once he gets outside. He tells you he doesn't want any trouble, he just wants to get home ok. What would you say? What would you do?

In this investigation, both the Direct Test and the Minimal Generalization Test were administered as part of the posttraining test battery, and then again after a five-week period as measures of skill maintenance. The Extended Generalization Test consisted of two simulated situations in which each participant was individually confronted by a peer who communicated information to which an optimal response would be to offer help.

The five-session course of Structured Learning provided condition I and II trainees following the procedures described in the *Structured Learning Trainers Manual for Adolescents*. Transfer programming was implemented by first pairing each condition I, II, and III participant with a liked peer in one of his classes. This procedure was responsive to the finding of Brown, Helm, and Tedeschi (1973) who reported that liked peers were highly effective social reinforcers in the context of verbal conditioning research. It was the task of each paired partner to observe his partner during the selected class period and provide social reinforcement and performance feedback when the partner offered help to others when appropriate. Certain record-keeping and teacher-checking steps were included in this procedure both to help standardize and to check on its accuracy as delivered by the peer partners.

The Brief Instructions Control condition (condition IV) was operationalized, as in our earlier studies, by means of information provided to the (nine) participants, immediately prior to the posttesting, which described the study skill and its behavioral steps, and encouraged the participants to implement the skill thus defined in their posttest responses. (As was the case in all other studies employing a Brief Control condition, persons assigned to all study Structured Learning conditions received the same instructions and encouragement just prior to post testing.)

The Attention Control condition sought to control for the possible effects on skill enhancement (in the Structured Learning groups) of receiving special attention from two adults over a period of time. For the same number of sessions during which Structured Learning was conducted, the two four-member Attention Control groups met with two group leaders and engaged in a series of discussions and debates whose focus was of inherent interest to adolescents, but which was irrelevant to the study's target skill and its acquisition.

Results and Discussion

Analyses of variance conducted to ascertain whether pretraining systematic differences existed as possible biases on dependent variable scores revealed no significant differences across experimental conditions on participant age, CARS score, or pretraining target skill level (Direct Test—pre).

Mean pre, post, and maintenance dependent variable scores, and standard deviations, by study experimental conditions are reported in Table 4.5. Analyses of variance were conducted across these and derivative scores as tests of the study hypotheses. These analyses sought first to discern Structured Learning main effects by comparison of conditions I + II versus III + IV. Significant main effects for Structured Learning emerged on (1) Direct Test (post − pre) difference ($F = 63.19$, df = 1, 31, $p < .01$) and Direct Test (post) ($F = 11.52$, df = 1, 62, $p < .01$) measures of skill acquisition, (2) Minimal Generalization Test ($F = 5.44$, df = 1, 31, $p < .05$) and Simulations Test ($F = 9.21$, df = 1, 31, $p < .01$) measures of skill transfer, and (3) Direct Test ($F = 7.2$, df = 1, 23, $p < .05$) and Minimal Generalization Test ($F = 8.84$, df = 1, 23, $p < .01$) measures of skill maintenance.

An analogous series of analyses of variance examined possible Transfer Programming main effects (Conditions I + III versus II + IV). None of these comparisons yielded significant results. Transfer Programming as operationalized in this investigation failed to enhance either skill transfer (on Minimal Generalization or Simulations) or skill maintenance (on Followup Direct Test and Minimal Generalization Test).

Greenleaf's (1978) data analysis also included a number of planned comparisons, analyzed by means of t tests. These results are reported in Table 4.6.

What may be said in commentary about these several ANOVA and planned comparisons? In contrast to its impact in the studies cited earlier, transfer programming as operationalized here had no discernible effect upon skill transfer or maintenance. Structured Learning, however, was itself powerful enough to yield consistent significant acquisition, transfer, and maintenance effects. We concur with Greenleaf's speculation that these results grew from two factors. First, as noted earlier, a number of procedures designed to

Table 4.5. Means and Standard Deviations for Study Dependent Measures.

Experimental Condition	Time of Testing	Direct Tests		Minimal Generalization Test		Simulation Test	
		Mean	S.D.	Mean	S.D.	Mean	S.D.
Structured Learning plus Transfer Programming	Pretest	4.94	2.04				
	Posttest	11.31	5.34	13.56	6.90	3.83	1.58
	Maintenance	10.41	4.02	11.44	2.82		
Structured Learning	Pretest	4.69	1.74				
	Posttest	11.81	3.40	11.50	3.30	3.81	1.29
	Maintenance	10.66	2.49	11.03	3.66		
Transfer Programming	Pretest	4.78	2.10				
	Posttest	8.91	3.13	9.88	3.04	1.88	1.73
	Maintenance	7.50	3.65	6.64	3.25		
Brief Instructions Control	Pretest	4.94	2.07				
	Posttest	7.93	2.36	8.22	2.90	2.28	2.08
	Maintenance	7.38	0.48	9.50	1.29		
Attention Control	Pretest	4.00	1.87				
	Posttest	6.75	2.04	7.22	2.34	2.00	1.28
	Maintenance	8.40	2.25	7.70	2.73		

Table 4.6. Planned Comparisons (t tests) on Study Dependent Measures.

Conditions Compared	Direct Test (post)	Minimal Generalizations (post)	Simulations (post)	Direct Test (maintenance)	Minimal Generalization (maintenance)
Structured Learning plus Transfer Programming (I) vs Attention Control (V)	2.69*	3.18*	2.32*	ns	2.17*
Structured Learning (II) vs Attention Control	2.99*	2.15*	2.29*	ns	ns
Transfer Programming (III) vs Attention Control (V)	ns	ns	ns	ns	ns
Structured Learning plus Transfer Programming (I) vs Structured Learning (II)	ns	ns	ns	ns	ns
Structured Learning plus Transfer Programming (I) vs Transfer Programming (III)	ns	ns	2.48*	ns	3.06*
Structured Learning (II) vs Transfer Programming	ns	ns	2.45*	ns	2.80*

$*p < .025$

enhance transfer and maintenance are built into Structured Learning in a variety of ways, and under certain circumstances transfer/maintenance ceiling effects may occur such that additional procedures, e.g., the transfer programming, cannot add further transfer enhancement. Such a ceiling effect, we would propose, occur when the target skill is both simple enough and prosocial enough that it is often enacted by the trainee, and pulls social reinforcement at high rates from those to whom it is directed. Our speculation and informal classroom observation suggest that this is precisely what occurred in this investigation in response to trainee classroom enactments of Helping Others.

In any event, this investigation adds considerably to our view of the skill enhancement usefulness of Structured Learning with skill-deficient adolescents. Transfer programming, in this instance at least, does not enhance the generalization of the newly acquired skill.

STUDY 9. TRANSFER ENHANCEMENT BY IDENTICAL ELEMENTS IN TRAINING ASSERTIVENESS TO PASSIVE AND AGGRESSIVE ADOLESCENTS (WOOD, 1977)

In our earlier examination of procedures demonstrated to function as effective transfer enhancers, we cited the long and positive history of identical elements. Across a variety of laboratory and, to some extent, real-life contexts, the greater the degree of similarity or explicitly shared characteristics between training and application, the greater the transfer from training to application. Although Structured Learning inherently possesses a number of real-life-like characteristics (see page 22), we felt it desirable to examine the transfer enhancement potency of even further operationalization in a Structured Learning context of identical elements. In the present investigation, in which assertiveness was the target skill, we sought to facilitate skill transfer by utilizing trainers and models similar in important characteristics to those types of persons who are likely real-life targets for trainee assertiveness, and by employing a training setting similar to the real-life settings in which trainees are likely to have opportunities to be assertive.

In addition to its concern with transfer enhancement, this investigation also reflected our interest in prescriptiveness. We selected both passive and aggressive youngsters as trainees in this investigation, in an effort to discern the relative effectiveness of Structured Learning with two types of trainees, both of whom were deficient in assertiveness, but in purportedly very different ways.

Procedure

This investigation was conducted in a suburban high school with a student population of approximately 1,500. Seventy-four ninth-grade youngsters constituted the study sample. In an accurate reflection of the school's total racial distribution, 72 study participants were white, 2 were black. Thirty-five were males, 39 were females; 33 were identified as aggressive, 41 were identified as passive. Their mean age was 14 years; their ages ranged from 13 to 15.

Screening for aggressiveness and passivity was conducted by the school's 12 ninth-grade teachers, who rated all students on the Syracuse Scales of Social Relations (Gardner & Thompson, 1959). Each of the 339 ninth-graders was rated on an array of items reflecting a passivity-assertiveness-aggression dimension relative to the (approximately) 27 other students in each of his four core classes (English, math, science, social studies) by his four teachers. The students selected for invitation into the study sample were those rated most extreme on the passive or aggressive items by at least two of these four teachers.

One factor reflected in this investigation's design, therefore, was passive-aggressive participants. The second operationally reflected identical elements. Since our later dependent variable measurement focused upon student assertiveness vis-à-vis *teachers*, we operationalized the identical elements similarity dimension by employing as Structured Learning trainers (1) teachers (high similarity), (2) parents (moderate similarity), and (3) students (low similarity). The 2 × 4 factorial design reflecting these two factors is depicted in Fig. 4.4.

The behavioral steps which operationalized assertiveness in this study were:
1. Pay attention to those body signals which help you know you are dissatisfied and would like to stand up for yourself.
2. Decide which outside events may have caused you to feel dissatisfied.
3. Consider ways in which you might stand up for yourself.
4. Take your stand in a direct and reasonable manner.

Participant   Training

	Structured Learning with Teacher Trainers	Structured Learning with Parent Trainers	Structured Learning with Student Trainers	Brief Instructions Control
Aggressive	I	II	III	IV
Passive	V	VI	VII	VIII

Fig. 4.4. Experimental design for identical elements—assertiveness study.

Measures and the measurement and training sequence for this investigation paralleled that employed in our other studies, namely Direct Test (pre), Training, Direct Test (post), Minimal and Extended Generalization Tests. The Direct and Minimal Generalization Tests, as before, required participants to respond to taped stimulus situations in response to which assertive behavior would be appropriate. The Direct Test situations were identical to those employed on the study's modeling tapes; those on the Minimal Generalization Test were new to each participant when presented. Some of these stimulus situations included:

1. *Teacher*: "Class, I've decided to give your test this Friday instead of next Monday."

2. *Parent*: "No. Absolutely not. I don't want you to hang around with Charlie. He's a bad influence on you. Why don't you hang around with John anymore? He's so nice and he listens to his parents."

3. *Peer*: "Hi. My friends are ahead of you. You don't mind if I skip in front of you, do you?"

The Extended Generalization Test, in this study termed the Hall Pass Test, was designed to serve the usual purpose for this type of measure in our research program, i.e., to provide a face-to-face opportunity for the participant to respond with the study skill in response to a live presentation of skill-relevant stimuli. The ninth-grade teachers and eight hall monitors were given a list of the names of study participants who were to be let out of predetermined classes at different scheduled times throughout the week of testing. (The classes were chosen for their concentration in one isolated wing of the school, which permitted confrontation with only one monitor, and which made for tighter control over extraneous situational influences.) At a prearranged time, participants were told, "You are to see Ms. Wood in the copy center office." A hall pass, which is regularly required of all students who travel in the school hallways during class periods, was not given to study participants. If a participant requested a pass, the teacher did not issue one but replied, "It's all right," or "You'll just be gone for a few minutes." As the participant proceeded down the hall, the hall monitor stopped him and asked, "Where's your pass? [*pause*] You know you can't go roaming around the halls without one." The hall monitor allowed up to 30 seconds for the participant to respond, then asked him his name, and said, "Okay, but next time please make sure you get a pass." Immediately after the participant entered the copy center, the hall monitor recorded the participant's verbatim response and its nonverbal accompaniments.

Results and Discussions

Study data were analyzed by means of multivariate analyses of variance which, when significant, were followed by ANOVA and then multiple cell

Table 4.7. Means and Standard Deviations for Experimental Conditions Across Study Measures of Assertiveness.

Experimental Condition		Direct Test (post)	Minimal* Gen'l #1	Minimal Gen'l #2	Minimal Gen'l #3	Extended Gen'l Test	Direct Test (post) Minus Direct Test (pre)
Structured Learning: Teacher Trainers	X	11.6	9.6	8.2	7.9	1.3	18.0
	SD	5.0	4.4	5.3	5.0	0.7	
Structured Learning: Parent Trainers	X	8.4	7.2	5.6	4.6	1.3	13.3
	SD	3.3	2.9	3.6	2.5	0.4	
Structured Learning: Student Trainers	X	8.8	8.7	7.2	5.8	1.2	14.0
	SD	3.9	3.4	4.0	3.9	0.6	
Brief Instructions Control	X	2.8	2.8	2.5	2.5	0.4	2.5
	SD	2.1	2.5	2.5	2.6	0.6	

* Consistent with the identical elements focus of this investigation, to discern whether minimal transfer would occur more or less readily to like stimuli, three separate scores were derived from this measure reflecting, respectively, (1) teacher, (2) parent, and (3) student instigations to assertiveness.

comparisons (Newman-Keuls) when appropriate. Analysis of variance on Direct Test (pre) data revealed no significant pretraining participant difference in target skill levels.

As in all the other investigations we have examined, a significant skill acquisition effect emerged. For Direct Test (post) minus Direct Test (pre) for training conditions versus control condition, all Structured Learning conditions showed significantly greater growth in assertiveness than did Brief Instructions control participants. Acquisition and transfer effects are further revealed by the means and standard deviations for all study conditions reported in Table 4.7, and means and standard deviations broken out by passive and aggressive participants, as reported in Table 4.8.

MANOVA results across these data revealed significant overall effects for both training and the passive-aggressive factor. Subsequent analyses of variance are reported in Table 4.9.

Newman-Keuls multiple cell comparisons following these MANOVAs revealed that, with the single exception of the parent-trained Structured Learning on Minimal Generalization Test subscore #3, all Structured Learning groups performed significantly better than Brief Instructions controls on all acquisition and transfer measures. Teacher-trained Structured Learning groups tended to perform with higher levels of assertiveness, and less aggression or passivity, than did parent- or student-trained groups on all five acquisition and transfer measures, but significantly so only on the Direct Test (post). Finally, comparisons of scores for passive and aggressive participants revealed that passive participants performed significantly better than aggressive participants on the Direct Test and Minimal Generalization Test (#2 and #3), but that the reverse was true (aggressive significantly exceeded passive) on the Extended Generalization Test.

In this investigation, Structured Learning led both passive and aggressive adolescents, whether trained by teachers, parents, or peers, to perform significantly better on acquisition and transfer measures of assertiveness than did youngsters not participating in Structured Learning. Being trained by teachers, in addition, led to greater skill acquisition and tended to enhance skill

Table 4.8. Means and Standard Deviations for Passive and Aggressive Participants Across Study Measures of Assertiveness.

Participants		Direct Test (post)	Minimal Gen'l #1	Minimal Gen'l #2	Minimal Gen'l #3	Extended Gen'l Test
Passive	X	8.7	7.4	6.5	6.0	0.9
	SD	5.3	4.8	5.1	4.5	0.7
Aggressive	X	6.3	6.2	4.7	3.8	1.2
	SD	3.8	3.1	2.9	2.7	0.6

Table 4.9. Analyses of Variance for Training and Passive-Aggressive.

Factor	Measure	df	F
Training:	Direct Test	3, 58	27.77***
	Minimal Gen'l #1	3, 58	15.97***
	Minimal Gen'l #2	3, 58	7.85***
	Minimal Gen'l #3	3, 58	7.73***
	Extended Gen'l	3, 58	9.22***
Passive-Aggressive:	Direct Test	1, 58	9.36**
	Minimal Gen'l #1	1, 58	2.23
	Minimal Gen'l #2	1, 58	4.31*
	Minimal Gen'l #3	1, 58	7.36**
	Extended Gen'l	1, 58	7.70**

*p < .05
**p < .01
***p < .001

transfer. This tendency was consistent but statistically not significant, suggesting that if implementations of identical elements are to have their hoped-for substantial transfer-enhancing effect, more powerful and sustained operationalizations of identical elements than characterized this study may be necessary.

Chapter 5
Child Trainees

The three major themes of our research program—skill acquisition, skill transfer, and prescriptive implementation—continuted to find major expression as our investigative focus shifted to yet another trainee population, children. This is a relatively recent focus for us, and the absolute number of Structured Learning studies with children is small. But we hope the conclusion will not therefore be drawn that we consider skill enhancement in children to be an unimportant goal. In fact, from a primary prevention or preparation-for-life perspective, child trainees patently appear to be among the most worthwhile groups to involve in such efforts. We are actively involved in additional research along such lines, beyond the promising studies reported in this chapter, and we hope others will join us in this effort. Clearly, the apparent effectiveness of a number of other recently developed skill training programs for children gives added impetus to this stance (Bash & Camp, 1980; Cartledge & Milburn, 1980; Rotheram, 1980; Sapen-Shevin, 1980; Spivack, Platt, & Shure, 1976).

STUDY 10. THE USE OF PRESCRIPTIVE COPING MODELING FOR TRANSFER ENHANCEMENT WITH PASSIVE AND AGGRESSIVE EDUCABLE MENTALLY RETARDED CHILDREN (FLEMING, 1976)

As part of the mainstreaming movement in American public education, there have been widespread attempts to integrate educable mentally retarded children into regular classes. Not infrequently, however, the youngster who is the target of such efforts is met with social rejection (Gottlieb, Cohen, & Goldstein, 1974) and is stereotyped as incompetent (Willey & McCandless, 1973). Lawrence and Winschel (1975) and Ross and Ross (1973) suggest that such youngsters often are in fact slow to develop social skill competence as a result of minimal stimulation, social play deprivation, familial overprotection, and general isolation from the social mainstream. Gottlieb and Budoff (1973) conclude, and we concur, that merely integrating a retarded child into a regular class setting is likely to enhance his social competence and acceptance rather little, and sometimes may even yield negative effects in these social regards, but that purposeful training in the skills requisite for successful interpersonal functioning has the potential for reversing this effect. Gott-lieb (1974) has also found that the competence-incompetence dimension was more predictive of youngster's social acceptance than the mental retar-dation–normal dimension, i.e., incompetent, nonlabeled children were more rejected than were those showing competence, even those with the label. Thus, we are in agreement with Fleming (1976), who comments, "Skill train-ing in the area of interpersonal social competence is . . . seen as a means to maximize the . . . attributes which could facilitate educable mental retar-dates' acceptance by normal peers" (p. 1). What particular psychological skills seem deficient in the educable mentally retarded youngster? In general, they appear to be skills designed to deal with precisely the same problem behaviors to which we have targeted Structured Learning efforts in other trainee populations—aggression (Baldwin, 1958; Johnson, 1950), passivity (Bruininks, Rynders, & Gross, 1974), and a number of school performance-related cognitive problem areas. It thus became apparent to us that a highly appropriate starting point in our effort to extend Structured Learning to child trainees would indeed be the educable mentally retarded youngster. Further, employing the same evidence and rationale as supported its use with passive and aggressive adolescents in Wood's (1977) study, the target skill employed in this investigation was assertiveness.

In a continuation of our effort to identify and examine the effectiveness of potential transfer-enhancing techniques, much of the investigative focus of this study was on prescriptive coping modeling. In 1971, Meichenbaum sought to examine the relative effectiveness of mastery versus coping model-ing in reducing avoidance behavior. The mastery model (as is used in Struc-tured Learning and most other programs with a modeling component) por-trays the desired or skilled behavior in its expert, complete, and usually errorless form. The coping model, in partial contrast, precedes his or her enactment of the skilled response by first also enacting the struggle, the errors, the difficulties experienced on the way to expertise. As Meichenbaum (1971) comments with regard to his avoidance behavior study:

> the models comment on their anxiety and fear, but at the same time attempt to cope with their fear. . . . They demonstrate not only desirable behaviors, but also coping cognitions, re-evaluations and ways of coping with feelings of frustration or self-doubt. [P. 376.]

The use of coping models has proven to be an effective innovation in a number of studies (Blanchard, 1970; Bruch, 1975; Debus, 1970; Ross, Ross & Evans (1971), a finding variously explained as resulting from (1) enhanced model-observer similarity (Meichenbaum, 1971; Ross, Ross, & Evans, 1971); (2) increased belief that the endpoint desired behavior is personally attain-able (Chan & Keogh, 1974; Madsen & Conner, 1973); (3) teaching specific cognitive coping skills (Kornhaber & Schroeder, 1975); and (4) making the trainee more aware of the chain of environmental situations and cognitive cues which trigger the undesirable or unskilled behaviors (Meichenbaum, 1975).

The present investigation, beyond its examination of the direct skill-acquisition potency of Structured Learning with this trainee sample, sought to discern the impact on both skill acquisition and transfer of coping modeling explicitly tailored to be prescriptively relevant to two discrete subsamples of educable mentally retarded youngsters. One, aggressive youngsters, viewed a model who displayed anger-coping frustrations and victories on his way to skilled behavior. The other subsample, consisting of passive youngsters, was corresponding exposed to a fear-coping model. Let us now look more fully at this study's procedures.

Procedure

Participants in this investigation were drawn from an urban elementary school servicing a primarily lower socioeconomic school district. The study sample consisted of 96 educable mentally retarded children aged nine to twelve, Binet or Wechsler I.Q. 55 to 75, 64 males and 32 females, 47 white and 49 black. These youngsters were drawn from eleven special classes in the three participating elementary schools, and screened into the study sample, first of all, by means of teacher ratings of his or her students on the Aggressive-Passive Rating Scale, a selection instrument developed for this purpose for this investigation. As in all of our investigations, once potential participants were identified, their actual joining of the study sample then became a joint function of their voluntary decision to do so plus parental permission. The 96 participating children were then randomly assigned, within the aggressive and passive factors, to study experimental conditions as shown in Fig. 5.1.

The evaluation and training sequence for this study, once again, consisted of a Direct Test (pre), Training, Direct Test (post), Minimal Generalization Test and Extended Generalization Test (immediate, post, and delayed). With the exception of the use of coping models in conditions I, II, V, and VI, the

	Structured Learning plus Anger Coping	Structured Learning plus Fear Coping	Structured Learning	Attention Control
Aggressive	I	II	III	IV
Passive	V	VI	VII	VIII

Fig. 5.1. Experimental design for coping model study.

training format followed those detailed in the *Structured Learning Manual for Adolescents* (see Appendix B). Six training sessions of 20 minutes each, with five trainees per group, were held to operationalize all Structured Learning conditions, such brevity of session length and smallness of group size reflecting prescriptive attempts on our part to be responsive to seemingly truncated participant attention span. The study's target skill, assertiveness, was operationally defined by the same behavioral steps which defined it in Wood's (1977) investigation, but was prescriptively reworded to fit the language comprehension level of this study's participants better. The behavioral steps were:

1. Realize you're mad about what just happened—"I'm mad!"
2. Think why you're mad—"Why am I mad?" "I'm mad because. . . ."
3. Think of things you might now do—"I could hit him, tell the teacher, ignore him, or tell him how I feel."
4. Choose to tell him your feelings and speak up—"I don't like it when. . . ."

The modeling displays that were utilized showed (on video) the model responding to an array of problematic, in-school situations (the same as those employed in both direct tests) with expert enactments of these behavioral steps. In addition, in all anger-coping condition Structured Learning groups (I and V), expert behavioral step enactment was preceded by portrayal by the model of successful coping with anger. An example of an assertion-relevant stimulus situation responded to with (1) anger coping, and (2) assertiveness is:

> You bring a new magazine to school. Later in the day, when you want to show it to a friend you realize your magazine is missing from your desk. You look around the room and you see Dave walking out the door carrying your magazine under his arm.
> *(That thief! I'm gonna break his head! Stealing my mazagine—what does he think it is—his birthday or something? I should steal his hat, or steal all his stuff from his desk and throw it all over the floor. But then, I might get in trouble with the teacher. Let's see—I'm mad. He shouldn't take my magazine without asking. I could just take all his stuff, that would fix him . . . or I could just wait—he'll probably bring it back. But I should tell him that I didn't like it that he took my magazine without asking.)*
> 1. "I really didn't like it that you took my magazine without asking me if you could see it."
> 2. "I'm sorry. Would you mind if I looked at it for a few minutes?"

A stimulus situation followed by fear coping and assertiveness is:

> You bring a new magazine to school. Later in the day, when you want to show it to a friend, you realize your magazine is missing from your desk. You

look around the room and you see Dave walking out the door carrying your magazine under his arm.

(*He didn't even ask if he could see my magazine! Oh well, I didn't want to look at it anyway. If I say something, he'll call me a baby for getting so upset. He'll say I'm selfish and won't let anyone use my things, then none of the kids will want to play with me. . . . Oh well. . . . But how does he know I wasn't going to use it? I'm mad. Who does he think he is, taking my magazine without asking? I'm going to tell the teacher on him. . . . or, maybe I shouldn't do anything—he was probably going to bring it back anyway. But I really should tell him that I didn't like it that he just took it that way.*)

1. "I really didn't like it that you took my magazine without asking me if you could see it."
2. "I'm sorry. Would you mind if I looked at it for awhile?"

Conditions II and VI participants heard parallel portrayals of fear coping. Attention control participants (IV and VIII) also met for six, 20-minute group sessions, in which videotapes of interpersonal behavior were shown, and no modeling, role playing, or other Structured Learning activities were employed.

The Direct and Minimal Generalization Tests followed our usual taped stimulus situations format. The study's two Extended Generalization tests, given as an immediate posttest and after a one-week delay, respectively, were contrived, face-to-face situations involving peers in which an appropriate participant response was assertiveness. One involved the confederate pushing ahead of the participant, out of turn. The other involved inappropriate criticism of the participant by the confederate while both played a ring toss game.

Results and Discussion

As our usual check on randomization efforts, an analysis of variance was conducted on between-group assertiveness skill across all study conditions, via Direct Test (pre) scores. No significant pretraining differences emerged. Two 2×4 ANOVAs across the two participant classifications crossed with four training conditions for Direct Test (post) and for Direct Test (post-pre) difference each yielded a significant effect ($F = 31.13$, df = 3,88, $p < .001$ and $F = 19.97$, df = 3,88, $p < .001$, respectively). A subsequent simple main effects analysis revealed that pre and post gain scores, i.e., Direct Test (post-pre), for all three experimental conditions were significant ($F = 106.94$, df = 1,88, $p < .001$ for anger coping; $F = 118.38$, df = 1,88, $p < .001$ for fear coping; $F = 123.62$, df = 1,88, $p < .001$ for Structured Learning alone). No similarly significant differences emerged on this skill-acquisition measure for the Attention Control groups.

Minimal Generalization Test results yielded a similar outcome. A significant overall difference emerged (F = 28.85, df = 3,88, p < .001) Subsequent analysis of variance revealed combined Structured Learning groups (Conditions I, II, III, V, VI, and VII) to show significantly higher minimal transfer of assertiveness than Attention Controls (IV and VIII). No Direct Test or Minimal Generalization Test comparisons among Structured Learning conditions, or between aggressive and passive youngsters yielded significant results. Further, analyses of Extended Generalization Test results, both immediate and delayed, revealed no significant effects in comparisons of (1) training conditions versus controls, (2) among training conditions, or (3) between types of trainees.

Thus, with the samples of educable mentally retarded trainees participating in this investigation, the significant effects which emerged were on skill acquisition and minimal transfer for youngsters participating in Structured Learning (compared to both their pretraining status and to Attention Controls), regardless of whether their sessions employed a coping or a mastery model. Fleming (1976) speculated that the failure of extended generalization in this investigation may have resulted from a low level of trainee motivation to employ assertiveness as the prepotent response to the situations presented, especially given their not infrequent history of success when employing alternative strategies, e.g., hitting, telling the teacher, etc. And further, she proposes, the coping-modeling interventions may have failed owing to a failure of the modeling displays either to stimulate a sufficient sense of model-observer similarity or to teach a sufficiently clear set of specific coping skills. While such speculation is of interest, and worthy of further study, the results of this investigation must in part be attributed to the nature of the trainee sample and the quality of the prescriptive match between trainee and training characteristics. The intellectual deficit characteristic of this study's trainees, as well as possible concurrent deficits in motivation and attention span, suggest that in order to move beyond the acquisition effects found in this study to reliable transfer effects, it may be necessary to alter "standard" Structured Learning training procedures much more extensively than merely providing coping models. More active trainers, use of tangible reinforcers, richer reinforcement schedules, later thinning of reinforcement, more repetitive implementation of modeling and role playing, more attention to simpler skills, and the further related suggestions offered in the *Structured Learning Trainers Manual for Adults* (see page 146) are among the types of prescriptive procedural alterations we would suggest. It is, we believe, only by means of such energetic and sensitive prescriptive responsiveness to trainee characteristics that the long-term skill-enhancement needs of populations such as the mentally retarded youngsters in the present investigation will be met.

STUDY 11. THE USE OF STIMULUS VARIABILITY FOR TRANSFER ENHANCEMENT WITH AGGRESSIVE CHILDREN (HUMMEL, 1980)

In the Lopez (1980) investigation presented in Chapter 3, we addressed ourselves to enhancement of transfer by means of overlearning, that is, by moderate levels of practice or repetition of correct skill responses. If attention is turned to the stimulus member of the event, it may be shown that transfer may also be enhanced by moderate or high levels of *variability* in the training stimuli to which the trainee is exposed. Kazdin (1975) has accurately articulated the rationale explaining why stimulus variability may function to enhance transfer:

> One reason that behaviors are not maintained and do not transfer to new settings is that the clients readily form a discrimination between conditions in which reinforcement (or punishment) is and is not delivered. Behavior becomes associated with a narrow range of cues. As soon as the program is withdrawn or the setting changes, clients discriminate that the desirable behavior is no longer associated with certain consequences. Thus, responses are not maintained and do not transfer to new situations. One way to program response maintenance and transfer of training is to develop the target behavior in a variety of situations and in the presence of several individuals. If the response is associated with a range of settings, individuals, and other cues, it is less likely to be lost when the situations change. [P. 211.]

These speculations have found empirical support in several diverse research contexts. Duncan (1958) has shown that on a paired associates task, transfer is substantially enhanced by a variety of training stimuli. Training on even only two stimuli was clearly better than training on a single stimulus. Callantine and Warren (1955) obtained similar results in research on concept attainment tasks, showing more rapid attainment and transfer when a variety of examples were utilized. Analogous positive effects for stimulus variability have emerged in studies examining the transfer of verbal learning (Slavin, 1967), prosocial behavior (Emshoff, Redd, & Davidson, 1976), impulse control (Kendall & Finch, 1976) and in less formal clinical explorations of the use of multiple therapists (Dreikurs, Schulman, & Mosak, 1952), multiple impact therapy (MacGregor, Ritchie, Serrano, & Schuster, 1964), round robin therapy (Holmes, 1971), rotational therapy (Slavin, 1967) and rotational group therapy (Frank, 1973). As we have noted in another context, "The implication is clear that in order to maximize positive transfer, training should provide for some sampling of the population of stimuli to which the response must ultimately be given" (Goldstein, Heller, & Sechrest, 1966, p. 220). Hummel (1980) sought to test this notion in the context of Structured Learning. In addition, for exploratory purposes, Hummel (1980) posited what he termed the Reciprocal Benefits Hypothesis. The majority of our Structured Learning investigations are empirical tests of the acquisition and transfer of single skills. While such a stratagem is appropriate and necessary for investigative purposes, real-life trainee needs almost always require learning of a number of (often related) skills. How many, which ones, and in what sequences remain interesting and unexplored parametric questions. In this spirit, Hummel proposed that under varied stimulus conditions, those trainees taught both study target skills—self-control and negotiation—would acquire and transfer each skill better than would trainees taught only self-control or only negotiation. Stated otherwise, it was predicted that the newly acquired self-control ability would be an aid to negotiation and, reciprocally, knowing how to negotiate would facilitate self-control ability—in contrast to the levels of one or the other skill in trainees taught *either* self-control *or* negotiation.

Procedure

As in a number of our investigations involving adolescent trainees, screening into this study's sample took place via (1) Classroom Adjustment Rating Scales (Lorian, Cowen, & Caldwell, 1975), completed across a large pool of potential participants by fourth, fifth, and sixth-grade teachers; (2) invitations to volunteer extended to the subsample of chronically aggressive youngsters thus identified; and (3) obtaining parental permission to participate from the parents of youngsters accepting our participation invitation. In this manner, 47 youngsters attending a public urban elementary school were selected for this study. Thirty were black, 17 were white; all were male, none mentally retarded, their mean age was 11 years, 8 months. This investigation's experimental design is depicted in Fig. 5.2.

Under varied stimulus conditions, participants were exposed to four different modeling displays and consistently changed role-play coactors over the course of their group's three Structured Learning sessions. Constant stimulus conditions were implemented by four exposures to the same model-

		Self Control	Negotiation	Self-Control and Negotiation
Stimulus Conditions	Varied	I	II	III
	Constant	IV	V	VI

Skill Taught

Fig. 5.2. Experimental design for stimulus variability study.

ing display, and by conducting all their role playing during their three sessions with the same coactor.

The study skills were operationally defined by means of the behavioral steps listed below:

Self-Control:
1. Figure out what made you feel hassled, and tune into what you feel in your gut or your head.
2. Count to ten, put the brakes on to stay out of trouble, slow down to stay out of hot water.
3. Picture a stop sign in your head, pretend you see a stop sign ahead, say "Stop."
4. Say, "I've got it under control so I can start to work it out." Tell yourself you did a good job.

Negotiation:
1. Say what you want.
2. Ask the other person to say what he wants, and listen.
3. Say back what the other person wants.
4. Say something in between, suggest a compromise.

The procedures which constituted all Structured Learning groups followed those described in the *Structured Learning Manual for Adolescents* (see Appendix B). As per our other investigations, Hummel's measurement and training sequence was Direct Test (pre), Training, Direct Test (post), Minimal Generalization Test, Extended Generalization Test. Two of the stimulus situations used on the Direct Test were:

1. Two boys are in the hallway. The first boy, the main boy, is carrying some books. The other boy knocks the books out of his arms. They smash on the first boy's foot. Other kids are looking on and laughing as the two boys argue. If you were the first boy, the main person, what would you think, say, and do in that situation?

2. Two boys are in the gym, and they are trying to get a kickball game started. Both boys want the same boy, Bill, to be on their team. The first boy, the main boy, wants to get the game started. The other boy is acting real fresh, and is trying to boss the situation. If you were the first boy, the main person, what would you think, say, and do in that situation.

Two Minimal Generalization tests were employed, one involving peers as stimulus figures, the other involving student-teacher conflicts. Extended Generalization was measured via a contrived, prearranged conflict event involving a student accomplice. In its enactment, it involved two students (a participant and the accomplice), one chair, and experimenter instructions to sit down. Its resolution would be facilitated by use of self-control and/or negotiation skill.

Table 5.1. Analyses of Variance (F) for Acquisition and Transfer
of Self-Control and Negotiation.

Source	Direct Test (post)	Min. Gen'l #1	Min. Gen'l #2	Extended Gen'l
Self-Control[a]	60.38***	56.29***	19.90***	5.97*
Negotiation[b]	8.90*	4.07*	4.79*	17.97**

[a]Study conditions I + III versus IV + VI
[b]Study conditions II + III versus V + VI
  *p < .05
 **p < .01
***p < .001

Results and Discussion

No significant between-conditions differences existed for participants in terms of age, race, CARS score, or Direct Test (pre) scores for the two study skills.

Analyses of variance conducted to discern the effects of varied versus constant stimulus conditions revealed consistently significant effects favoring stimulus variability across both skills and all study measures of acquisition and transfer. These results are presented in Table 5.1.

Study results bearing upon the notion of reciprocal benefits or mutual facilitation of skill transfer when learning two (or more) skills were mixed. Youngsters who learned both self-control and negotiation obtained significantly higher transfer scores on negotiation than did youngsters learning only negotiation. A parallel facilitation effect of self-control plus negotiation on the transfer of self-control did not emerge. These findings are presented, by means of t statistics, in Table 5.2.

As has been found in a number of other therapeutic, training, and laboratory contexts, stimulus variability as operationalized by Hummel in the context of Structured Learning yielded a robust and consistent transfer-enhancing effect. Its future study and present incorporation into Structured Learning both appear deserved.

Table 5.2. Reciprocal Benefits Effects on Skill Transfer.

	Min. Gen'l #1	Min. Gen'l #2	Extended Gen'l
Self-Control plus Negotiation versus Negotiation Alone	4.02*	3.21*	3.57*
Self-Control plus Negotiation versus Self-Control Alone	1.0	.41	.54

*p < .025

That this study found one skill (self-control) to facilitate transfer of another (negotiation) is not a surprise. A "Skill" as a behavior unit is, after all, an artificial slice of an ongoing behavioral stream. Successful commerce with the interpersonal environment requires an ever-changing series of intrapersonal (e.g., self-control) adjustments to accommodate to interpersonal (e.g. negotiation) demands. In fact, we have often conceptualized our skill subseries[1] as hierarchically arranged building blocks, the mastery of one to at least an appreciable extent dependent upon the prior mastery of a presumptively "earlier" or "easier" or "lower-order" skill. We have not yet empirically examined this hierarchical supposition but, as the findings of the present study suggest, to do so might greatly further the applied utility of Structured Learning.

---

1. *Adults* Conversations: Beginning Skills, Conversations: Expressing Oneself, Conversations: Responding to Others, Planning Skills, Alternative to Aggression. *Adolescents* Beginning Social Skills, Advanced Social Skills, Dealing with Feelings, Alternatives to Aggression, Dealing with Stress, Planning Skills.

Chapter 6
Change Agent Trainees

There exists no prescriptive or other a priori reason to believe that the skill enhancement utility of Structured Learning is limited to the client or client-like trainees—adult, adolescent, or child—examined thus far in this book. Nor, we believe, is its effectiveness limited to the classes of interpersonal or intrapersonal target skills whose investigation is reported in the preceding chapters. Numerous other domains of human behavior may be appropriately and conveniently conceptualized and operationalized in skill-enactment terms, including the behaviors of diverse types of change agents. Thus, it is our position that the role behaviors or interventions optimally performed by such persons as mental hospital staff, parents, counselors, teachers, and others may usefully be viewed in skill terms, and as such, attempts at correcting their deficit may appropriately be implemented by means of Structured Learning. The investigations reported in this chapter represent a comprehensive attempt to test this position, as we examine the effectiveness of Structured Learning for skill acquisition and transfer with an array of change agent trainees and change agent–relevant target skills.

HOSPITAL STAFF

STUDIES 12 AND 13. THE USE OF *IN VIVO* TRANSFER TRAINING FOR EMPATHY ENHANCEMENT (GOLDSTEIN & GOEDHART, 1973)

Though recent prescriptive research has made clear that high levels of helper empathy are not necessarily therapeutically facilitative with all types of clients, the potency of helper-offered empathy for client growth remains a robust finding across many types of helpees (Mitchell, Bozarth, & Krauft, 1977). Thus, with the probable exception of certain types of schizophrenic and delinquent clients, openness, self-disclosure, and a favorable change agent–helpee relationship generally seem to be facilitated by high levels of change agent–offered empathy (Mitchell, Bozarth, & Krauft, 1977).

Procedure 1

Participants in this investigation were 74 student nurses employed at a moderately sized, public mental hospital located near Amsterdam, Holland.

Their involvement in the study was voluntary, and in response to a somewhat detailed hospital-wide invitation to a ten-hour course in "conversation training." To obtain base rate, pretraining information regarding participants' empathy levels, the Direct Test (pre) was administered. This measure consisted of patient and hospital-relevant stimulus situations (also used in the study's modeling displays and Direct Test [post]) to which an appropriate and optimal response would be a statement reflecting high levels of nurse empathy. Participants were then randomly assigned to one of two conditions, experimental (Structured Learning) or control (no training, wait period). Experimental condition participants were constituted into five Structured Learning groups of six to eight trainees each. The ten hours of Structured Learning training, for administrative reasons, was implemented as two five-hour meetings on consecutive days for each training group. Stimulus situations employed in the modeling displays (and Direct Tests), and the model responses, included:

1. Nurse: Here is your medicine, Mr. ——.

    Patient: I don't want it. People here are always telling me to do this, do that, do the other thing. I'll take the medicine when I want to!

    Nurse (model): So it's not so much the medicine itself, but you feel you're bossed around all the time. You're tired of people giving you orders.

2. Patient: You remind me of a cousin of mine that I really like a lot. I'm very comfortable and relaxed when I talk to her also.

    Nurse (model): Thank you, I hear you saying something very warm and friendly to me.

3. Patient: This is a hospital, a place where you're supposed to get better. But the doctor hasn't seen me for weeks and weeks. How is someone supposed to get better if the doctor never sees them?

    Nurse (model): You feel you'd really like to get his help, and you're a little angry he hardly ever sees you.

4. Patient: All I know is that the blue pill helped me a lot the last time I felt this way. Why can't you let me have one now?

    Nurse (model): You sort of feel I'm keeping something from you that would really make you feel better, and you can't understand why.

Following the Structured Learning sessions, the Direct Test (post) and the study's Minimal Generalization Test (same testing format, new items) were administered. These same measures were administered pre and post an equivalent series of waiting periods for the 37 control group nurses.

Four head nurses also participated in this empathy training program. Each served first as an (additional) participating trainee in one of the five Structured Learning groups, and then as a nonparticipating observer in a second such group. It was our intention in implementing this procedure to discern whether such persons could, following this training and exposure, serve as effective Structured Learning trainers themselves. Thus, as the second major phase of this study's procedures, the 37 student nurses previously assigned to the control condition then met with two of these now trained head nurses for a ten-hour training program identical in format and content to that received by experimental condition trainees. One month after completion of their respective training sessions, all trainees (experimental condition and the later-trained control condition) responded a second time to the Minimal Generalization Test, given this time as a maintenance measure.

Results and Discussion

Tests of four predictions were addressed to the study's data. A significant increase in the level of displayed empathy during the investigation's first phase was predicted for the experimental condition nurses, in contrast to that evidenced by the control group members during their no-training wait period. A comparison of Direct Test (post-pre) change scores for the two conditions yielded the predicted effect ($t = 19.86$, $p < .001$). Experimental condition trainees also displayed significantly higher levels of empathy than did control condition nurses on the Minimal Generalization Test ($t = 20.94$, $p < .001$).

Our third prediction sought to examine the effectiveness of the Structured Learning conducted during the study's second phase by the four head nurses. The score comparison made concerned the change in empathy level displayed by members of the original control group as a function of their training (phase two) in comparison to that evidenced by them during the wait period (phase one). (These nurses, therefore, served as an equivalent control group for the nurse sample trained during phase one, as well as own controls for themselves.) This comparison, too, yielded a significant increase in the level of empathy displayed ($t = 15.21$, $p < .001$).

Finally, our study measure of skill maintenance administered to all participants one month after their training, when compared to trainee base rate levels, revealed that the enhanced empathy levels had sustained ($t = 10.01$, $p < .001$).

Procedure 2

A second investigation was conducted at a large American state mental hospital, and was essentially a replication and extension (to the issue of transfer) of the first study. Psychiatric hospital personnel were again the sample; empathy enhancement was again the target skill. Ninety participants were utilized: 20 staff nurses, 40 attendants, and 30 other high patient-contact personnel (e.g., occupational therapists, recreational therapists, etc.) Our experimental procedures and materials included but elaborated upon those employed in Study 12. Specifically, three, equal-sized experimental groups were randomly constituted: (1) Structured Learning plus transfer training; (2) Structured Learning, and (3) no training control.

Procedures and materials for groups 2 and 3 were exact replications of that used for the experimental and control groups in the Dutch student nurse study. Group 2 underwent a ten-hour Structured Learning program for empathy enhancement. Group 3 participated in no such training, but responded to the study measures at pre, post, and followup points in time.

Group 1 participants, in addition to their participation in the ten-hour program, engaged in procedures intended to augment the likelihood that training gains would find reliable expression in the participant's real-life environment (the ward) subsequent to the initial training. The procedure utilized toward this end was *in vivo* performance feedback. Concretely, two senior nurses who had participated as both trainees and observers in the initial Structured Learning training of empathy were assigned on a full-time basis for a two-week period to the two wards on which the 30 Group 1 participants worked. Their task, in general terms, was to provide *in vivo* Structured Learning; that is, each transfer trainer spent two hours per day observing the actual on-the-ward interactions of staff participants and patients.

Each participant, further, met daily with one of the two trainers for an individual 15-minute session. The participant was asked to bring verbatim notes of interactions she had had with patients that day with her to these meetings. These notes and the trainer's observations formed the session's training stimuli. Those interactions reported by the trainee or observed by the trainer in which the trainee offered the patient an empathic response (levels 3, 4 or 5) on the Truax and Carkhuff (1967) Empathy Scale were responded to by the trainer with social reinforcement. When the trainee had provided a level 1 or 2 response, the trainer offered further modeling (e.g., "What you might have said was . . .") and role playing (e.g., "Now, why don't you tell me what you might say if the patient says to you . . .").

Our measurement procedures required all participants to complete the Direct Test for base rate measurement purposes prior to their participation in Structured Learning; Direct Test and Minimal Generalization Test at the completion of such training; and to respond two weeks later to 15 tape-recorded "patient" statements constructed in such a manner as to represent our measure of transfer. Items for this latter measure were derived from actual staff-patient interactions occurring on the three wards on which the study participants worked. That is, we sought to approximate a measure of subject response to the actual patients with whom they interacted daily.

Results and Discussion

Analysis of variance for empathy revealed (1) a replication of the significant acquisition effect of Structured Learning on empathy enhancement (F = 143.5; df = 2, 86; p < .01); (2) a replication of the significant effect of Structured Learning on the generalization of empathy enhancement to new stimuli, not present at either premeasurement or in training (F = 126.1; df = 2, 86; p < .01); and (3) a significant transfer-training effect for *in vivo* performance feedback (F = 93.0; df = 2, 83; p < .01).

In vivo transfer training, a successful transfer enhancer in this study, will be recognized by the reader as a combination of the use of identical elements (the setting and patient stimuli) plus trainer-provided prompting and coaching. We may thus tentatively add this variant of the identical elements approach to the growing number of successful transfer enhancers already described in connection with studies reported earlier.

STUDY 14. THE USE OF GENERAL PROBLEM-SOLVING PRINCIPLES FOR SKILL ACQUISITION AND TRANSFER OF CONTINGENCY MANAGEMENT SKILLS (LACK, 1975)

In laboratory settings, especially in research concerned with skill acquisition, transfer of training has been shown to be facilitated by providing the learner, experimental participant, or trainee with the general mediating principles which govern satisfactory performance on both the original and the transfer tasks. He is given the rules, strategies, or organizing principles that can lead to successful performance. In the earliest research dealing with transfer enhancement by means of general principles, Judd (1902) sought to teach boys to shoot darts at a target submerged in water. Boys thus instructed about the principle of refraction did better at the task than boys not so instructed. This finding was later replicated on a related task by Hendrickson and Schroeder (1941). In both studies, positive transfer was attributed to the acquisition of the general principles governing successful task performance. Other experiments have further confirmed this conclusion. Woodrow (1927) was able to produce improved performance in memorization on transfer tasks requiring memorizing poetry, prose, and factual material by instructing subjects in specific principles and techniques of memorization. Ulmer (1939) found that a special geometry curriculum designed to arouse critical thinking both connected and unconnected with geometry resulted in better performance on later transfer tasks. Duncan (1959), Goldbeck, Bernstein, Hellix, and Marx

(1975) and Miller, Heise, and Lichten (1951) are others who have reported similar results. Recent interest in the "New Math" is a more current example of anticipated transfer of training mediated by general principles.

This general finding, that mediating principles for successful performance can enhance transfer to new tasks and contexts, has furthermore been reported in a number of other domains of psychological research. These include studies of labeling, rules, mediated generalization, advance organizers, learning sets, deutero-learning, and, as is the case for the present investigation, problem solving. The enhancement of transfer via the provision of general problem-solving principles, while a robust laboratory finding, has only infrequently been studied in applied contexts. A few approaches to psychotherapy employ this notion creatively, but also informally and unsystematically—Kelly's (1955) fixed-role therapy, Haley's (1976) problem-solving therapy, Phillips' (1956) assertion-structured therapy, Loveless and Brody's (1974) cognitive psychotherapy, and Watkins' (1972) therapeutic use of cognitive maps—but its systematic study in such settings is quite rare. In the present investigation, a sequence of problem-solving steps derived from the work of Miller, Pribram, and Galanter (1960), and of D'Zurilla and Goldfried (1971) was taught to trainees and examined for its possible transfer-enhancing utility.

To evaluate further the effectiveness of Structured Learning as a change-agent training technique, in addition to the presence versus absence of problem-solving training, this study's second factor, training technique, compared Structured Learning training of the study's target skills against a very commonly used approach to change-agent training: didactic techniques.

In contrast to the empathy skills which were the training target of the Goldstein and Goedhart (1973) studies, Lack's (1975) investigation sought to teach mental hospital staff an array of contingency-management skills—the use of behavioral assessment, instructions, reinforcement, extinction, modeling, and shaping. This choice was in response to the widespread use of contingency-management techniques by nursing and other hospital staff in token economy and related types of programs in a great many American hospitals and clinics.

Procedure

Forty-nine staff members at a large state mental hospital served as participants in this investigation. Most were nurses, with a small number of occupational and recreational therapists also included. There were 25 females and 24 males, ranging in age from 20 to 53. Participants, all of whom were volunteers, were randomly assigned to one of five study conditions, which are schematically illustrated in Fig. 6.1.

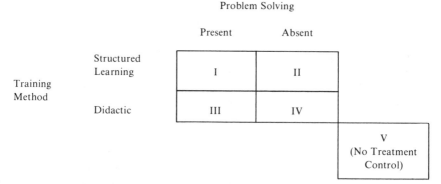

Fig. 6.1 Experimental design for problem-solving principles study.

Thus, Condition I participants engaged first in a period of explicit training in problem-solving principles and techniques, and their application in defining, selecting, and implementing the target skill contingency-management procedures. They then engaged in a five-session sequence of Structured Learning training of contingency management techniques. Condition II participants also engaged in this Structured Learning sequence, but without the problem-solving pretraining. Participants assigned to the didactic experimental conditions underwent a five-session lecture series in which the same contingency management target skills were the focus, but in which no modeling, role playing, or performance feedback was employed. In addition, Condition III participants received the problem-solving pretraining, while those assigned to Experimental Condition IV did not. The No Treatment Control group simply participated in all study pre- and posttesting.

The study's dependent measures included (1) pre- and posttraining Direct Tests consisting of videotaped in-hospital stimulus situations constructed by us in response to which staff initiation and implementation of contingency-management procedures would be appropriate; (2) a live Minimal Generalization Test consisting of previously unseen stimulus situations, to which the trainee was required to provide a skilled response in writing, and (3) an Extended Generalization Test similar to (2) but requiring a live, face-to-face skilled response to undesirable behavior by an actor "patient" (e.g., drinking water by dipping his hand in a pitcher, although glasses were available; buttoning his shirt incorrectly; spitting on the floor).

Results and Discussion

The result of this investigation yielded only minimal support for the transfer-enhancement potency of problem-solving principles as operationalized herein. Direct Test comparisons yielded no problem-solving or interaction effects, and a significant acquisition effect for Structured Learning only on the skills of Instructions and Modeling.

The significant Minimal Generalization Test effects which emerged were mostly in the realm of behavioral assessment skills. Participants receiving Structured Learning combined with problem-solving principles (Experimental Condition I) proved superior to the Didactic and Control condition participants in the ability to identify both excessive and absent behavior targetable for treatment, and superior to Controls in defining treatment alternatives and defining treatment goals. In the live-assessment context, the Extended Generalization Test, no problem-solving effects emerged and the Structured Learning conditions, as on the Direct Test, had its significant impact on Instructions and Modeling only—not the assessment skills and not the other intervention skills.

Research on the training and transfer implications of providing trainees with general principles and problem-solving strategies and rules is both considerable in extent and robust in positive findings. Its study in clinical contexts such as that of the present study is quite rare, and Lack's (1975) effort should be viewed as an important beginning effort. Its general lack of positive results strongly suggests, however, that it is indeed naught but a beginning, and that additional effort and creativity must be forthcoming in further implementation and study of general principles as a potential transfer enhancer.

PARENTS

STUDY 15. THE USE OF IDENTICAL ELEMENTS FOR TRANSFER ENHANCEMENT IN PARENT EMPATHY TRAINING (GUZZETTA, 1974)

Disordered parent-child relationships, while springing from multiple and often complex roots, often have a failure to understand and communicate accurately about each other's feelings at the heart of the disorder. This empathic deficiency was seen by Offer (1969) as a major contibutor to the so-called generation gap, which might be closed by "open and flowing communication [and] a willingness to empathize with each other's emotional position" (p. 208). Truax and Carkhuff (1967) have similarly stressed the likely value of high levels of empathy in this context, as has Guerney (1977) who made parent empathy training the central feature of his Filial Therapy, a therapy/training approach designed to remediate parent-child difficulties. The potential value of interventions such as Guerney's is underscored by a substantial series of supportive investigations including, for example, the work of Irving (1966) who found that not only do well-adjusted adolescents perceive their parents as more empathic than do poorly adjusted youngsters, but that the parents of well-adjusted adolescents are, in fact, more empathic. Esty (1967), Gordon (1970), and Reif and Stollak (1972) report concurring results, and stress the likely value, in both preventive and corrective senses, of teaching parents to be more empathic with their own children. It was in the spirit of these findings and recommendations that the Guzzetta (1974) study was undertaken. In addition, as will be seen, she also implemented training conditions in such a manner that the study provided a further test of the value of identical elements as a transfer-enhancing procedure.

Procedure

This investigation was conducted in a largely rural community of mostly lower-middle-class Italian-American families. The study sample consisted of 37 mothers of sixth, seventh and eighth-grade students who attended the area's central junior-senior high school or its middle school. These mothers were volunteers who responded to announcements in both schools and the area's newspapers and on its local radio station that a mini-course entitled "Communicating With Your Teenager" was going to be offered.

To implement the study goals of testing the efficacy of Structured Learning for empathy-training purposes and the efficacy of identical elements for transfer-enhancement purposes, participants were assigned to four experimental conditions. It will be recalled that the essential finding in support of identical elements as a transfer enhancer holds that the greater the similarity between characteristics of the training and application, the greater the purported transfer. As can be seen from the depiction of these conditions in Fig. 6.2, we arranged the training procedures to be responsive to this notion by varying the degree to which the mother trainees learned and practiced empathic responding in their Structured Learning groups with the same person (their child) with whom they hoped to interact empathically in their application (home) settings.

The participating mothers in Conditions I, II, and III all served as trainees learning the skill Empathy by means of the training procedures described in the *Structured Learning Trainers Manual for Adults* (see Appendix A). In

Mother and her teenager trained together	Mother and her teenager trained separately	Mother only trained	Wait period Control
I	II	III	IV

Fig. 6.2. Experimental design for identical elements—empathy study.

Condition I, their role-play coactor was their own child who, as part of his or her group participation, was also exposed to discussions about empathy and its value in a parent-child context. Condition II mothers received the same Structured Learning training in empathy, using each other as role-play coactors in the usual Structured Learning format. Their youngsters were not part of these mothers' groups, but met separately in teenager groups in which empathy and its value were discussed along with other positive aspects of parent-child communication. Condition III mothers received the same empathy training as those in Condition II, but their youngsters did not participate in the investigation. Finally, mothers randomly assigned to Condition IV constituted a No Treatment Control Condition, whose empathy training was postponed until after study posttesting.

Three two-hour Structured Learning sessions were held separately for Condition I, II and III trainees. Pretesting (Direct Test-pre), the training itself, and the posttesting (Direct Test, Minimal, and Extended Generalization Tests) targeted on the skill Empathy, defined by the behavioral steps:
1. What is the teenager feeling?
2. How can I best communicate to him/her that I understand his/her feelings?

Direct Test and Minimal Generalization Test content (on tape) and Extended Generalization Test content (portrayed live by the trainee's own teenager) required trainee response to such stimulus statements as:
1. Why do you have to know every little thing I do? You don't trust me at all!
2. Gee, everybody's been invited to the party but me.
3. You never *listen* to me! You've got your mind made up before I say anything?
4. Guess what! Our class might go on a trip to Washington this Easter!
5. I just *can't* do any better in school, that's all! Whenever I get a low grade you get mad, but you hardly say anything when I do good!

Results and Discussion

As a check on random assignment of trainees to experimental conditions, and in particular to be sure that systematic differences did not exist between conditions in terms of parent-child communication, the Parent-Adolescent Communication Inventory was administered to the teenagers of study trainees, before training commenced. A single factor, analysis of variance conducted across these data revealed no significant between-group pretraining differences.

Our study analysis of the effects of Structured Learning on the acquisition and transfer of empathy skill proceeded by means of Dunnett's t statistic, a statistic for systematically comparing experimental treatments with a control condition. These results are presented in Table 6.1

These findings indicate that all Structured Learning study conditions yielded significantly greater empathy skill levels than was true for control group mothers. Therefore, in terms of acquisition of the target skill, its minimal transfer, as well as its transfer to a role-play enactment involving her own youngster, all mothers participating in Structured Learning demonstrated higher skill levels than did those not participating.

Analyses of variance conducted to discern differences between Structured Learning conditions failed to yield any significant effects. In particular, and contrary to our identical elements predictions, undergoing training (I) with the central application setting target person failed to yield greater minimal or extended transfer than did training (II or III) with the target person absent.

These two sets of findings must be reconciled. All Structured Learning groups led to significant skill transfer; the intended transfer-enhancing procedures failed to augment this effect differentially. Guzzetta (1974) claims:

> Far from providing evidence for lack of transfer, therefore, the absence of differences on the behavioral measure between the treatment groups suggests that Structured Learning training was so effective that the parents in all groups were able to transfer the new skill to situations role played by their own children. [P. 89.]

Guzetta (1974) may be correct in her conclusion. There may well exist populations and target skills on which successful transfer can occur as a function of Structured Learning although no special transfer enhancers are added to those inherent in the modeling, role playing, performance feedback sequence as we have operationalized. Although we most certainly welcome such training outcomes, we believe it is much more likely that they are the exception rather than the rule. It is, we believe, more useful as well as more parsimonious to view the combined transfer findings of this study as possibly

Table 6.1. Dunnett's t Comparisons for the Effects of Structured Learning on Empathy Acquisition and Transfer

Experimental Condition	Direct Test		Minimal Gen'l		Extended Gen'l	
	Mean	t_D	Mean	t_D	Mean	t_D
I. Mother & Youngster	2.73	8.98*	2.62	8.36*	2.58	6.15*
II. Mother/Youngster	2.89	9.88*	2.84	9.58*	2.56	6.09*
III. Mother	2.94	10.69*	2.83	10.00*	2.78	7.43*
IV. Control	1.06	—	1.07	—	1.18	—

*p < .01

constrained by a measurement ceiling effect. Perhaps, we would speculate, if the study's Extended Generalization Test more demandingly required for its success that generalization stretch over a broader gradient of similarity and/ or time, Condition I might well have exceeded Conditions II and III in terms of skill transfer. But these are only speculations, offered here in part from awareness of the robustness of the findings in other studies (Structured Learning and otherwise) of the transfer-enhancing potency of identical elements. Clearly, its further experimental scrutiny seems most worthwhile, especially with regard to discerning which of its operationalizations are prescriptively effective with which types of trainees and target skills.

STUDY 16. MASTERY INDUCTION AND HELPER STRUCTURING AS TRANSFER ENHANCERS IN TEACHING SELF-CONTROL TO ABUSIVE PARENTS (SOLOMON, 1978)

The past 20 years have witnessed a burgeoning of awareness and concern with child abuse in the United States. In both public and professional media, incidence, causes, and treatments are increasingly featured. A substantial portion of this literature consistently describes a large percentage of child-abusing parents as markedly skill deficient—in interpersonal, intrapersonal, parenting, and especially, in self-control skills (Cicchetti, Taraldson, & Egeland, 1976; Gelles, 1973; Justice & Justice, 1976; Tracy, Ballard, & Clark, 1975). A broad array of psychiatric, psychological, and social interventions have been directed toward such persons, including a small number of efforts aimed directly at skill remediation. Patterson (1974) and Sadler and Seyden (1976) have employed a number of contingency-management techniques in an effort to reduce the reliance of such parents on physical punishment as a control technique, and to increase their skill in the use of nonassaultive tactics. Parke and Collmer (1975) describe the use of modeling for similar skill-enhancement purposes, and speculate that direct anger-control techniques such as Novaco's (1976) may also be useful in this regard. It was in the spirit of these few skill-oriented interventions, plus our pilot use of Structured Learning in informal clinical-educational trials with abusive parents, that led to our formal scrutiny of its value in the present investigation.

In addition to continuing our research program's basic strategy of testing the skill-acquisition effectiveness of Structured Learning with different populations (abusive parents) and different skills (self-control), we also continued in this study to pursue our aim of implementing and evaluating the widest possible range of potential transfer-enhancing procedures.

A major direction taken by the behavior modification movement in recent years, as part of its dual focus upon cognitive variables and self-instructional techniques, has been procedures aimed at helping the individual develop a sense of control and even mastery over difficult or threatening circumstances that he or she may be facing. Bandura's (1973) notion of self-efficacy, Frank's (1978) views on avoidance of demoralization, and Kazdin and Wilcoxon's (1976) perspective on the importance of the individual's expectancy for change are examples of this stance. A number of persons have sought to relate this perspective to transfer. If, they hold, the individual not only sees his overt coping behavior working but, in addition, he attributes the success to his own efforts and skills, he is much better able in subsequent problem confrontations to have the motivation and self-confidence to be successful again. Consistent with this view is Lang's (1968) proposal that failure to transfer is a direct result of failure to alter cognitive sets when changing an individual's overt behavior. In response to this view, D'Zurilla and Goldfried (1971) sought to counteract failures of transfer by a technique they termed cognitive restructuring. Here, past situations which have been explained in person-as-victim terms are relabeled with more rational, often mastery explanations. In the subsequent problem situation, the individual is encouraged to make appropriate control and mastery ("can do") self-statements which serve to cue adaptive behavioral responses.

This effect of a sense of control and mastery on the transfer of positive behaviors is not without experimental support. Goldfried and Trier (1974) found that representing relaxation training to clients as a self-control procedure increased maintenance of therapeutic gains more effectively than did portraying relaxation as an automatic anxiety-reducing technique. Liberman (1977), whose procedures were the mastery manipulation we used in the present investigation, falsely informed a sample of psychotherapy outpatients that their success on a series of tasks was due to their own efforts. These patients maintained their therapeutic improvement on a three-month followup, while those not subjected to this mastery manipulation did not. Nisbett and Schachter (1966) and Valins and Ray (1967) have reported analogous results in other experimental contexts. The present investigation examined the transfer-enhancing potency of this self-attribution process in the context of skill training for self-control in an abusive parent sample. In a beginning effort to discern the joint impact of combinations of potential transfer-enhancing techniques, the mastery manipulation experimental conditions were crossed with a second factor, helper structuring, which it will be recalled proved promising for transfer-enhancing purposes in Litwack's (1976) investigation reported earlier.

Procedure

Study procedures were operationalized in a 2 × 2 plus Brief Instructions control group factorial designed, as schematically depicted in Fig. 6.3.

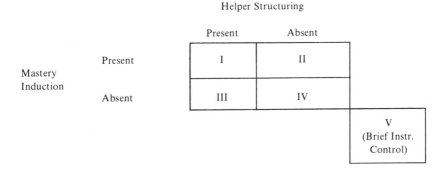

Fig. 6.3 Experimental design for mastery induction—helper structuring study.

Participants in this investigation were 40 child-abusing parents affiliated with a child abuse service agency in a large metropolitan area. Of the 31 women and 9 men (assigned randomly, not proportionately to study conditions), 38 were white and two were black. Nineteen were married and 21 were single. Study participation, as in all of our investigations, was on a volunteer basis following a detailed description to all potential trainees of study procedures and goals. (To facilitate study participation, for persons whose life circumstances often makes such participation quite difficult, the child abuse agency involved in this investigation provided transportation, babysitting, and related services.)

The study's target skill, Self-control, was operationalized by the following behavioral steps:

1. Think about what is happening to make you feel that you are about to lose control.
2. Think about what you could do that would help you control yourself.
3. Consider what might happen if you did each of these things.
4. Choose the best way to control yourself and do it.

Study assessment procedures followed our more or less standard Direct Tests (pre and post), Training, Minimal Generalization Test, and Extended Generalization Test format. Direct Test and Minimal Generalization Test stimulus situations included:

1. You're sitting in the living room watching your favorite soap opera. Its been a long day and you're really tired. Your child starts whining and says: "I'm hungry, get me something to eat. I want something to eat now!"
2. Its breakfast time and you've just put a bowl of cereal on the table for your child. You turn around to pour yourself a cup of coffee and when you turn back you see the bowl broken into pieces with milk and cereal all over the floor.

3. It's about time for you to leave for school. You are all ready to go and you hear the news report that the day care center where your kids go will be closed because of a watermain break. You are really angry about this and say: "Go to your room and play." But the kids won't listen and start fighting.

4. It's noon and your child has just come back from the day care center. You're fixing his lunch when he says, "I don't want that shit for lunch. Give me something else."

Each study participant, as a part of agency procedures for all of its clients, was assigned to a parent aide who functioned in the participant's home in a variety of helping capacities. Extended Generalization Test information for this investigation was obtained from these parent aides who were trained by us to make reliable observations of the presence and absence of self-control behaviors in response to real-life, in-the-home stimuli which chronically function as instigators of loss of self-control.

Participants assigned to study Conditions I-IV participated in two two-hour Structured Learning sessions targeted to Self-control. Prior to training, participants assigned to the two Mastery Induction cells (I and II) underwent a procedure designed after that developed by Liberman (1977). Essentially, it was a reaction time task in which they had to discriminate between light stimuli of different colors. In describing the task, the experimenter led the parents to believe that it was directly related to self-control and that success with this task would lead to, or be indicative of, improvement in his or her ability to maintain self-control in difficult situations. The instructions were as follows:

> In this task you will learn to improve your control over your feelings and actions. You will know when you are starting to get angry and will be able to stop yourself from acting on it and getting in trouble. As you improve in this skill you will be able to be more in control and make good choices about what to do when you get tense. This way you can find other ways to blow off steam that won't hurt you or anyone else. This skill plus your own control over yourself will help you improve relationships with others. You may find it easier to get along better with members of your family and may feel better about yourself. As you gain more control over yourself you may have better control over the way you are with others and improve the way you get along with them.

Then the experimenter explained the reaction time task in the following way:

> In front of you there is a panel with four different colored lights and four buttons. One button is in front of each light. What I would like you to do is to rest your hand in front of the panel. When the light comes on I want you to push the button that matches the light as fast as possible. Try to push the

button as soon as you can after the light comes on. You will be given a few practice trials and then I will begin to record whether you pushed the correct button and how fast you are. Remember to try to go as fast as you can. Get ready and we will take a few practice trials.

Each parent was given three practice trials and asked if there were any questions. Then he or she was given ten recorded trials. At the end of this session, the experimenter gave the parent feedback on his or her performance. The feedback, however, was unrelated to actual performance. Instead, it was structured to indicate progressive improvement over the course of the reaction time task sessions. The reaction time task was given once more during training but prior to any posttesting. For the first reaction time session the parent was told that on four trials his or her reaction time was faster than average but that on six trials it was too slow. For the second reaction time session the parent was told that his or her reaction times were faster than that of the average population on all of the trials. The experimenter attributed the "improved" performance to something the person must have been doing, that is, his or her own efforts at doing it more quickly and that it was expected that he or she would maintain this improvement. The experimenter added that this control would be useful for controlling feelings and actions in general.

Helper Structuring induction (Cells I and III) directly paralleled Litwack's (1976) instructions:

There are others who would like help in learning how to better control themselves in difficult situations. We think you could be helpful to them by teaching them the skills that you learn. Being a member of this group will prepare you to be able to be good helpers. (p. 39)

During the subsequent Structured Learning training itself, the expectation of later serving as a helper was reiterated, e.g., prior to tape listening, the trainer would say, "Remember to listen carefully to the tape because you will be teaching this to another person," or after successful role playing, "That was really good, learning the steps so well will help you teach it to others."

Results and Discussion

Means and Standard Deviations for each experimental condition on all study measures are presented in Table 6.2.

As has proven to be the case in almost all of our investigations, participation in Structured Learning (I-IV) led to significantly higher levels of skill acquisition than did a No Training (Brief Instructions) control experience. Of greater import, however, are this study's other between-condition differ-

Table 6.2. Means and Standard Deviations for Study Conditions.

Condition	Direct Test (pre)	Direct Test (post)	Minimal Gen'l	Extended Gen'l
I Mastery plus Helper				
X	5.18	25.13	21.13	16.63
SD	1.77	7.40	6.13	5.66
II Mastery				
X	8.25	19.63	17.50	15.38
SD	2.49	6.50	5.63	5.40
III Helper				
X	5.13	13.75	14.38	9.13
SD	2.75	2.44	2.39	5.03
IV No Mastery-No Helper				
X	6.50	13.50	13.00	6.50
SD	2.20	3.02	2.50	2.78
V Brief Instruction				
X	4.88	5.25	4.25	3.00
SD	3.23	3.88	3.37	0.00

ences, which bear upon the issue of transfer enhancement. Analyses of variance across conditions (2 × 2) are reported in Table 6.3.

These analyses of variance reveal a significant overall effect for mastery induction on the acquisition and transfer of self-control on all three study dependent measures. Post hoc Newman-Keuls cell comparisons across these data reveal that parents receiving both mastery induction and helper structuring (cell I) show levels of self-control significantly greater than all other study conditions at acquisition and minimal generalization. On extended generalization, both mastery induction plus helper structuring, and mastery induction alone, led to significantly greater target skill level than the other study conditions. As shown in Table 6.2, helper-structuring effects were consistently in the direction predicted, but were not statistically significant.

It seems appropriate, given these findings, to conclude our consideration of this investigation by quoting Solomon's (1978) summary observation:

Table 6.3. Analysis of Variance (F) for Study Conditions.

Source	Direct Test (post)	Minimal Gen'l	Extended Gen'l
Mastery	19.69*	12.46*	25.95*
Helper	.12	2.46	1.45
Mastery × Helper	.73	.50	.18

*$p < .01$

The present study offers further support for the clinical utility of attribution theory. The results suggest that when a patient views himself as responsible for his improvement in therapy he is more likely to maintain the gains made. . . . Parents in this study receiving the Mastery manipulation developed an increased sense of mastery over one part of their environment and in doing so may have developed more positive expectations regarding competent performance in areas where they had previously met with little success. Their belief that they were responsible for changes in their behavior on the reaction time task may have fostered the belief that their sucess at self-control in the groups were due to their own efforts. Thus, they were more likely to apply this skill to new situations than parents who did not receive the mastery component. The implication for therapy with abusive parents is that the inculcation of the expectation of the efficacy of one's own efforts in changing the abusive pattern may be the essential element in generalizing therapeutic gains. [pp. 49–50.]

COUNSELORS

Prior to or concurrent with our own attempts to apply Structured Learning to the counselor skill training domain, a number of creative psychologists sought in a systematic manner to conceptualize and implement counselor training in skill development terms (Carkhuff, 1969; Danish & Hauer 1973; Ivey & Authier 1978; Kagan, 1970). These efforts have blossomed into major research and training programs which, in our view, speak well for the current viability and future prospects of counselor (and other helper) training. In our own facet of this enterprise, as the Structured Learning study which follows exemplifies, we have maintained our tripartite interest in acquisition, transfer, and prescriptiveness.

STUDY 17. CONCEPTUAL LEVEL AS A PRESCRIPTIVE CRITERION IN COUNSELOR TRAINING (ROSENTHAL, 1975)

In earlier chapters we sought to articulate and to examine a prescriptive perspective toward skill training in which the training method employed is modified in such a manner as to be responsive to those trainee characteristics which influence how effectively he or she is able to learn the target skills. The present investigation was a further attempt to implement this strategy.

In an educational context, Hunt (1971) sought to coordinate teaching methods and learner characteristics by matching the structuredness and autonomy of teaching methods to learner conceptual level. Conceptual level, according to Hunt and his colleagues, is a person dimension reflecting a developmental hierarchy of increasing self-responsibility, independence, and ability to generate concepts (Hunt, 1970, 1971; Hunt & Sullivan, 1974). Levels on this dimension, hierarchically arranged, are Level A—immature, unsocialized, and unable to generate own concepts; Level B—dependent and conforming, concerned with rules, categorical thinking; Level C—independent and self-reliant, cognitively complex, able to consider experiences from different viewpoints. In relating these person conceptual levels to optimal teaching methods, Hunt hypothesized that those learners classified as low in conceptual level profit more from a highly structured learning approach, while those individuals high in conceptual level will either benefit most from a minimally structured training approach or, at times, may be unaffected by the training environment's degree of structure. To examine the relevance of these notions to Structured Learning, Rosenthal (1975) implemented two versions of it, namely, the standard, highly structured Structured Learning, and a self-guided, much more independently administered form of Structured Learning, and examined the relative effectiveness of these variants with high and low conceptual level counselor trainees.

Procedure

Participants in this investigation were 58 graduate students enrolled in an introductory counseling methods course. This study sample contained 24 males and 34 females, ages 22 to 55. Their conceptual level (high or low) was determined by scores on the Paragraph Completion Test (Hunt, 1970). Participants were then randomly assigned, within conceptual levels, to the three study treatments, as shown in Fig. 6.4.

The Guided Instruction version (or "standard") Structured Learning consisted of three two-hour sessions held a week apart. In the Self-instruction format, (a) trainees worked independently at a self-paced rate and without the assistance of a trainer; (b) trainees engaged in self-contained role play of the study skill; and (c) trainees relied upon self-reinforcement, rather than peer or trainer approval. Length of this self-paced training necessarily varied

		Structured Learning: Guided Instruction	Structured Learning Self-instruction	Attention plus Brief Instructions Control
Conceptual Level	High	I	II	III
	Low	IV	V	VI

Fig. 6.4. Experimental design for conceptual level study.

somewhat within this (individualized) condition, but averaged two, 90-minute sessions. The Attention plus Brief Instructions control participants spent two two-hour sessions in a discussion of school-revelant problem situations, engaging in self-awareness exercises, and receiving skill-relevant content and motivational brief instructions.

The target skill for this investigation was the effective counseling skill, Confrontation. Confrontation occurs when a counselor points out to a client that there is a contradiction or inconsistency in what the client is communicating. Two types of confrontations have been distinguished. A content-affect confrontation is directed at the discrepancy between the words of the client and the manner in which they are spoken. A content-content confrontation points out an inconsistency between what the client is saying now and has said previously. Both types of confrontation can and should be delivered with counselor warmth and sincerity, and should be distinguished from attack or similar distancing behaviors. Johnson (1970) and Mainord, Burk, and Collins (1965) have shown high levels of counselor confrontation skill to have positive consequences for client change.

Direct Test and Minimal Generalization Test format followed our usual taped stimulus situation—verbal trainee response format. Examples of these situations, to all of which counselor-trainee confrontation would constitute an optimal response, included:

1. Yeah, my Dad got a big raise and promotion. Now all he does is work! He's not interested in us anymore. We used to go places together; we used to play football and baseball. Now I get a lot of things like a stereo and guitar. Boy, its great that Dad got a promotion and gets more money.

2. I'm never getting married! Men are just chauvinist pigs. All of them, they're all alike. They all see women as some kind of sex symbol. I'm lucky Rob and I broke up. Believe me, that Sue is welcome to him. I'm certainly glad he's found someone else. It gets lonely sometimes, but I know I'll find another guy.

3. No, I'm not upset! It will only hurt me if I get angry at Joe. Whenever you get angry at others you wind up hurting yourself. I don't care what he does. He can go to Alaska for all I care; it won't bother me. Bob came over last night and we talked for a while. He seems like a nice guy. I like him.

This study's Extended Generalization Test required trainees to conduct a 15-minute interview with a male, coached-client experimental accomplice who was trained to provide three content-content discrepancies and three content-affect discrepancies during the interview.

In almost all of our other investigations, participant dependent variable scores were represented in terms of ratings reflecting the number and quality of the target skill's behavioral steps expressed in response to Direct, Minimal Generalization, or Extended Generalization Test stimulus situations. In the present study, participant Confrontation skill scores were determined by judges who rated trainee responses on the three dependent variable tests against the definitions and examples of levels of this skill depicted in Carkhuff's (1969) Confrontation in Interpersonal Process Scale.

Results and Discussion

Trainee performance on study dependent measures is shown in Table 6.4. Analysis of these data by means of Dunn's multiple planned comparison test revealed, as predicted, consistent overall significant effects for the presence of Structured Learning compared to its absence, across trainee conceptual levels. Both Structured Learning in Guided Instruction (G.I.) format and Structured Learning in Self-Instruction (S.I.) format yielded significantly higher levels of confrontation acquisition ($d_{G.I.}$ = 1.24, $d_{S.I.}$ = 1.12) minimal transfer ($d_{G.I.}$ = 1.43, $d_{S.I.}$ = 1.25) and extended transfer ($d_{G.I.}$ = .88, $d_{S.I.}$ = 8.6) as compared to Attention-Brief Instruction control trainees.

Perhaps of finer-grained interest than the overall effects of Structured Learning described above was the differential impact of Structured Learning training method on trainees differing in conceptual level. Mean scores and standard deviations for all study dependent measures, by type of Structured Learning instruction and conceptual level, are reported in Table 6.5.

As the data in Table 6.5. suggest, and as subsequent planned comparison analyses confirm, self-instruction employed by high conceptual level trainees led to significantly greater target skill acquisition (d = 1.15) and minimal transfer (d = .88), though not extended transfer, than its effect for low conceptual level trainees. In complement with this effect, it was also the case that within the low conceptual level sample, those receiving guided instruction in Structured Learning acquire (d = .80) and minimally transfer (d = .53) the target skill to a significantly greater degree than do those receiving Structured Learning training via self-instruction. In constrast, and as predicted, high conceptual level trainees appear to acquire and to transfer

Table 6.4. Means and Standard Deviations for Study Measures of Confrontation.

Study Condition	Direct Test (pre)		Direct Test (post)		Minimal Generalization		Extended Generalization	
	X	SD	X	SD	X	SD	X	SD
SL-Guided Instruction	1.61	.18	2.98	.09	2.97	.10	2.52	.53
SL-Self-Instruction	1.57	.33	2.82	.47	2.79	.40	2.54	.38
Attention-Instruction Control	1.64	.20	1.77	.33	1.54	.32	1.66	.33

Table 6.5. Means and Standard Deviations by Instruction Method and Conceptual Level.

Study Condition		Direct Test (pre)		Direct Test (post)		Minimal Gen'l		Extended Gen'l	
		X	SD	X	SD	X	SD	X	SD
SL-Guided Instruction:	High CL	1.53	.16	2.98	.18	2.99	.16	2.36	.59
	Low CL	1.71	.25	2.97	.15	2.95	.11	2.70	.50
SL-Self- Instruction:	High CL	1.58	.31	3.04	.18	3.02	.10	2.66	.26
	Low CL	1.60	.23	2.45	.55	2.42	.59	2.28	.52

the target skill approximately equally well under guided or self-instruction training conditions.

The investigation and identification of trainee characteristics of reliable prescriptive utility—such as conceptual level—is still in a highly primitive stage. We believe that the efficacy of training will (some day) be optimized when its procedures and contents are differentially tailored to not one, but to a wide array of relevant trainee characteristics. Consistent with Kiesler's (1969) grid model, Lazarus' (1971) personalistic therapy perspective, Magaro, Gripp, and McDowell's (1978) prescriptive tree, and our own (Goldstein & Stein, 1976) tridifferential factorial model, outcome variance is conceptualized as having multiple prescriptive determinants associated with trainer, trainee, and training method characteristics. Current research, which must be seen as but beginning prescriptive research, has focused more or less necessarily on single potentially relevant and potentially active ingredients, e.g., social class (Goldstein, 1973), premorbid personality (Magaro, 1969) or, as in the case of the present investigation, conceptual level (Rosenthal, 1975). We applaud these efforts, and eagerly wish to promote their further complexification into multidimensional, three-way factorial studies and research programs in which several trainer × trainee × training method characteristics are cojointly examined for their prescriptive impact on the acquisition and transfer of training objectives. In doing so, we urge the prescriptive investigator to be highly tentative and cautious in his differential generalizations. As part of our research program, Gilstad (1978) sought to replicate certain major aspects of Rosenthal's (1975) investigation. He examined guided instruction and self-instruction versions of Structured Learning used to train skill in empathy to high and low conceptual level teachers. Thus, both the target skill (empathy) and the trainee population (teachers) differed from Rosenthal's training of confrontation skill to counselors. Gilstad's results did demonstrate significant overall acquisition and transfer effects for Structured Learning versus control group, and self-instructed high conceptual level trainees were (nonsignificantly) the highest on the target skill after training, but there was not a successful demonstration of the significant conceptual level by training method interaction which Rosenthal had found. Why this difference in results occurred is a matter for speculation. Perhaps the learning of the skill confrontation demands greater levels of cognitive ability or cognitive complexity than does empathy, and thus conceptual level was relevant to Rosenthal's outcome but not to Gilstad's. Or perhaps there exist other confrontation versus empathy or counselor versus teacher differences relevant to the differential results. The point, we believe, is clear. Once one has identified a reliable prescriptive predictor, one must systematically test the limits of its utility in parametric studies which separately test its predictive efficacy with those differing trainer $\times$ trainee $\times$ training method combinations which correspond to the real world trainer $\times$ trainee $\times$ training method combinations which functionally exist or might ideally exist.

Chapter 7
Other Trainees

Certain of the applications of Structured Learning, while they are directed at societally important trainee populations, have not yet received extended research scrutiny. Included here are police, industrial managers, teachers, and the use of Structured Learning by the general public on a self-help basis—all of which areas we consider in the present chapter. We do so in the belief that these applications have made a useful contribution to the functioning skill levels of the trainees involved, and that future research may go beyond our current impressionistic evidence on these populations and aid us in making Structured Learning of even greater value to these and related trainee groups.

POLICE

Crisis Intervention

Surveys completed in several police departments across the United States have revealed that only about 20 percent of the typical officer's time is spent in criminal apprehension or related crime control activities. Approximately 80 percent of the time, the average police officer is involved in service calls primarily requiring social regulation or what has been termed order maintenance. Our main training concern in utilizing Structured Learning in several American police departments has been those order maintenance calls involving crisis intervention. These are calls for police assistance in dealing with family fights, mentally disturbed or intoxicated citizens, suicide attempts, and the victims of accidents, assaults, rape, or other offenses. Such crisis calls have certain important and skill-relevant similarities.

First, one or more highly emotional citizens are likely to be involved, though the particular emotion will tend to vary with the type of crisis— family dispute (anger), suicide and accident (anxiety, depression), rape and assault (hysteria), mental disturbance or intoxication (agitation, confusion).

In part because of their highly emotional nature, a second similarity among most crisis calls is their high level of unpredictable danger, including substantial threats to the responding officer's safety. Forty percent of all police injuries occur on crisis calls, and family disputes are particularly dangerous, accounting for 103 of the 786 police officers killed in the United

States in a recent ten-year period. One of the main purposes of our Structured Learning training with police was to teach safety-enhancing, threat-reducing skills which might function to reduce or minimize the danger associated with crisis intervention.

Calming an aggressive, confused, anxious, or hysterical citizen is frequently a difficult task. Such persons must be calmed, not only for their own comfort and safety and for that of others at the crisis scene, but also to permit the responding officer to get on with the job of resolving the crisis and restoring order. Thus, a second major purpose of our police training was to teach a variety of skills useful in calming highly emotional individuals. Once the officer has calmed the individuals involved, and taken precautions to guard his own safety, he can begin to gather relevant information and take appropriate, crisis-resolving police action. These two final steps in crisis resolution, i.e., information gathering and taking effective action, were also central targets for our police training programs. More fully, our Structured Learning police training for crisis intervention competence has consisted of the following target skills:

I.   Observing and protecting against threats to your safety:
    1. Consider your prior experience on similar calls.
    2. Anticipate that the unexpected may actually happen.
    3. Form a tentative plan of action.
II. Calming the situation:
    1. Observe and neutralize threats to your safety.
    2. Create a first impression of nonhostile authority.
    3. Calm the emotional citizen.
III. Gathering relevant information:
    1. Explain to the citizen what you want him to discuss with you and why.
    2. Interview the citizen so as to get details of the crisis as clearly as possible.
    3. Show that you understand the citizen's statements and give accurate answers to his questions.
    4. Revise your plan of action if appropriate.
IV. Taking appropriate action:
    1. Carefully explain your plan of action to the citizen.
    2. Check that the citizen understands and agrees with your plan of action.
    3. Carry out your plan of action.

These safety-maintaining, calming, information-gathering, and actional skills, and their training and implementation, are described in full detail in our *Structured Learning Manual for Police Officers* (Appendix C) and in *Police Crisis Intervention* (Goldstein, Monti, Sardino, & Green, 1977).

Hostage Negotiation

In the mid-1970s, law enforcement agencies in the United States and elsewhere began to have to face on a substantial scale a new type of criminal activity, which heretofore had confronted them only rarely. Hostage taking—by terrorists, criminals, or the mentally deranged—seemed to become an almost weekly event as skyjacking, embassy takeovers, and bank robberies involving hostages occurred time and again. Gradually, through the wisdom of experienced law enforcement sources (Bassiouni, 1975; Clutterbuck, 1975; Parry, 1976) and behavioral science research on negotiation and persuasion (Cohen, 1966; Karlins & Abelson, 1970; Rubin & Brown, 1975) a coherent and effective response to hostage taking emerged. Cast into Structured Learning skill terms, effective resolution of hostage-taking situations consists sequentially of:

1. Safety skills.
2. Choosing negotiation strategies.
3. Skills for calming the perpetrator.
4. Building rapport skills.
5. Information-obtaining skills.
6. Persuading the perpetrator skills.

A detailed presentation and examination of these hostage resolution skills appears in Appendix D and in *Hostage* (Miron & Goldstein, 1979).

Elderly Citizens

Police officers face special problems in their dealings with elderly citizens. Fear of crime, crime prevention, investigative problems, and a number of other special law enforcement issues exist vis-à-vis the elderly citizen, and must be dealt with in a skilled, sensitive, and, in a sense, prescriptive manner by the effective police officer. What these issues are, and how their management may be expressed and taught in skill training terms has recently been explicated by us in *Police and the Elderly* (Goldstein, Hoyer, & Monti, 1979), to which we refer the interested reader.

INDUSTRIAL MANAGERS

In the early 1970s, we began implementing Structured Learning in industrial contexts, primarily for teaching management skills to foremen and first-line managers. These efforts, described in detail in *Changing Supervisor Behavior* (Goldstein & Sorcher, 1974), had as their goal not only efficient and humanitarian managerial behavior, but especially management skill in dealing with special worker populations, e.g., minorities, women supervised by men, men supervised by women, etc. The specific skills for which we developed modeling displays, listed below, provide a more concrete sense of the training goals of this work:

Industrial Management Skills Taught by Structured Learning

1. Orienting a new employee.
2. Teaching the job.
3. Motivating the poor performer.
4. Correcting inadequate work quantity.
5. Correcting inadequate work quality.
6. Reducing absenteeism among disadvantaged workers.
7. Reducing turnover among disadvantaged workers.
8. Handling the racial discrimination complaint.
9. Handling the reverse discrimination complaint.
10. Reducing resentment of the female supervisor.
11. Discussing personal work habits with an employee.
12. Discussing formal corrective action with an employee.
13. Giving recognition to the average employee.
14. Overcoming resistance to change.
15. Reducing evaluation resistance.
16. Delegating responsibility.
17. Conducting a performance review.

Our early studies on this application of Structured Learning were encouraging. In one investigation, we obtained evidence demonstrating significantly less turnover among disadvantaged employees when they and their foremen underwent Structured Learning (for skills 1, 3, 6, 13, 14 in the above list), as compared to groups not participating (Goldstein & Sorcher, 1973). In a second investigation, a significant difference in productivity emerged favoring workers of trained foremen versus those whose foremen had not undergone Structured Learning (Sorcher & Goldstein, 1972).

Other studies soon followed. Burnaska (1975) at General Electric taught an array of nine managerial skills to 62 middle-level managers from six company locations, and randomly assigned 62 others to a no-training control condition. Behavioral (role-play) dependent variable measurement for skill acquisition (immediate posttesting) and skill maintenance (four-month followup) yielded significant effects favoring the trained managers. Analysis of data, however, gathered on employee perceptions of trained versus untrained managers at the four-month followup point generally failed to demonstrate significant differences.

At AT&T, Moses and Ritchie (1975) taught most of the above-listed skills to a sample of 90 first-level supervisors, with 93 others assigned to a no-training control group. Following training, all supervisors (trained and untrained) participated in role-play behavioral assessment, on both previously trained and new situations (absenteeism, discrimination, theft). Across test situations, all of which were administered two months after training, trained supervisors performed in a significantly more skilled manner according to independently made behavioral ratings, than did the untrained supervisors.

At IBM, Smith (1975) compared (1) Structured Learning plus *in vivo* practice, (2) Structured Learning, (3) traditional (memos, guides, etc.) managerial training, and (4) a no-training control group on customer satisfaction and sales performance. At the completion of training, the Structured Learning trainees (groups [1] and [2]) significantly surpassed the traditionally trained and untrained study participants on the customer satisfaction criterion, but this effect had faded by the four-month followup. Sales performance, however, was significantly better in these two trained groups as much as a year after the Structured Learning training.

Latham and Saari (1979), in the final industrial examination of Structured Learning we have been able to locate, conducted a nine-week Structured Learning program which sought to teach most of the above skills to 20 first-level supervisors in a large company (name unspecified). Twenty other supervisors were assigned to a no-training control condition. As in the studies described above, on behavioral acquisition and followup measures of skill proficiency, experimentals significantly exceeded controls.

These half-dozen studies are a useful beginning. Their designs tend to be rather rudimentary; most of them rarely deal with the crucial issues of transfer-enhancement or prescriptive utilization at all, and certain of them suffer from a number of substantial methodological weaknesses which have been perceptively identified and discussed by McGhee and Tullar (1978). But we applaud this research as an important start, especially in the hope that more (and more sophisticated) research will follow. The utilization of Structured Learning in industry has far outpaced its investigation. Under such names as behavior modeling, interaction modeling, supervisory relationships training, and others, Structured Learning is finding especially widespread application in industry. While we find this a welcome development, we hope such use will be matched increasingly by careful and creative scrutiny by skilled and energetic researchers.

TEACHERS

In addition to the Gilstad (1978) comparison of guided-instruction versus self-instruction Structured Learning at different conceptual levels, which we briefly examined earlier, there have been two applications of Structured Learning to teacher populations. Mudd and his students have prepared a *Teacher-Student Relationships Training Manual* (Mudd, 1979) which deals at length with all applied aspects of utilizing Structured Learning with teacher trainees. In doing so, they have operationally defined a series of useful teacher-student skills, including:

I.   Encouraging the average student:
  1. Compliment the student on something he/she has done recently.
  2. Explain why this was important to you.
  3. Ask what things you could do to make the class more interesting for him/her.
  4. Specify followup of any reasonable suggestions.
II. Reducing fear of public presentation:
  1. Describe to the student what you've seen and why it concerns you.
  2. Explain why this was important to you.
  3. Show understanding of the student's problem.
  4. Explore things that each of you could do to make the situation better.
III. Reducing tardiness:
  1. Ask the student for reasons for the tardiness and listen openly.
  2. Show that you understand the student's feelings and reasons.
  3. Review school policy and explain why it is important to be on time.
  4. Together, discuss ways to avoid tardiness and agree on a solution to the problem.
  5. Followup and reinforce punctuality.

Their informal evaluation of these and related materials in a junior high school context appeared favorable, a conclusion supported in the more formal study conducted by Schneiman (1972), which we wish to consider at greater length. Schneiman selected certain principles of contingency management relevant to a classroom setting as the training target for his study. The application of behavioral assessment and behavioral treatment strategies and procedures has emerged in recent years as a major force in the management of classroom behavior (e.g., Buckley & Walker, 1972; O'Leary & O'Leary, 1972). Becker, Madsen, Arnold, and Thomas (1967) sought to alter the disruptive classroom behavior of ten children by training their teachers to implement systematically the principles of Rule making, Ignoring, and Praising. Rule making meant regularly making explicit to the child what behaviors were expected of him during each class period. Ignoring was defined as having the teacher avoid paying attention to any behaviors by the child that interfered with the teaching-learning process, except any behaviors that might result in injury. Praise required the teacher to attend overtly to, and comment favorably on, those behaviors by the child that facilitated learning. Apparently as a function of these procedures, classroom observation revealed a substantial and consistent decrease in deviant behavior for almost all the participating children.

Madsen, Becker, and Thomas (1968) both replicated and extended these findings. Rule making, Ignoring, and Praising again proved effective in reducing disruptive classroom behavior, and there was some evidence that the major contribution stemmed from the teacher's use of praise and related expressions of social reinforcement. Lorr (1970) substituted Mild Disapproval (a corrective statement that specifies the inappropriate behavior and presents an acceptable alternative) for Ignoring and found even more satisfactory behavioral outcomes. Thus, it was the ability to implement the principles of Rule making, Mild Disapproval and Praise adequately that formed the training goal for the Schneiman investigation. We have held that Structured Learning appears to be appropriately prescriptive for lower-class and working-class populations. In the present study we sought to examine the restrictiveness or breadth of this "prescription" by training and comparing both lower-class and middle-class teacher's aide samples.

Procedure

Subjects for this investigation were 30 lower-class teacher's aides randomly selected from the population of such persons in a moderately large city school district, and 30 middle-class teacher's aides drawn randomly from a suburban school district.

Following pretesting on the study target skills, and utilizing a 2×3 factorial design, aides were randomly assigned (within social class groupings) to three experimental conditions:

1. Structured Learning. Aides met in groups of ten each for one three-hour Structured Learning session.

2. Didactic Learning. Aides assigned to this experimental condition participated in a three-hour lecture and group discussion session, led by the same E who had served as Structured Learning leader. Rule making, Mild Disapproval, and Praise were defined and (verbally) exemplified at considerable length. Their role in the broader context of classroom management was elaborated. Group discussion focused on both the foregoing, as well as concrete examination of how the three principles might most effectively be utilized with specific children in the participant's classes.

3. No-Treatment Control. The ten middle-class and ten lower-class teacher's aides assigned to this experimental condition participated in the study's pretesting and posttesting only. They were exposed to no Structured or Didactic Learning procedures.

In addition to Direct Test (pre and post) information, study-dependent measures included two forms of behavioral assessment of study skills. One was a Minimal Generalization Test which was a standardized stimulus situation in which each aide, in turn, had to respond to a child actor who initiated three disruptive behaviors during the five-minute test period. These were refusal to sit with the aide, failure to pay attention to the aide when seated next to her, and disruptive noise making when the aide was reading aloud. The second, an Extended Generalization Test, consisted of 30 minutes of actual classroom observation of each aide.

The major findings in this investigation are presented in Table 7.1. These results indicate a rather clear and consistent pattern. The analyses of the Direct Test (post-pre) data reveal that across social class levels, both Structured and Didactic Learning are superior to no instruction in enhancing acquisition of the target skills—at least as far as participant ability to verbalize such skills is concerned. Of greater applied consequence is the aides' ability actually to enact the skill behaviors. Can they, first of all, perform the behaviors immediately after training and while still in the training setting? Results for the role-played behavioral testing reveal an affirmative answer, again across social class levels, but only for those aides trained by Structured Learning. That is, both middle- and lower-class aides receiving Structured Learning performed significantly more adequately on all three target skills (separately and combined) than did either Didactic Learning or no-treatment participants. Across treatments it appears that middle-class aides demonstrated significantly more adequate performance than did their lower-class counterparts on two of the three skill dimensions.

Of greatest importance among these results is not what the aides say they would do, nor their immediate posttraining performance. Most consequential is their overt skill performance in the classroom. The Classroom Observation Instrument results do indicate substantial positive transfer from the training to application setting. In both their appropriate use of Mild Disapproval, and in their use of the three skills combined, aides receiving Structured Learning evidence performance superior to those receiving Didactic Learning or no treatment. While these findings also held separately for both social class groupings, there is again related evidence that middle-class aides perform more adequately than do lower-class aides.

The Gilstad (1978), Mudd (1979), and Schneiman (1972) efforts are an encouraging series. They combine with the several more elaborate studies presented in Chapters 4 and 5 to suggest that Structured Learning can indeed have an important place in high school and elementary school contexts, for both student-training and teacher-training purposes.

SELF-INSTRUCTION

As noted earlier, two of our investigations indicated that a self-instructional version of Structured Learning could indeed enhance skill proficiency, espe-

Table 7.1. Analyses of Variance (F Values) and t Tests for Rule Making,
Mild Disapproval, and Praise.

Measure	Source[a]
Direct Test	
1. Rule making	
a. between treatments (F = 32.86**)	SL > NT
	DL > NT
2. Mild disapproval	
a. between treatments (F = 86.28**)	SL > NT
	DL > NT
3. Praise	
a. between treatments (F = 10.18**)	SL > NT
	DL > NT
4. Total	
a. between treatments (F = 67.97**)	SL > NT
	DL > NT
Minimal Generalization Test	
1. Rule making	
a. between treatments (F = 24.23**)	SL > DL
	SL > NT
b. between social classes (F = 17.06**)	MC > LC
2. Mild disapproval	
a. between treatments (F = 33.79**)	SL > DL
	SL > NT
3. Praise	
a. between treatments (F = 17.67**)	SL > DL
	SL > NT
b. between social classes (F = 10.05**)	MC > LC
4. Total	
a. between treatments (F = 59.84**)	SL > DL
	SL > NT
b. between social classes (F = 15.56**)	MC > LC
Extended Generalization Test	
1. Rule making	
a. between social classes (F = 10.78**)	MC > LC
2. Mild disapproval	
a. between treatments (F = 4.53*)	SL > DL
	SL > NT
3. Praise	
a. between social classes (F = 10.11**)	MC > LC
4. Total	
a. between treatments (F = 4.56*)	SL > DL
	SL > NT

[a] Source key: SL—Structured Learning; DL—Didactic Learning; NT—No treatment; MC—Middle class; LC—Lower class.
* p < .05
** p < .01

cially in high conceptual level individuals (Rosenthal, 1975; Gilstad, 1976). Stimulated by these findings, and by the widespread self-help movement in the United States, we have prepared a Structured Learning self-help text, *I Know What's Wrong, But I Don't Know What To Do about It* (Goldstein, Sprafkin, & Gershaw, 1979). In order to utilize the main procedures which constitute Structured Learning on a self-help basis, we found it necessary to alter somewhat the specific events which made up modeling, role playing, performance feedback, and transfer training. These procedures, renamed behavioral description, behavioral rehearsal, behavioral feedback, and behavioral transfer in this self-help version, are described in detail in Appendix E.

Our self-instructional, self-help version of Structured Learning, as is true of almost all of the many self-help books which have appeared in this era of "giving psychology away," has not been evaluated in a rigorous, systematic manner. Even when a therapy or training or educational approach has been thoroughly tested in its therapist- or teacher-led form, its self-help version has almost invariably not been. It cannot be assumed that the absence of the change agent makes no difference, at least for most target populations, and thus direct empirical tests of such self-help versions must be performed.

Chapter 8
Issues in Skill Training: Resolved and Unresolved

As we bring to a close our presentation and examination of this research skills-training program, there remains a series of issues worth further consideration. We consider these issues in this final chapter as a means of explicitly pointing to relevant problems yet to be resolved and, thus, to useful directions for further research.

TRANSFER ENHANCEMENT

We have visited the topic of transfer enhancement many times in the preceding chapters, and do not wish to dwell upon it at length here. Our view of its crucial importance as an investigative and training goal has been amply stated, and perhaps can best be summarized by the following quotation from Goldstein and Kanfer (1979):

> Examination of both relevant clinical reports and therapy outcome research findings reveals that maintenance and transfer of gain is not a common outcome and, in fact, is much more the exception than the rule in treatment results. In the large majority of psychotherapeutic encounters—be they psychodynamic, behavioral, existential, or otherwise—patient improvement neither persists nor generalizes to new settings (Ford & Urban, 1963; Goldstein, Heller, & Sechrest, 1966; Kazdin, 1975; Marholin, Siegel, & Phillips, 1976). This contention is readily supported by the results of an extensive number of therapy outcome studies which are summarized in Table 1.1. Though the number of studies in Table 1.1. reporting positive therapeutic outcomes at the termination of treatment is high (85%), only 14% of the studies conducted report maintenance or transfer of therapeutic gains. The total sample of studies, furthermore, was selected on criteria reflecting high levels of methodological soundness, thus adding further to the tenability of the conclusion that transfer is a relatively uncommon psychotherapeutic outcome. It is true, of course, that follow-up evaluation of therapeutic outcome was absent in many of these studies. Thus, the 14% rate of response maintenance and positive transfer *may*, in fact, be artificially low and a truer rate *may* be somewhat higher. We think this to be unlikely, however. Keeley, Shemberg, and Carbonell (1976) examined an essentially different series of therapy outcome studies

Table 1.1. Therapy Outcome Study Results on Termination and Transfer.

Diagnosis	Number of studies	Number with positive results on termination	Number with positive results on transfer
Psychoneuroses			
Phobic reaction	55	45	11
Obsessive-Compulsive	6	3	0
Hysteria	3	3	1
Depression	7	6	1
Psychophysiological disorders			
Bronchial asthma	8	6	1
Ulcerative colitis	5	4	1
Hypertension and hypertensive headaches	4	4	1
Sexual deviations			
Sexual orientation disturbance	14	8	0
Orgasmic dysfunctioning	7	5	0
Fetishism and tranvestism	5	4	2
Exhibitionism	2	1	0
Antisocial behavior	15	11	1
Obesity	12	9	3
Insomnia	4	4	2
Schizophrenia	45	28	4
Totals	192	163	28

and came to the same conclusion as we have. They focused on the 146 investigations of operant interventions reported in a series of behaviorally oriented journals during 1972–1973. Even moderately long-term concern with transfer was rare. For the total number of investigations examined, follow-up (response maintenance), stimulus generalization, and response generalization each appear to occur in approximately 3% of the studies surveyed. They comment: "It seems clear that workers are not seriously researching operant interventions beyond prosthesis. Only 8 of the 146 studies analyzed present hard data collected at least 6 months past termination, and short term generalization data are conspicuously absent [p. 302]." Based on surveys of outcome investigations such as these, it appears appropriate to maintain that positive maintenance and transfer of therapeutic gain is much more often the exception than the rule, a conclusion also emerging in the therapeutic writings of many, many other investigators and theorists (Ayllon & Azrin, 1968; Bandura, 1969; Bijou & Redd, 1975; Burchard, 1971; Davidson & Seidman, 1974; DeMeyer & Ferster, 1962; Grindee, 1964, 1965; Kazdin, 1975; Marholin, Siegel, & Phillips, 1976; Meichenbaum, Bowers & Ross, 1968; Meyer & Crisp, 1964; O'Leary, Becker, Evans & Saudargas, 1969; Reiss, 1973). Nonmaintenance and nontransferability of therapeutic gains appears to occur as frequently as it does because psychotherapy theorists and practitioners either assume it will occur automatically or, if aware that transfer-enhancing procedures must be purposefully built into ongoing treatment, do not yet know how to do so adequately enough. [Goldstein & Kanfer, 1979, pp. 2-4.]

We would propose that the several transfer-enhancing procedures studied in the present research program are a heuristic beginning answer to this search. To review, these include:

1. Overlearning (Lopez, 1980)
2. Helper role structuring (Litwack, 1976; Solomon, 1978)
3. Identical elements (Wood, 1977; Guzzetta, 1974)
4. Coping modeling (Fleming, 1976)
5. Stimulus variability (Hummel, 1980)
6. General principles (Lopez, 1980; Lack, 1975)
7. Programmed reinforcement (Gutride, Goldstein, & Hunter, 1973; Greenleaf, 1978)
8. *In vivo* feedback (Goldstein & Goedhart, 1973)
9. Teaching skills in tandem (reciprocal benefits) (Hummel, 1980)
10. Mastery induction (Solomon, 1978)

Two texts have recently appeared which discuss these and numerous other potential transfer-enhancing techniques at considerable length, *Maximizing Treatment Gains: Transfer Enhancement in Psychotherapy* (Goldstein & Kanfer, 1979), and *Improving the Long-Term Effects of Psychotherapy* (Karoly & Steffen, 1980). We strongly urge careful examination of the procedures described therein and hope for their continued experimental scrutiny. In doing so, we hope it will prove more possible than it has in many of our investigations to examine the effectiveness of attempts at transfer and maintenance enhancement on a long-term basis and in a variety of real-life application contexts.

PRESCRIPTIVENESS

This topic, too, has already been dealt with in some depth by us both in earlier chapters and elsewhere (Goldstein & Stein, 1976; Goldstein, 1978). There are but a few summary observations we wish to add. A highly important subtask in the pursuit of optimally prescriptive trainee × trainer × training method combinations is the identification of potentially active ingredients. *Which* trainee characteristics, for example, are predictive of skill acquisition given a particular type of trainer and training method. The Hoyer et al. (in press) multiple regression investigation described in Chapter 3 is an example of the type of study which can yield such active ingredients information. It will be recalled that this investigation yielded mental status and anxiety as predictors of response to Structured Learning in chronic, adult, mental patient trainees. Another member of our research team conducted a parallel study seeking to identify characteristics of young children predictive of response to Structured Learning (Anderson, 1981). None of the participant characteristics examined in this manner proved, in fact, to be predictive, including (1) social maturity, (2) verbal ability, (3) cognitive and affective role-taking ability, (4) peer popularity, (5) age, and (6) sex. We are currently preparing to conduct analogous multiple regression research with adolescent trainees. Clearly, such studies are a necessary component of any effort to construct effective, prescriptive interventions. In conducting such research, we hope that investigators will go beyond the remedial strategy implicit in certain of our studies—in which we focused upon persons already displaying long-term skill deficiencies—and respond more to a preventive strategy by seeking to identify persons at risk and training them in a preparatory manner to confront future skill-demanding situations as they arise. Concretely, we refer here to the identification of outcome-relevant characteristics of such trainees as young children, and adults profitably taught premarital, parenting, preretirement, or other developmental stage-relevant skills.

A related question concerns what might be termed "combination prescriptions." Not only would it seem fruitful to pursue the path of studying the outcome relevance of components of interventions, but also of combinations of interventions. What is the impact, as we asked in the Gutride et al. (1973) study in Chapter 3, of jointly receiving Structured Learning training and psychotherapy? What other psychotherapeutic, educational, or related interventions can function in an additive, mutually facilitative manner? This, too, seems to be a worthwhile investigative path.

Finally, in operationalizing Structured Learning with different trainee populations, one might usefully consider not only prescriptively determined procedural adaptations, but also modifying or tailoring the materials utilized in Structured Learning in accordance with trainee learning styles and preferred channels of accessibility. In our work with adolescents, for example, extended observation of what such youngsters prefer to do if given the freedom of choice yielded such preferred activities as watching television, listening to rock music, reading comic books, and playing board games. In prescriptive response to these observations, our Structured Learning interventions with adolescents (1) always utilize visual modeling displays (live or filmstrip), (2) contain rock music theme songs (which also have the skill's behavioral steps as part of their lyrics), and (3) are supplemented with a skill-training board game ("Making It") and with comic books that we have developed in prototype. Similarly trainee-specific materials can and should be developed in response to the needs and preferences of other trainee populations.

EXPERIMENTAL DESIGNS

With relatively few (mostly multiple regression) exceptions, our research program has relied upon factorial experimental designs as its investigative means, a reliance we chose largely because of the potential utility of such designs in prescriptively oriented research. While we feel this to be a sound decision on which we plan to continue to act, we do not wish to devalue the potential of other design orientations to the understanding and improvement of psychological skill-training efforts. Studies employing single-case designs, for example, have been shown by Bellak and Herson (1979) to be able to shed considerable light on the skill-training process, and thus are to be encouraged. Even at the rudimentary, case-study level, we have found that experiences with single groups of special types of trainees—depressed college students (O'Brien, 1981), convicted felons (Weiss, 1979), blind individuals (Meyer, 1978)—tell us much of value about the trainees themselves, about Structured Learning, and about the psychological skill-training process in general.

Analog studies have long been a preferred companion research strategy of ours (Goldstein & Dean, 1966). We have conducted a subseries of Structured Learning analog investigations and found their outcomes to be sufficiently productive that, in companion with nonanalog research, we feel their further use would be quite valuable. In this manner, we have examined the usefulness of Structured Learning in teaching change agents how to recognize trainee fearfulness (Berlin, 1974), anger (Healy, 1975) and certain paralinguistic affective cues (Lopez, 1977); and we have examined which types of trainees are optimally matched in a Structured Learning-like context with trainers who are high in hostility-guilt (Edelman, 1977), high in need to control (Robertson, 1977), high in aggression tolerance (Sturm, 1979), or high on certain compatibility indices (O'Brien, 1977). At early parameter-identifying stages of a research program, in particular, analog research seems especially useful, and might well be considered as one of the tactics of choice as Structured Learning research ventures into new terrain at the hands of additional investigators.

STRUCTURED LEARNING TRAINERS

Though we have had relatively little to say about Structured Learning trainers throughout this book, we wish to point out that trainer characteristics and behavior are equal to trainee and method dimensions in their importance in the trainee × trainer × training method match. As Kiesler (1966) observed several years ago, we must no longer operate under the beliefs of a therapist uniformity myth. Trainers differ from one another, and are probably different in ways that substantially influence training outcome (e.g., see the analog studies cited above). Systematic identification and investigation of such trainer characteristics seem to us to be an especially valuable research goal. Consistent with such an aspiration, we might note that the array of types of change agents who have seemingly functioned as effective Structured Learning trainers is quite broad—psychologists; social workers; teachers; nurses; occupational and recreational therapists; graduate, undergraduate, and high school students; home aides; parent aides; teacher aides; and people who, by dint of their own (since overcome) skill-deficient history, might be called "been theres." Type of profession or level of credentials have not, it is our impression, been terribly important in determining who is or is not an effective Structured Learning trainer. Though we have provided our impressions of requisite general and specific trainer skills necessary for skilled leadership (see Appendix A), which characteristics do in fact lead to effective Structured Learning group leadership, to functionally skill-enhancing leadership, remains largely a domain for future investigation.

We have in this book sought to describe our research program in detail. Psychological skill training in general, and Structured Learning in particular, remain a relatively new venture. It is hoped that its beginning contribution to human satisfaction and effectiveness will be viewed both as a stimulus to its further implementation and study, and as a promise that such further scrutiny may well yield yet further benefit to diverse populations of skill-deficient individuals.

Appendices

Appendix A
Structured Learning Trainer's Manual for Adult Trainees

Arnold P. Goldstein,
Syracuse University

N. Jane Gershaw,
Veterans Administration

Robert P. Sprafkin,
Veterans Administration

CONTENTS

INTRODUCTION

The primary purpose of this trainer's manual is to provide detailed guidelines for effectively conducting Structured Learning Therapy groups. Structured Learning is a therapy approach which has been demonstrated to be successful in teaching psychiatric outpatients, inpatients, and a variety of other trainees, skills helpful to them in leading satisfying and effective lives. It is an approach which focuses on the teaching of personal and interpersonal coping and mastery skills, including such skills as initiating, carrying out, and ending a conversation; listening; initiating and responding to a complaint; negotiation; role taking; asking for help; self-control; stress rehearsal; problem solving; affective perception; aggression reduction, and a host of other skills relevant to the interpersonal and planning components of the work, social, financial, and personal aspects of daily living.

Structured Learning consists of four components, each of which is a well-established behavior-change procedure. These procedures are modeling, role playing, social reinforcement, and transfer training.

In each training session, a group of six to twelve patients: (1) listens to a brief audiotape (or watches live persons) depicting scientific skill behaviors shown to be helpful in dealing with common problems of daily living (MODELING)[1]; (2) is given extensive opportunity, encouragement, and training to rehearse or practice the effective behaviors which have been modeled behaviorally (ROLE PLAYING); (3) is provided corrective feedback and approval or praise as their role playing of the behaviors becomes more and more similar to the tape model's behavior (SOCIAL REINFORCEMENT); and (4) discusses Homework Reports completed between sessions as but one of a variety of procedures used to encourage the transfer of the newly learned behaviors from the training setting to a real-life setting (TRANSFER TRAINING).

Before describing the procedures involved in organizing and actually running Structured Learning sessions in further detail, we wish to mention briefly what Structured Learning is not. First, it is important to stress that the behavioral steps which make up each skill portrayed on each audiotape should not be viewed as the one and only way to enact the skill effectively. The goal of Structured Learning Therapy is to help build a flexible repertoire of socially effective and satisfying behaviors which can be adjusted to the demands of the patients' life situations. Thus, we urge the reader to consider the taped behaviors as good examples, as they indeed have been shown to be, but not as the only effective way to perform the skill involved.

---

1. See Addendum 1, Tables 3 and 4, for a complete listing of the Structured Learning Therapy modeling tapes.

A second caution may be stated by noting that the Structured Learning modeling tapes are not instructional tapes in the usual sense. An instructional tape is most typically played to an audience which listens to it passively and then, at some later date, is supposed to do what was played. Such passive learning is not likely to be enduring. Thus, the Structured Learning modeling tapes should not be played alone—i.e., without following them with role playing and feedback. We have demonstrated experimentally that all four components of our training approach are necessary and sufficient for enduring behavior change, and these results should be reflected in the use of these materials and procedures. Finally, Structured Learning is not an approach that can be effectively used by all possible trainers. Later in this manual, we shall describe in detail the knowledge, skills, and sensitivities which a trainer must possess to be effective with this approach.

ORGANIZING THE STRUCTURED LEARNING GROUP

Selection of Patients

Each Structured Learning group should consist of trainees who are clearly deficient in whatever skill is going to be taught. If possible, trainees should also be grouped according to the degree of their deficiency in the given skill. The optimal group size for effective Structured Learning sessions is six to twelve trainees plus two trainers. In order for both learning and transfer to occur, each trainee must have ample opportunity to practice what he has heard or seen modeled, must receive feedback from other group members and from the trainers, and must discuss his attempts to apply what he has learned in the therapy sessions at home, on the job, or on the ward. Yet, each session should typically not exceed two hours in length, since Structured Learning is intensive and trainees' efficiency of learning diminishes beyond this span. A group size of six to twelve, therefore, is optimal in that it permits the specific therapy tasks to be accomplished within the allotted time period. If most trainees in a given group show a particularly brief span of attention, the session can be shortened to as little as one half-hour, although in this instance it is advisable to meet more often than the usual two or three times per week.

The trainees selected need not be from the same ward (if inpatients) nor from the same community area (if outpatients). Again to maximize transfer, however, trainees are asked to "set the stage" when role playing by enacting the modeling tape's specific behaviors, or behavioral steps, as they fit their real situation on the ward, at home, or at work. Each role play involves at least two participants, the trainee himself (main actor) and another trainee (coactor) chosen by him to play the role of wife, boss, nurse, or whatever role is appropriate for the given skill problem. We ask the main actor playing himself to describe in detail an actual situation in which he is having or could be having difficulty performing the skill behaviors which have been modeled. The coactor plays the part of the other person in the main actor's life who is involved in the skill problem area. In this way, the role playing becomes real—i.e., rehearsal for solving real-life problems. Thus, while participants need not come from the same ward or community, they should be familiar enough with one another's real-life situations so that they can role-play these situations realistically.

Number, Length, and Spacing of Sessions

The Structured Learning modeling tapes and associated procedures typically constitute a training program from three to fifteen sessions long, depending on the level of the group and the number and complexity of the skills being taught. For each interpersonal or personal skill we have sought to teach, we have developed a different modeling tape.[2] The specific behavioral steps comprising the skills are concretely demonstrated on each tape. The order in which the modeling tapes are utilized should (1) give trainees a sense of making progress in skill mastery (thus, the easier skills should come first); and (2) provide them (in each session) with useful knowledge that can be applied in real-life settings between sessions.

It is most desirable that treatment occur at a rate of two or, at the most, three times per week. Spacing is crucial. Most trainees in all therapy or skill-training programs learn well in the training setting. Most, however, fail to transfer this learning to where it counts—to the ward, the home, at work, or in the community. As will be seen below, Structured Learning includes special procedures which maximize the likelihood of transfer of training, including between-sessions "homework." For there to be ample opportunity for trainees to try out what was learned in the training setting in real-life, sessions must be well spaced. One sequence of modeling, several role plays, feedback, and assignment of homework is ideally covered in each training session of one to two hours in length. The following session should open with a review of the previous session's homework.

TRAINERS

The role-playing and feedback activities which constitute most of each Structured Learning session are a series of "action-reaction" sequences in which

---

2. Modeling tapes for Goldstein, A. P., Sprafkin, R. P., & Gershaw, N. J. *Skill training for community living* (New York: Pergamon Press, 1976).

effective skill behaviors are first rehearsed (role playing) and then critiqued (feedback). As such, the trainer must both lead and observe. We have found that one trainer is very hard pressed to do both of these tasks well at the same time, and we therefore recommend strongly that each session be led by a team of two trainers. Their professional credentials are largely irrelevant; on the other hand, their group leadership skills, interpersonal sensitivity, enthusiasm, and the favorableness of the relationship between them appear crucial to the success of treatment. Furthermore, proficiency in two types of skills are required of Structured Learning trainers.

The first might best be described as General Trainer Skills—i.e., those skills requisite for success in almost any training or therapy effort. These include:

a. oral communication and group discussion leadership;
b. flexibility and capacity for resourcefulness;
c. enthusiasm;
d. ability to work under pressure;
e. empathic ability;
f. listening skill;
g. broad knowledge of human behavior, demands of community living, etc.; and
h. group management skills.

The second type of requisite skills are Specific Trainer Skills—i.e., those germane to Structured Learning in particular. These include:

a. knowledge, in depth, of Structured Learning—its background, procedures, and goals;
b. ability to orient both patients and supporting staff to Structured Learning;
c. ability to initiate and sustain role playing;
d. ability to present material in concrete, behavioral form;
e. ability to reduce trainees' resistance; and
f. sensitivity in providing corrective feedback.

For both trainer selection and development purposes, we have found it most desirable to have potential trainers participate, as if they were actual trainees, in a series of Structured Learning sessions. After this experience, we have had them co-lead a series of sessions with an experienced trainer. In doing so, we have shown them how to conduct such sessions, given them several opportunities to practice what they have seen, and provided them with feedback regarding their performance. In effect, we have used Structured Learning to teach Structured Learning. To aid in this regard, we have developed and utilized a series of Trainer Preparation tapes[3] portraying Initial, Advanced, and Resistive Structured Learning Therapy sessions.

---

3. Trainer Preparation tapes for Goldstein, A. P., Sprafkin, R. P., & Gershaw, N. J. *Skill training for community living* (New York: Pergamon Press, 1976).

THE STRUCTURED LEARNING SESSIONS

The Setting

One major principle for encouraging transfer from the therapy to the real-life setting is the rule of identical elements. This rule states that the more similar the two settings—i.e., the greater number of identical physical and social qualities shared by them—the greater the transfer. Therapy in a fancy office or at a mountaintop work-play retreat may be great fun, but it results in minimal transfer of training. We urge that Structured Learning be conducted in the same general setting as the real-life environment of most participating trainees and that the treatment setting be furnished to resemble or simulate as much as possible the likely application settings.

The horseshoe seating arrangement, illustrated in Fig. 1, is one good example of how furniture might be arranged in the therapy room. Participating trainees may sit at a desk or at tables so that some writing space is provided. Two chairs are placed up front for the role players. Behind and to the side of one of the role players is a chalkboard on which is written the behavioral steps for the skill being worked with at that time. If possible, other parts of this same room should be furnished with props which resemble (at least in rudimentary form) a kitchen, a store counter, an office, a bedroom, or other relevant application setting. When no appropriate furniture or materials are available to "set the scene," substitute or even imaginary props can readily be used.

We have found it useful in the majority of Structured Learning Therapy groups to provide each trainee with a simplified and structured guide which explains group procedures and which is useful for taking notes during and between training sessions. This guide, the *Trainee's Notebook for Structured Learning Therapy*,[4] outlines the procedural details for Structured Learning Therapy and provides note pages for the trainee to write behavioral steps, role-play observations, and homework assignments. The notebook also serves as a convenient reference for trainees as they build a repertoire of skills.

The Introduction

The trainers open the initial session first introducing themselves and having each trainee do likewise, being sure that every trainee has the opportunity to tell the group something about his background and training goals. After such an initial warmup or familiarization period, the trainers introduce the program by providing trainees with a brief description of its rationale, training

---

4. See Appendix B for Table of Contents of Goldstein, A. P., Sprafkin, R. P. & Gershaw, N. J., *Trainee's Notebook for Structured Learning Therapy* (New York: Pergamon Press, 1976).

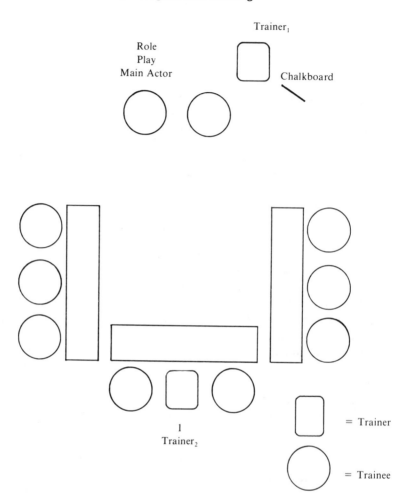

Fig. 1. A functional room arrangement for Structured Learning Therapy.

procedures, targets, and so forth. Typically, the introduction also covers such topics as the centrality of interpersonal skill for effective and satisfying community living, the value of skill knowledge and skill flexibility on the part of the trainee, the variety of skills needed in relation to the complex demands made in contemporary society, and the manner in which training focuses on altering specific behaviors and not on attitude change. The specific training procedures (modeling, role playing, etc.) are then described, as is the implementation (dates, time, place, etc.) of these procedures. A period of time is spent discussing these introductory points, and then the actual training begins.

Modeling

Trainers describe the first skill to be taught and hand out cards (SKILL CARDS), on which the name of the skill and its behavioral steps are printed, to all trainees. The first modeling tape is then played. Trainees are told to listen closely to the way the actors in each vignette on the tape follow the behavioral steps.

To ease trainees into Structured Learning, it is recommended that the first skill taught be one that trainees can master with relative ease. It is particularly important that a trainee's first experience with Structured Learning be a successful one.

All modeling audiotapes begin with a narrator setting the scene and stating the name of the skill and the behavioral steps that make up that skill. Sets of actors portray a series of vignettes in which each behavioral step is clearly enacted in sequence. The narrator then returns, makes a summary statement, restates the behavioral steps, and urges their continued use. In our view, this sequence of narrator's introduction, modeling scenes, and narrator's summary constitutes the minimum requirement for a satisfactory modeling audiotape. We have described in detail elsewhere (see Goldstein, 1973) those tape, model, and patient characteristics that usually enhance or diminish the degree of learning that occurs. We refer the reader interested in developing modeling displays to this source. We have found that live modeling by trainers can also often provide those elements that promote satisfactory learning by trainees.

Role Playing

A brief spontaneous discussion almost invariably follows the playing of a modeling tape. Trainees comment on the behavioral steps, the actors, and, very often, on how the situation or skill problem portrayed occurs in their own lives. Since our primary goal in role playing is to encourage realistic behavioral rehearsal, a trainee's statements about his individual difficulties using the skill being taught can often develop into material for the first role play. To enhance the realism of the portrayal, have him (now the main actor) choose a second trainee (coactor) to play the role of the significant other person in his life who is relevant to the skill problem. One trainer should be responsible for keeping a record of who has role-played, which role, and for which skill, to be sure that all trainees participate about equally.

It is of crucial importance that the main actor seek to enact the behavioral steps he has just heard modeled. He is told to refer to his skill card on which the behavioral steps are printed. As noted, the behavioral steps should also be written on a chalkboard for him to see while role-playing. Before role-playing begins, the following instructions should be delivered:

1. *To the main actor*: Follow and enact the behavioral steps. Do so with the real skill problem you have chosen in mind.
2. *To the coactor*: Respond as realistically as possible, doing what you think the actual other person in the main actor's real-life situation would do.
3. *To the other trainees in the group*: Observe how well the main actor follows the behavioral steps and take notes on this for later discussion.

The main actor is asked briefly to describe the real skill problem situation and the real person(s) involved in it, with whom he could try these behavioral step behaviors in real life. The coactor should be called by the name of the main actor's significant other during the role play. The trainers then instruct the role players to begin. It is the trainers' main responsibility at this point to be sure that the main actor keeps role-playing and that he attempts to follow the behavioral steps while doing so. If he "breaks role" and begins making comments, explaining background events, etc., the trainers should firmly instruct him to resume his role. One trainer should position himself near the chalkboard and point to each behavioral step, in turn, as the role play unfolds, being sure none is either missed or enacted out of order. If the trainers or actors feel the role play is not progressing well and wish to start it over, this is appropriate. Trainers should make an effort to have the actors complete the skill enactment before stepping down. Observers should be instructed to hold their comments until the role play is completed.

The role playing should be continued until all trainees have had an opportunity to participate (in either role) and preferably until all have had a chance to be the main actor, even if all of the same behavioral steps must be carried over to a second or third session. Note that while the framework (behavioral steps) of each role play in the series remains the same, the actual content can and should change from role play to role play. It is the problem as it actually occurs, or could occur, in each trainee's real-life environment that should be the content of the given role play. When completed, each trainee should be better armed to act appropriately in the given reality situation.

A few further procedural matters relevant to role playing should be noted, as each will serve to increase its effectiveness. Role reversal is often a useful role-play procedure. A trainee role-playing a skill problem may have a difficult time perceiving his coactor's viewpoint, and vice versa. Having them exchange roles and resume the role playing can be most helpful in this regard.

At times, it has been worthwhile for the trainer to assume the coactor role, in an effort to expose trainees to the handling of types of reactions not otherwise role-played during the session. It is here that the trainer's flexibility and creativity will certainly be called upon. We might add in this context that while we sometimes suggest that trainers play the coactor role, we urge them to be especially cautious when taking on the main actor role. Errors in the enactment of this live modeling role can be most serious, can destroy trainer credibility, and can severely decrease his value as a trainer for that group of trainees.

Real-life problems very often require effective use of a combination of Basic Skills for their satisfactory solution. To reflect this fact in our training procedures, we have developed a series of modeling Application Tapes which portray sequences and combinations of Basic Skills necessary to deal with such daily living matters as finding a place to live, job seeking, marital interactions, and dealing with crises.[5] The procedures utilized with the Application Skill tapes are essentially the same as those used for the Basic Skill tapes, though individualized skill combinations will have to be constructed prior to role playing. Application groups, using Basic Skills in combination, should only be started once trainees have a firm grasp of Basic Skills used separately.

Feedback

Upon completion of each role play, a brief feedback period should ensue. The goals of this activity are to let the main actor know how well he followed the behavioral steps or in what ways he departed from them, to explore the psychological impact of his enactment on his coactor, and to provide him encouragement to try out his role-play behaviors in real-life. To implement this process, the recommended feedback sequence is:

A. The coactor is asked, "How did your (friend, husband, wife, boss, etc.) make you feel?" "What were your reactions to him?" "What would you be likely to do if you really were _____?"

B. The observing trainees are asked, "How well were the behavioral steps followed?" "What specific behaviors did you like or dislike?" "How was the coactor helpful?"

C. The trainers should comment in particular on the following of the behavioral steps, and provide social reinforcement (praise, approval, encouragement) for close following. To be most effective, reinforcement provided by the the trainers should be offered in accordance with the following rules:

    1. Provide reinforcement at the earliest appropriate opportunity after role plays which follow the behavioral steps;

    2. Provide reinforcement only after role plays which follow the behavioral steps;

---

5. See Addendum 1 (Table 4) for a complete list of Application Tapes (Application Tapes for Goldstein, A. P., Sprafkin, R. P., & Gershaw, N. J. *Skill training for community living.* [New York: Pergamon Press, 1976]).

3. Vary the specific content of the reinforcements offered;
4. Provide enough role-playing activity for each group member to have sufficient opportunity to be reinforced;
5. Provide reinforcement in an amount consistent with the quality of the given role play;
6. Provide no reinforcement when the role play departs significantly from the behavioral steps (except for "trying" in the first session or two);
7. In later sessions, space out the reinforcement you provide so that not every good role play is reinforced.

D. The main actor is asked to comment on his own enactment, on the comments of others, and on his specific expectations regarding how, when, and with whom he might attempt the behavioral steps in his real-life environment.

In all these critiques, it is crucial that the behavioral focus of Structured Learning be maintained. Comments must point to the presence or absence of specific, concrete behaviors, and should not take the form of general evaluative comments or broad generalities. Feedback, of course, may be positive or negative in content. At minimum, "poor" performances (major departures from the behavioral steps) can be praised as "good tries" while being criticized for their real faults. If at all possible, trainees who fail to follow the relevant behavioral steps in their role play should be given the opportunity to re-role-play these same behavioral steps after receiving corrective feedback. At times, as a further feedback procedure, we have audiotaped or videotaped entire role plays. Giving trainees later opportunities to observe themselves on tape can be an effective aid to learning, by enabling them to reflect on their own behavior.

Since a primary goal of Structured Learning is skill flexibility, a role-play enactment which departs markedly from the behavioral steps may not be "wrong." That is, it may in fact "work" in some situations. Trainers should stress that they are trying to teach effective alternatives and that the trainees would do well to have the behavioral steps in their repertoire of skill behaviors available to use when appropriate.

As the final feedback step, after all role playing and discussion are completed, the modeling tape can be replayed. This step, in a sense, summarizes the session and leaves trainees with a final review of the behavioral steps.

Transfer Training

Several aspects of the training sessions described above had, as their primary purpose, augmentation of the likelihood that learning in the therapy setting will transfer to the trainee's actual real-life environment. We would suggest, however, that even more forthright steps need to be taken to maximize transfer. When possible, we would urge a homework technique which we have used successfully with most groups. In this procedure, trainees are openly instructed to try the behavioral step behaviors they have practiced during the session in their own real-life settings. The name of the person(s) with whom they will try it, the day, the place, etc., are all discussed. The trainee is urged to take notes on his first transfer attempt on Homework Report 1 (see Addendum 4) provided by the trainers. This form requests detailed information about what happened when the homework assignment was attempted, how well the relevant behavioral points were followed, the trainee's evaluation of his performance, and his thoughts about what his next assignment might appropriately be.

As is true of our use of the modeling tapes, it has often proven useful (to ensure success experiences) to start with relatively simple homework behaviors and work up to more complex and demanding assignments as mastery is achieved. The first part of each session is devoted to a presentation and discussion of these homework reports. Trainers should meet patient failure to "do their homework" with some chagrin and expressed disappointment. When trainees do attempt to complete their homework assignments, however, social reinforcement (praise, approval, encouragement) should be provided by the trainers. It cannot be stressed too strongly that without these, or similar attempts to maximize transfer, the value of the entire therapy effort is in severe jeopardy.

Of the several principles of transfer training for which research evidence exists, the principle of performance feedback is clearly most consequential. A trainee can learn very well in the therapy setting, do all his transfer homework, and yet the training program can be a performance failure. "Learning" concerns the question, Can he do it? "Performance" is a matter of, Will he do it? Trainees will perform as trained if and only if there is some "payoff" for doing so. Stated simply, new behaviors persist if they are rewarded and diminish if they are ignored or actively challenged.

We have found it useful to implement several supplemental programs outside of the Structured Learning Therapy setting which can help to provide the rewards or reinforcements trainees need so that their new behaviors are maintained. These programs include provision for both external social reward, provided by people in the trainee's real-life environment, and self-reward, provided by the trainee himself.

In several hospitals and agencies, we have actively sought to identify and develop environmental or external support by holding orientation meetings for hospital staff and for relatives and friends of trainees—i.e., the real-life reward and punishment givers. The purpose of these meetings was to acquaint significant others in the trainee's life with Structured Learning Therapy theory and procedures. Most important in these sessions is the presentation of procedures whereby staff, relatives, and friends can encourage and reward trainees as they practice their new skills. We consider these orientation sessions for such persons to be of major value for transfer of training.

Frequently, environmental support is insufficient to maintain newly learned skills. It is also the case that many real-life environments in which trainees work and live will actively resist a trainee's efforts at behavior change. For this reason, we have found it useful to include in our transfer efforts a method through which trainees can learn to be their own rewarders. Once a new skill has been practiced through role playing, and once the trainee has made his first homework effort and has received group feedback, we recommend that trainees continue to practice their new skill as frequently as possible. It is at this time that a program of self-reinforcement can and should be initiated. Trainees can be instructed in the nature of self-reinforcement and encouraged to "say something and do something nice for yourself" if they practice their new skill well. Homework Report 2 (see Addendum 4) will aid both trainers and trainees in this effort. On this form, trainees can specify potential rewards and indicate how they rewarded themselves for a job well done. Trainees' notes can be collected by the trainer in order to keep abreast of independent progress being made by trainees without consuming group time.

Resistance and Resistance Reduction

As happens in all treatment and training approaches, trainees participating in Structured Learning Therapy will sometimes behave in a resistive manner. In one or more of a variety of ways, they may seek to block or avoid trainer efforts to conduct the session as we have defined it throughout this Manual. We have identified 18 different ways in which such resistance may occur. These types of resistance are listed in Table 1, along with brief mention of the general approaches to reducing such resistance which we have found useful. These several means for dealing effectively with trainee resistance are identified more fully in Table 2.

Table 1. Types of Trainee Resistance

I.   Active resistance to participation
      1. participation, but not as instructed
      2. refusal to role-play
      3. lateness
      4. walking out
      5. cutting
Reduce this resistance by: (a) empathic encouragement, (b) threat reduction, (c) instruction.

II. Inappropriate behavior owing to pathology
   1. inability to remember
   2. inattention
   3. excessive restlessness
   4. bizarre behavior
Reduce this resistance by: (a) simplification, (b) termination of responses, (c) instruction.
III. Inactivity
   1. apathy
   2. falling asleep
   3. minimal participation
   4. minimal ability to understand
Reduce this resistance by (a) threat reduction, (b) elicitation of responses, (c) instruction
IV. Hyperactivity
   1. interruption
   2. monopolizing
   3. trainer's helper
   4. jumping out of role
   5. digression
Reduce this resistance by: (a) empathic encouragement, (b) termination of responses, (c) threat reduction.

Table 2. Method for Reducing Trainee Resistance

I. Simplification Methods
   1. Reinforce minimal trainee accomplishment.
   2. Shorten the role play.
   3. Have the trainee read a script portraying the behavioral steps.
   4. Have the trainee play a passive role (responder or even nonspeaking) in role playing.
   5. Have trainee follow one behavioral step.
   6. Have trainer "feed" sentences to the trainee.
II. Threat Reduction Methods
   1. Have live modeling by the trainer.
   2. Reassure the trainee.
   3. Clarify any aspects of the trainee's task which are still unclear.
III. Elicitation of Responses Methods
   1. Call for volunteers
   2. Introduce topics for discussion.
   3. Ask specific trainee to participate, preferably choosing someone who has made eye contact with leader.
IV. Termination of Responses Methods

1. Interrupt ongoing behavior.
2. Cause extinction through inattention to trainee behavior.
3. Discontinue contact and get others to participate.
4. Urge trainee to get back on correct track.

V.   Instruction Methods
   1. Coach and prompt.
   2. Instruct in specific procedures and applications.

VI. Empathic Encouragement Method

Step 1. Offer the resistant trainee the opportunity to explain in greater detail his reluctance to role-play, and listen nondefensively.

Step 2. Clearly express your understanding of the resistant trainee's feelings.

Step 3. If appropriate, respond that the trainee's view is a viable alternative.

Step 4. Present your own view in greater detail, with both supporting reasons and probable outcomes.

Step 5. Express the appropriateness of delaying a resolution of the trainer-trainee difference.

Step 6. Urge the trainee to try tentatively to role-play the given behavioral steps.

Prescriptive Utilization

While Structured Learning Therapy has been shown to be effective with many different types of psychiatric populations varying greatly in their initial levels of skill deficit, its effectiveness may be enhanced even further by responsiveness on the part of trainers to special characteristics of the trainees with whom they are working. For example, with long-term hospitalized patients, whose attention span is short and whose motivation for skill enhancement is low, we have adapted the procedures set forth earlier in this manual by (1) having the trainers be more active and participate more actively in role playing; (2) having the trainers offer social (token and material) reinforcement more frequently and for lesser skill increments; (3) having the trainers begin thinning of reinforcements later; (4) having shorter and more repetitive group sessions; (5) having fewer trainees per group; (6) paying more relative attention to simpler levels of a given skill; (7) allowing more total time per skill; and (8) requiring less demanding homework assignments. We urge those using Structured Learning Therapy to consider implementing analogous alterations in any and all aspects of this approach as a function of the special needs, potentialities, or limitations of the trainees they are trying to assist.

ADDENDUM 1

Table 3. Structured Learning Therapy Modeling Tapes: Basic Skills

Series I.	Conversations: Beginning Skills
	Skill 1. Starting a conversation
	Skill 2. Carrying on a conversation
	Skill 3. Ending a conversation
	Skill 4. Listening
Series II.	Conversations: Expressing Oneself
	Skill 5. Expressing a compliment
	Skill 6. Expressing appreciation
	Skill 7. Expressing encouragement
	Skill 8. Asking for help
	Skill 9. Giving instructions
	Skill 10. Expressing affection
	Skill 11. Expressing a complaint
	Skill 12. Persuading others
	Skill 13. Expressing anger
Series III.	Conversations: Responding to Others
	Skill 14. Responding to praise
	Skill 15. Responding to the feelings of others (Empathy)
	Skill 16. Apologizing
	Skill 17. Following instructions
	Skill 18. Responding to persuasion
	Skill 19. Responding to failure
	Skill 20. Responding to contradictory messages
	Skill 21. Responding to a complaint
	Skill 22. Responding to anger
Series IV.	Planning Skills
	Skill 23. Setting a goal
	Skill 24. Gathering information
	Skill 25. Concentrating on a task
	Skill 26. Evaluating your abilities
	Skill 27. Preparing for a stressful conversation
	Skill 28. Setting problem priorities
	Skill 29. Decision making
Series V.	Alternatives to Aggression
	Skill 30. Identifying and labeling your emotions
	Skill 31. Determining responsibility
	Skill 32. Making requests
	Skill 33. Relaxation
	Skill 34. Self-control

Skill 35. Negotiation
Skill 36. Helping others
Skill 37. Assertiveness

Table 4. Structured Learning Therapy Modeling Tapes: Application Skills

Skill 38. Finding a place to live (through formal channels)
Skill 39. Moving in (typical)
Skill 40. Moving in (difficult)
Skill 41. Managing money
Skill 42. Neighboring (apartment house)
Skill 43. Job seeking (typical)
Skill 44. Job seeking (difficult)
Skill 45. Job keeping (average day's work)
Skill 46. Job keeping (strict boss)
Skill 47. Receiving telephone calls (difficult)
Skill 48. Restaurant eating (typical)
Skill 49. Organizing time (typical)
Skill 50. Using leisure time (learning something new)
Skill 51. Using leisure time (interpersonal activity)
Skill 52. Social (party)
Skill 53. Social (church supper)
Skill 54. Marital (positive interaction)
Skill 55. Marital (negative interaction)
Skill 56. Using community resources (seeking money)
Skill 57. Using community resources (avoiding red tape)
Skill 58. Dealing with crises (inpatient to nonpatient transition)
Skill 59. Dealing with crises (loss)

ADDENDUM 2

Trainee's Notebook for Structured Learning Therapy

Contents

ADDENDUM 3

Modeling Tape Format

I.   Narrator's Introduction
  1. Introduction of self:
     a. Name and title;
     b. High status position—e.g., hospital director.
  2. Introduction of skill:
     a. Name;
     b. General (descriptive) definition;
     c. Behavioral (behavioral steps) definition.
  3. Incentive statement—how and why skill-presence may be rewarding
  4. Discrimination statement—examples of skill-absence, and how and why skill-absence may be unrewarding;
  5. Repeat statement of behavioral steps and request for attention to what follows.
II. Modeling Displays. Ten brief vignettes of the behavioral steps, each vignette providing the complete set of the steps which constitute the given skill. A variety of actors (models) and situations are used. Model characteristics (age, sex, apparent socioeconomic level, etc.) are similar to typical trainee characteristics; situation characteristics should also reflect common trainee real-life environments. The displays portray both overt model behaviors as well as ideational and self-instructional behavioral steps. Models are provided social reinforcement for skill enactment.
III. Narrator's Summary
  1. Repeat statement of behavioral steps;
  2. Description of rewards to both models and actual trainees for skill usage;
  3. Urging of trainees to enact the behavioral steps in the Structured Learning Therapy session which follows and subsequently in their real-life environments.

ADDENDUM 4

Homework Reports

Homework Report 1
NAME: _____ DATE: _____
GROUP LEADERS: _____
FILL IN DURING THIS CLASS:
1. Homework assignment:

2. Behavioral steps to be followed:

FILL IN BEFORE NEXT CLASS:
3. Describe what happened when you did the homework assignment:
4. Behavioral steps you actually followed:
5. Rate yourself on how well you used the skill (check one):
   a. Excellent _____
   b. Good   _____
   c. Fair   _____
   d. Poor   _____
6. Describe what you feel should be your next homework assignment.

Homework Report 2
NAME: _____ DATE: _____
GROUP LEADERS: _____
FILL IN BEFORE DOING YOUR HOMEWORK:
1. Homework assignment:

2. Behavioral steps to be followed:

3. Rewarding yourself:
   a. An excellent job will be rewarded with:

   b. A good job will be rewarded with:

   c. A fair job will be rewarded with:

FILL IN AFTER DOING YOUR HOMEWORK
4. Describe what happened when you did the homework assignment:

5. Behavioral steps you actually followed:

6. Rate yourself on how well you used the skill (check one):
   a. Excellent _____
   b. Good   _____
   c. Fair   _____
   d. Poor   _____
7. Describe how you rewarded yourself:

8. Describe what you feel should be your next homework assignment:

Appendix B
Structured Learning Trainer's Manual for Adolescents

Robert P. Sprafkin,
Veterans Administration

N. Jane Gershaw,
Veterans Administration

Arnold P. Goldstein,
Syracuse University

Paul Klein,
Syracuse School District

CONTENTS

This trainer's manual will acquaint you with Structured Learning, a highly effective method for teaching interpersonal, personal, and planning skills to adolescents who may be weak or lacking in such skills.

This manual is addressed to teachers, trainers, or other helpers who work in such settings as schools, community centers, residential centers, or other places where young people learn important skills for living. By learning to use the tools and techniques described here, you, the teacher, will be able to conduct Structured Learning classes with teenagers who share a common need to learn skills which can help them lead more effective and satisfying lives.

INTRODUCTION

Why Social Skills Training?

Throughout the history of education there has been an ongoing debate as to what should be taught and how to teach it. At various periods there has been an emphasis on teaching "basics"—on teaching such traditional subject areas as reading, writing, arithmetic, or on teaching related technological skills. Such an emphasis is generally accomplished by a didactic approach to instruction, along with the belief that such concerns as values, morals, social skills, and the like are not the responsibility of the school, but of the home or place of worship.

At other periods in the history of education, when the pendulum has swung to the other extreme, there has been a greater emphasis on using the schools to enrich the emotional life of the young person. School time is spent dealing with feelings, emotional growth, social concerns, and self-exploration. The teaching of traditional academic subjects is often deemphasized. Teaching methods tend to be less didactic and more experiential. Tests, grades, and assessment by rote performance are employed less frequently.

Regardless of which period of education one lives in, many teachers, counselors, and others concerned with the education and development of young people often find themselves wishing for some type of balance between both extremes. Such a balance would enable the teaching of "basics" as well as foster emotional development. These educators often wish to combine the best of both didactic and experiential approaches to teaching in a variety of educational settings.

Recently, there has been a great deal of interest in teaching interpersonal competency skills in educational settings as a partial resolution to this traditional educational debate. Youngsters are being taught how to interact more effectively with others; how to deal with fear, anger, and other feelings; taught alternative skills for handling stressful situations, and so forth.

Through the teaching of such specific skills, useful in school as well as outside the educational setting, the best of didactic and experiential techniques can be combined. In such a way, the acquisition and performance of the range of behaviors necessary for effective and satisfying functioning in academic and nonacademic pursuits through the adolescent years can be enhanced. This trainer's manual introduces you to Structured Learning, a highly effective method for teaching these important skills to young people. As you will see, the approach is systematic, sequential, and measurable.

What Is Structured Learning?

Structured Learning is a highly successful approach to skill training. It consists of four components—modeling, role playing, feedback, and transfer training—each of which is a well-established behavior change procedure. While the terms may be new to you, you'll recognize the components, as they are basic to the learning process.

Modeling refers to providing small groups of students with a demonstration or example of the skill behaviors we wish youngsters to learn. If the skill to be learned was negotiating, we would present students with a number of vivid audiotaped, videotaped, filmed, or live displays (geared to maximize attention and motivation to learn) of adolescents who use the skill effectively. In the display, the skill of negotiating would be broken down into a series of behavioral steps which make up negotiation (see Addendum 2 for behavioral steps), and each example presented or modeled illustrates the use of these behavioral steps. Thus, students would see and hear the models negotiating successfully in a variety of relevant settings: at home, at school, and with peer groups.

Once the models have been presented, the next step in learning the skill is role playing. Role playing is behavioral rehearsal or practice for eventual real-life use of the skill. To use our example of negotiation, individuals in the group are asked to think about times in their own lives when they would benefit from using the skill they have just seen modeled or demonstrated. In turn, each youth is given the opportunity to practice using the skill (i.e., the steps which make up the skill) as he or she might eventually use it in real life. This role playing is accomplished with the aid of other group members, as well as the group leaders, who simulate the real-life situation. The teenager who enacts a scene in which there is negotiation with a friend regarding where to go after school might role-play the scene with another group member who acts out the part of the friend.

Feedback, the third component in Structured Learning, refers to providing the youngster with an evaluation of the role-played rehearsal. Following each role play, group members and trainers provide the role player with praise (and sometimes material rewards) as his or her behavior becomes more and more like that of the model. During this part of the group, adolescents are given corrective instruction which will enable them to continue to improve their skill use.

The last element in Structured Learning is transfer of training. This refers to a variety of procedures used to encourage transfer of the newly learned behaviors from the training setting to the real-life situation. Homework assignments, use of real or imaginary props and procedures to make role playing realistic, and re-role-playing a scene even after it is learned well (i.e., overlearning) are some of the several transfer-enhancing procedures which are part of Structured Learning. In a real sense, transfer of training is the most important and often the most difficult aspect of Structured Learning. If the newly learned behavior does not carry over to the real-life environment, then a lasting and meaningful change in the youngster's behavior is extremely unlikely to occur.

For our purposes here, the Structured Learning approach can be broadly applied to teaching a wide range of interpersonal, personal, and planning skills or behaviors which can be classified as Beginning Social Skills, Advanced Social Skills, Skills for Dealing with Feelings, Skill Alternatives to Aggression, Skills for Dealing with Stress, and Planning Skills (the complete Skill List is found on pages 164-165). Within these categories, adolescents in a Structured Learning group might learn the beginning skill of "Listening" or "Starting a Conversation." At a more advanced level, as a prosocial alternative to aggression, they might learn "Sharing," "Self-control" or "How to negotiate." All of the skills taught through Structured Learning groups are skills which are relevant to the interpersonal, personal, and planning components of the daily lives of adolescents in school, at home, and in peer group settings.

This trainer's manual provides the Structured Learning group leader with detailed guidelines for effectively conducting Structured Learning classes with adolescents in a variety of settings. These settings might include a secondary school, a residential or nonresidential treatment center, an after-school program, or other place where adolescents may gather in order to learn skills which will help them lead effective and satisfying lives.

What Structured Learning Is Not

Before describing the specific procedures involved in organizing and running Structured Learning classes, we'd like to mention what Structured Learning is not. First, Structured Learning should not be conceived of as a dynamic psychotherapy, aimed at uncovering a youngster's deep-seated conflicts. Rather, Structured Learning is aimed at teaching skills or behaviors to a wide range of young people who may be deficient or need practice in the particular skills being taught. Structured Learning classes are quite task-oriented, making use of specific, sequential procedures. Rather than unstructured open-ended discussions about "problems," discussion in the Structured Learning class is goal-oriented and limited in scope to the skill being taught. Emphasis is not placed on diagnosing, labeling, and referring a youngster for "treatment," but rather on identifying strengths and weaknesses in various skill areas, and providing training in those areas which need improvement.

Second, it is important to stress the fact that you should not view the behavioral steps portrayed for each skill as the only way to enact that skill effectively. The goal of Structured Learning is to help youngsters build flexible repertoires of socially effective and satisfying behaviors which can be adapted to the demands of their lives. Thus, we urge you to consider the behavioral steps shown in the modeling displays as good examples, but not as the only way to perform the skills effectively.

A third caution must also be noted. The Structured Learning audiovisual modeling displays are not instructional tapes in the usual sense. An instructional tape is most typically played to an audience which passively listens to it and then, at some later date, is supposed to perform what was played. Such passive learning is not likely to be enduring. Thus the Structured Learning modeling tapes should not be played alone, i.e., without following them with role playing and feedback. It is the active, "learning by doing," that is critically important for learning and retaining new skills. We have demonstrated experimentally that all four components of our training approach (modeling, role playing, feedback, and transfer of training) are necessary and sufficient for enduring behavioral change, and results of this research should be reflected in the use of these materials and procedures.

Finally, Structured Learning is not an approach which can be used effectively by all possible trainers. Later in this manual we will describe in detail the knowledge, skills, and sensitivities which a trainer must possess in order to be effective with Structured Learning.

ORGANIZING THE STRUCTURED LEARNING GROUP

Selecting Participants

Each Structured Learning group should consist of students who are clearly deficient in whatever skills are going to be taught. If possible, students should also be grouped according to the degree of their deficiency in the given skill. You may find it helpful to use the Skill Checklist (see Addendum 2) in an initial grouping effort. On that instrument, each student can be rated on how well he or she uses the various skills. You can select students who are all deficient on certain common groups of skills, as assessed by the checklist.

Defining which skills to work on may determine the behavioral objectives for the students in the class. You can record each youngster's progress toward learning each skill, and thus measure individual and class mastery of the behavioral objectives (see Addendum 2). The optimal size group for effective Structured Learning sessions consists of five to eight students[1] plus two trainers. The students selected for a Structured Learning group need not be from the same class or even the same grade. However, since behavioral rehearsal or role playing in the group is most beneficial when it's as realistic as possible, it's often useful to include students whose social worlds (family, school, peer groups) have some important elements of similarity. In this way, when a participant is asked to role-play a part, this part can be role-played in a reasonably accurate fashion.

There are times when it won't be possible to group students according to shared skill deficits. Instead, you may want to group according to naturally occurring units, such as school classes, residential cottages, etc. If you decide to use naturally occurring units, the group members will probably reflect some range of skill strengths and weaknesses. In this case, you'll find it helpful to fill out a Skill Checklist for each student in order to obtain a class profile. You should select as starting skills those in which many of the class members show a deficiency. In such a potentially diverse group, it's likely that one or two class members will be proficient in the use of whatever skill might be taught on a given day. In that case, you can use these more skillful youngsters in helper roles, such as coactors or providers of useful feedback.

Number, Length, and Spacing of Sessions

The Structured Learning modeling tapes and associated procedures typically constitute a training program which can be broken into segments matching part or all of the semesters of the school or training setting. It is most desirable that training should occur at a rate of one or two times per week. Spacing is crucial. Most students in skill training or other programs learn well in the training setting. Most, however, fail to transfer this learning to where it counts—at home, in school, with friends, in the community. As you'll see below, Structured Learning includes special procedures which maximize the likelihood that learning will transfer. (One such transfer procedure is between-session homework.) In order to provide ample opportunity for students to try out in real life what they've learned in the training setting, sessions must be spaced carefully.

---

1. We recognize that most classes in school settings are much larger than is desirable for a Structured Learning class. Often it is possible for two or more teachers to combine their classes for a period or two and have one teacher take the larger group while a smaller group of five to eight students participates in Structured Learning.

Typically, each training session should focus on learning one skill. As such, it should include one sequence of modeling, several role plays, feedback, and assignment of homework. Each session should be scheduled for one half-hour to one hour in length. Session length should be determined by a number of factors, such as attention span, impulsivity, verbal ability, etc. If most students in a given group show particularly brief attention spans, the session can be as brief as twenty minutes. In such cases, more frequent sessions are advisable. Sessions longer than an hour are possible with students whose capacity for sustained attention is greater. Since Structured Learning is intensive, we recommend that sessions not last beyond one and a half hours, as learning efficiency tends to diminish beyond that length of time.

TRAINER PREPARATION

The role-playing and feedback activities which make up most of each Structured Learning session are a series of "action-reaction" sequences in which effective skill behaviors are first rehearsed (role-played) and then critiqued (feedback). As such, the trainer must both lead and observe. We have found that one trainer is hard pressed to do both of these tasks well at the same time, and thus, we strongly recommend that each session be led by a team of two trainers. Two types of trainer skills appear crucial for successfully conducting a Structured Learning group.

The first might best be described as General Trainer Skills—i.e., those skills requisite for success in almost any training or teaching effort. These include:

a. Oral communication and teaching ability;
b. Flexibility and capacity for resourcefulness;
c. Enthusiasm;
d. Ability to work under pressure;
e. Interpersonal sensitivity;
f. Listening skills; and
g. Broad knowledge of human behavior, adolescent development, etc.

The second type of requisite skills are Specific Trainer Skills—i.e., those germane to Structured Learning in particular. These include:

a. Knowledge of Structured Learning—its background, procedures, and goals (see Recommended Readings);
b. Ability to orient both students and supporting staff to Structured Learning;
c. Ability to initiate and sustain role playing;
d. Ability to present material in concrete, behavioral form;
e. Ability to deal with classroom management problems effectively; and
f. Sensitivity in providing corrective feedback.

For both trainer selection and development purposes, potential trainers should first participate, in the role of students, in a series of Structured Learning sessions. These sessions are led by two experienced trainers. After this experience, beginning trainers can then co-lead a series of sessions with an experienced trainer. In this way, trainers can be given several opportunities to practice what they have seen and also receive feedback regarding their performance. In effect, we recommend the use of the Structured Learning procedures of modeling, role playing, and feedback as the method of choice for training Structured Learning trainers.

In school settings, trainers and cotrainers are often regular classroom teachers, aides, guidance counselors, psychologists, resource or special education teachers, volunteers, or even students themselves. The particular job title of the trainer depends largely on the setting in which Structured Learning is used. What we consider more important than the job title of the trainer is that the trainer possesses the kind of characteristics described above, and that he or she apply the Structured Learning techniques appropriately.

THE STRUCTURED LEARNING SESSIONS

The Setting

One major principle for encouraging transfer from the classroom and training room to the real-life setting is the rule of identical elements. This rule states that the more similar or identical the two settings—i.e, the greater the number of physical and interpersonal qualities shared by them—the greater the transfer from one setting to the other. We urge that Structured Learning be conducted in the same general setting as the real-life environment of most participating students and that the training setting be furnished to resemble or simulate as much as possible the likely application settings. In a typical classroom you can accomplish this simply through the creative use of available furniture and supplies. Should a couch be needed for a particular role play, several chairs can be pushed together to simulate the couch. Should a television set be an important part of a role play, a box, a chair, or a drawing on the chalkboard can, in imagination, approximate the real object. If actual props are available, for example in the form of an actual TV set, store counter, living room furniture, etc., they should certainly be used in the role-play scenes.

The horseshoe seating arrangement, illustrated in Fig. 1, is one good example of how furniture might be arranged in the training room. Participating students sit at desks or tables so that some writing space is provided. Role playing takes place in the front of the room. Behind and to the side of one of the role players is a chalkboard displaying the behavioral steps (Specific skill behaviors) which make up the skill being worked with at that time.

1. screen
2. role play, main actor
3. role play, co-actor
4. trainer 1
5. chalkboard
6. projector   7. trainer 2

Fig. 1. Typical arrangement for a Structured Learning Session

In this way the role player can glance up at the steps during the role play. If film strips or other visual modeling displays are used, the screen should be easily visible to all.

Pre-meeting Preparation of Students

Preparation of students individually prior to the first meeting of the Structured Learning class may be helpful. This orientation or structuring should be tailored to the individual needs and maturity of level of each student. It should be designed to provide each group member with heightened motivation to attend and participate in the group, as well as to provide the student with accurate expectations of what the activities of the group will be like. Methods of student preparation might include:

a. Mentioning what the purposes of the group will be, as they relate to the specific skill deficits of the youngster. For example, the trainer might say: "Remember when you got into a fight with Billy, and you wound up restricted for a week? Well, in this class you'll be able to learn how to stay out of that kind of trouble so you don't get restricted."

b. Mentioning briefly and generally what procedures will be used. The student must have an accurate picture of what to expect and not feel as if he/she has been tricked. You might say something like, "In order to learn to handle (these kinds of) situations better, we're going to see and hear some examples of how different kids do it well, and then actually take turns trying some of these ways right here. Then we'll let you know how you did, and you'll have a chance to practice them on your own."

c. Mentioning the benefits to be gained from participation, stating that the group will help the student work on particular relevant issues such as getting along in school, at home, and with peers.

d. Mentioning the tangible or token (e.g., points, credits, etc.) rewards which students will receive for participation (see Recommended Readings for additional discussions of token economies and other reward systems).

e. Using the trainer-student relationship to promote cooperation. For example, the trainer might ask the youngster to "Give it a try. I think you'll get something out of it."

f. Presenting the Structured Learning class as a new part of the curriculum in which the student is expected to participate. Along with the message of expected participation, students should also understand that the group is not compulsory and that confidentiality will be respected. A verbal commitment from the youngster to "give it a try" is useful at this point.

g. Mentioning the particular skills that the youngster is likely to identify as his/her major felt deficiency, and how progress might be made in working on such skills.

The Opening Session

The opening session is designed to create student interest in the group as well as to educate the group regarding the procedures of Structured Learning. The trainers open the session by first introducing themselves and having each student do likewise. A brief familiarization period of warmup follows, with the goals of helping students to become comfortable interacting with the group leaders and with one another in the class. Content for this initial phase should be interesting as well as nonthreatening. Next, trainers introduce the Structured Learning program by providing students with a brief description of what skill training is about. Typically, this introduction covers such topics as the importance of interpersonal skills for effective and satisfying living, examples of skills which will be taught, and how these skills can be useful to students in their everyday lives. It is often helpful to expand upon this discussion of everyday skill use, so as to emphasize the importance of the undertaking and its personal relevance to the participants. The specific training procedures (modeling, role playing, etc.) are then described at a level which the group can easily understand.

New trainers should note that although this overview is intended to acquaint students with Structured Learning procedures, frequently students will not grasp the concepts described until they actually get involved in the training process. Because of this, we do not advise trainers to spend a great deal of time describing the procedures. Instead, we recommend that you describe procedures briefly, as introduction, with the expectation that students will actually experience and understand the training process more fully once they have actually started. The procedures which ideally make up this opening session are described, step by step, in Addendum 1 of this manual (page 175).

Modeling

As your first step, describe the skill to be taught and hand out cards (SKILL CARDS) to all students on which the name of the skill and its behavioral steps are printed. The first modeling tape is then played. Students are told to watch and listen closely to the way the actors in each vignette on the tape portray the behavioral steps.

To ease students into Structured Learning, we recommend that the first skill you teach be one that students can master with relative ease. It is particularly important that a student's first experience with Structured Learning be a successful one. As mentioned earlier, filling out a Skill Checklist (see Addendum 2) for each youngster can help you in selecting which skill to use. The skills for adolescents taught by Structured Learning are listed below:

Skill List

Group I.   BEGINNING SOCIAL SKILLS
      1. Listening
      2. Starting a conversation
      3. Having a conversation
      4. Asking a question
      5. Saying thank you
      6. Introducing yourself
      7. Introducing other people
      8. Giving a compliment
Group II. ADVANCED SOCIAL SKILLS
      9. Asking for help
      10. Joining in
      11. Giving instructions
      12. Following instructions
      13. Apologizing
      14. Convincing others
Group III. SKILLS FOR DEALING WITH FEELINGS
      15. Knowing your feelings
      16. Expressing your feelings

17. Understanding the feelings of others
18. Dealing with someone else's anger
19. Expressing affection
20. Dealing with fear
21. Rewarding yourself

Group IV. SKILL ALTERNATIVES TO AGGRESSION
22. Asking permission
23. Sharing something
24. Helping others
25. Negotiating
26. Using self-control
27. Standing up for your rights
28. Responding to teasing
29. Avoiding trouble with others
30. Keeping out of fights

Group V. SKILLS FOR DEALING WITH STRESS
31. Making a complaint
32. Answering a complaint
33. Sportsmanship after the game
34. Dealing with embarrassment
35. Dealing with being left out
36. Standing up for a friend
37. Responding to persuasion
38. Responding to failure
39. Dealing with confusing messages
40. Dealing with an accusation
41. Getting ready for a difficult conversation
42. Dealing with group pressure

Group VI. PLANNING SKILLS
43. Deciding on something to do
44. Deciding what caused a problem
45. Setting a goal
46. Deciding on your abilities
47. Gathering information
48. Arranging problems by importance
49. Making a decision
50. Concentrating on a task

Role Playing

You should direct discussion following the playing of the modeling display toward helping students relate the modeled skill use to their own lives. Invite comments on the behavioral steps and how these steps might be useful in the real-life situations which students encounter. Focus on dealing with specific current and future skill use by students rather than only on general issues involving the skill.

It is important to remember that role playing in Structured Learning is viewed as behavioral rehearsal or practice for future use of the skill. As such, trainers should be aware that role playing of past events which have little relevance for future situations is of limited value to students. Discussion of past events involving skill use, however, can be relevant in stimulating students to think of times when a similar situation might occur in the future. In such a case, the hypothetical future situation rather than the past event would be selected for role playing.

Once a student has described a situation in his or her own life in which skill usage might be helpful, that student is designated the main actor. He or she chooses a second student (the coactor) to play the role of the significant other person (e.g., mother, peer, etc.) in his or her life who is relevant to the skill problem. The student should be urged to pick as a coactor someone who resembles the real-life person in as many ways as possible. The trainer then elicits any additional information from the main actor needed to set the stage for role playing, for example, a description of the physical setting, a description of the events immediately preceding the role play, a description of the coactor's mood or manner, etc.

It is crucial that the main actor seek to enact the behavioral steps which have been modeled. The trainer should go over each step as it applies to the role-play situation prior to any actual role playing being started, thus aiding the main actor in making a successful role-play effort. The main actor is told to refer to the skill card on which the behavioral steps are printed. As noted previously, the behavioral steps should also be written on a chalkboard visible to the main actor during role playing. Before the role playing begins, you should remind all of the participants of their roles: the main actor should be told to follow the behavioral steps; the coactor, to stay in the role of the other person; and the observers, to watch carefully for the enactment of the behavioral steps. For the first several role plays, it is helpful for you to coach the observers as to what kinds of cues to observe, e.g., posture, tone of voice, content of speech, etc. This also provides an opportunity to set a positive example for feedback from the observers.

Next, instruct the role players to begin. It's your main responsibility, at this point, to provide the main actor with whatever help or coaching he or she needs in order to keep the role playing going according to the behavioral steps. Urge students who "break role" and begin to explain their behavior or make comments to get back into role and explain later. If the role play is clearly straying from the behavioral steps, stop the scene, provide needed instruction, and begin again. One trainer should be positioned near the chalkboard and point to each behavioral step, in turn, as the role play unfolds, thus helping the main actor (as well as other students) to follow each step in order.

The role playing should be continued until all students have had an opportunity to participate (in either role) and preferably until all have had a chance to be the main actor. Sometimes this will require two or three sessions for a given skill. We again suggest that each session begin with two or three modeling vignettes for a skill, even if the skill is not new to the group. It's important to note that while the framework (behavioral steps) of each role play in the series remains the same, the actual content can and should change from role play to role play. It is the problem as it actually occurs, or could occur, in each youngster's real-life environment that should be the content of the given role play. When completed, each student will thus be better armed to act appropriately in a real situation requiring skill use in his or her own life.

You should also note a few further procedural matters relevant to role playing which will serve to increase the effectiveness of the role playing. Role reversal is often a useful role-play procedure. A student role-playing a skill may on occasion have a difficult time perceiving his or her coactor's viewpoint, and vice versa. Having them exchange roles and resume the role playing can be most helpful in this regard.

You can assume the coactor role, in an effort to expose youngsters to the handling of types of reactions not otherwise role-played during the session. For example, it may be crucial to have a difficult adult role realistically portrayed in the role play. It is here that your flexibility and creativity will certainly be called upon. This may be particularly helpful when dealing with less verbal or more hesitant students.

Feedback

A brief feedback period should follow each role play. This helps the main actor to find out how well he or she followed or departed from the behavioral steps, to explore the psychological impact of his or her enactment on the coactor, and to provide encouragement to try out the role-play behaviors in real-life. To implement this process, ask the main actor to wait until he or she has heard everyone's comments before talking.

Then ask the coactor about his or her reactions first. Next ask the observers to comment on the behavioral steps and other relevant aspects of the role play. You and your cotrainer should comment in particular on how well the behavioral steps were followed, and provide social reinforcement (praise, approval, encouragement) for close following. To be most effective with your use of reinforcement, you should follow the guidelines listed below:

Guidelines for Positive Reinforcement
1. Provide reinforcement at the earliest appropriate opportunity after role plays which follow the behavioral steps.
2. Always provide reinforcement to the coactor for being helpful, cooperative, etc.
3. Provide reinforcement only after role plays which follow the behavioral steps.
4. Vary the specific content of the reinforcements offered, i.e., praise particular aspects of the performance, such as tone of voice, posture, phrasing, etc.
5. Provide enough role-playing activity for each group member to have sufficient opportunity to be reinforced.
6. Provide reinforcement in an amount consistent with the quality of the given role play.
7. Provide no reinforcement when the role play departs significantly from the behavioral steps (except for "trying" in the first session or two).
8. Provide reinforcement for an individual student's improvement over his or her previous performance.

After the main actor hears all the feedback, invite him or her to make comments regarding the role play and the comments of others. In this way, he or she can learn to evaluate the effectiveness of his or her skill enactment in the light of evidence from others as to its success or lack of success.

In all aspects of feedback, it's crucial that you maintain the behavioral focus of Structured Learning. Your comments must point to the presence or absence of specific, concrete behaviors, and not take the form of general evaluative comments or broad generalities. Feedback, of course, may be positive or negative in content. Negative comments should always be followed by a constructive comment as to how a particular fault might be improved. At minimum, a "poor" performance (major departures from the behavioral steps) can be praised as "a good try" at the same time as it is being criticized for its real faults. If at all possible, youngsters failing to follow the relevant behavioral steps in their role play should be given the opportunity to re-role-play these same behavioral steps after receiving corrective feedback. At times, as a further feedback procedure, we have audiotaped or videotaped entire role plays. Giving students later opportunities to observe themselves on tape can be an effective aid to learning, enabling them to reflect on their own behavior.

Since a primary goal of Structured Learning is skill flexibility, role-play enactment which departs markedly from the behavioral steps may not be "wrong." That is, a different approach to the skill may in fact "work" in some situations. You should stress that you're trying to teach effective alternatives and that the students would do well to have the behavioral steps in their repertoire of skill behaviors available to use when appropriate.

Transfer of Training

Several aspects of the training sessions we've described above have, as their primary purpose, augmenting the likelihood that learning in the training setting will transfer to the youngster's actual real-life environment. We would suggest, however, that even more forthright steps need to be taken to maximize transfer. When possible, we would urge a homework technique which we have found to be successful with most groups.

In this procedure, students are openly instructed to try in their own real-life settings the behaviors they have practiced during the session. The name of the person(s) with whom they will try it, the day, the place, etc., are all discussed. The student is urged to take notes on his or her first transfer attempt on Homework Report 1 (see Addendum 2) provided by the trainers. This form requests detailed information about what happened when the student attempted the homework assignment, how well he or she followed the relevant behavioral steps, the student's evaluation of his or her performance, and his or her thoughts about what the next assignment might appropriately be.

As is true of our use of the modeling tapes, it has often proven useful (to ensure a success experience) to start with relatively simple homework behaviors and, as mastery is achieved, work up to more complex and more demanding assignments. This provides you with an opportunity to reinforce each approximation of the more complex target behavior. Often it is best to make a first homework assignment something that can be done close by, i.e., in the school, community center, or wherever the class is taking place. It may then be possible to forewarn and prepare the person(s) with whom the youngster is planning to try out his new skill, in order to ensure a positive outcome. For example, a student's homework assignment might be to ask the gym teacher a particular question. You might then tell the gym teacher to expect the student's question so that he or she will be prepared to answer in a positive way.[2] These success experiences in beginning homework attempts are crucial in encouraging the student to make further attempts at real-life skill use. The first part of each session is devoted to presenting and discussing these homework reports. When students make an effort to complete their homework assignments, you should provide social reinforcement (praise, approval, encouragement). You should meet students' failure to do their homework with some chagrin and expressed disappointment. It cannot be

---

2. Trainers should be cautioned, however, that breach of confidentiality can damage a teenager's trust in the trainer. If persons outside of the group are to be informed of specific training activities, youngsters should be told of this, and their permission should be asked, early in the group's life.

stressed too strongly that without these, or similar attempts to maximize transfer, the value of the entire training effort is in severe jeopardy.

External Support and Self-Reward

Of the several principles of transfer training for which research evidence exists, the principle of performance feedback is clearly most consequential. A youngster can learn very well in the training setting and do all his or her transfer homework, and yet the training program can be a performance failure. "Learning" concerns the question, Can he do it? "Performance" is a matter of will he do it? Students will perform as trained if and only if there is some "payoff" for doing so. Stated simply, new behaviors persist if they are rewarded, diminish if they are ignored or actively challenged.

We have found it useful to implement several supplemental programs outside of the Structured Learning training setting which can help to provide the rewards or reinforcements students need so that their new behaviors are maintained. These programs include providing for both external social re-ward (provided by people in the student's real-life environment) and self-re-ward (provided by the student him- or herself).

In several settings, we have actively sought to identify and develop environmental or external support by holding orientation meetings for school staff and for relatives and friends of youngsters—i.e., the real-life reward and punishment givers. These meetings acquaint significant others in the young-ster's life with Structured Learning, the skill being taught, and the steps which make up these skills. The most important segment of these sessions involves presenting the procedures whereby staff, relatives, and friends can encourage and reward students as they practice their new skills. We consider these orientation sessions for such persons to be of major value for transfer of training. In such sessions you should provide the significant others with an overview of Structured Learning, much like the overview previously de-scribed for use with a new group of students. You should give them an accurate picture of what goes on in a Structured Learning class, what proce-dures are typically used, and why. Most important, you should inform and instruct them as to how they might help in the transfer effort, and why their contributions are so necessary to the success of the program. Typically, such potential reward givers should be given instructions in how to reinforce appropriate behaviors, or the approximations of such behaviors. You might tell them what specific responses on their parts would be appropriate for the skills being covered in the Structured Learning class. It is often worthwhile to engage these significant others in role-playing the kinds of responses they might make, so they can have practice and feedback in these behaviors. References to further discussions of procedures useful in reinforcing appro-priate behaviors can be found in the Recommended Readings section.

Frequently, environmental support is insufficient to maintain newly learned skills. In fact, many real-life environments in which youngsters work and live actually actively resist a youngster's efforts at behavior change. For this reason, we have found it useful to include in our transfer efforts a method through which students can learn to be their own rewarders—the method of self-reinforcement or self-reward.

Once a new skill has been practiced through role playing, and once the student has made his or her first homework effort and has received group feedback, we recommend that students continue to practice their new skill as frequently as possible. It is at this time that a program of self-reinforcement can and should be initiated. Students can be instructed in the nature of self-reinforcement and encouraged to "say something and do somethig nice for yourself" if they practice their new skill well. Homework Report 2 (see Addendum 2) will aid both trainers and students in this effort. On this form, students can specify potential rewards and indicate how they rewarded themselves for a job well done. Self-rewards may be both things that one says to oneself and things that one does for oneself. The student should be taught to evaluate his or her own performance, even if his or her efforts don't meet with the hoped for response from others. For example, if the youngster follows all of the steps of a particular skill well, he or she might be taught to reward him- or herself by saying something (e.g., "I really did that well. I'm proud of myself") and doing something (e.g., "I'll play basketball after school") as a special reward. It is important that these self-rewards are indeed special, i.e., not things that are said or done routinely, but things that are done to acknowledge and reinforce special efforts. Students' notes can be collected by the trainer in order to keep abreast of independent practice only when it is clear that he or she can successfully do what is being asked.

As an additional aid to transfer, it is important to acknowledge the power of peer group pressure on the behaviors of adolescents. The natural peer leader is often far more influential in a youngster's life than any adult trainer could hope to be. In this regard, it is sometimes possible to capitalize on the natural leadership qualities of some adolescents. Hence, you may want to select a peer (adolescent) cotrainer whom you can train and use instead of a second adult trainer. If a peer cotrainer is selected, it is important, of course, that he or she be proficient in the particular skill being taught.

GROUP MANAGEMENT PROBLEMS AND RESISTIVE BEHAVIOR

As happens in training approaches of all types, a variety of things can interfere with your efforts to conduct Structured Learning sessions according to prescribed procedures. We have identified a number of methods for you to use in order to deal with a broad range of resistive and problem behaviors on the part of students in a Structured Learning group. In general, we recommend that you remain sensitive and alert to the problems that students are having in following the prescribed training program. Students having difficulty might exhibit apathetic or indifferent attitudes in class, disruptive behavior as they are called upon, or a variety of other behaviors geared to disguise the real problem. In all cases, the first question you should ask is, Why is the student having this particular problem? Answers to this question might include: the material being covered is too difficult or complex; the material is too simple; the student is afraid of making a mistake or otherwise failing in front of his or her classmates; the student is responding to peer pressure not to participate as instructed, and so forth. Depending upon the answer to this question, you can select and carry out an appropriate remedial technique.

In this section we will describe a number of behavioral approaches to handling such problem behaviors. In all cases of problem behavior, we would advise trainers to give a minimum of class time to dealing with the student who is having difficulty. The Structured Learning class, being task-oriented, should have a certain pace and plan for accomplishing a particular goal on a particular day. Sacrificing that goal to one or two students who are having problems of one sort or another will have an effect on other group members, and trainers will find themselves hard pressed to return to "business as usual" in future sessions. Another reason for spending minimal class time on problem behavior is that, frequently, attention to problem behavior can serve as a reinforcement or reward for just that behavior you're seeking to diminish or eliminate. As such, the disruptive youngster who learns that he or she receives class time and attention for his or her behavior may become increasingly disruptive in future classes.

We've listed below a number of approaches for dealing with disruptive behaviors which can interfere with effective participation in a Structured Learning class.

Encourage with empathy. In many situations involving problem behavior on the part of the student, the trainer should make an effort to show empathic understanding of the difficulty the student is having. This technique is a stepwise method for you to let the resistant student know that his or her feelings are understood. Following the use of this stepwise method, the trainer may then utilize one or more of the other methods described in this section. The steps for empathic encouragement are:

1. Offer the student the opportunity to explain in greater detail his/her difficulty in participating as instructed, and listen nondefensively.
2. Clearly express your understanding of the student's feelings.
3. If appropriate, respond that the student's view is a viable alternative.
4. Present your own view in greater detail, with both supporting reasons and probable outcomes.

5. Express the appropriateness of delaying a resolution of the trainer-student difference.
6. Urge the student tentatively to try to participate.

Reinstruct and simplify. Once it becomes clear to you that the student is having such difficulty, the student's task should be modified in such a way that he or she is capable of succeeding at the task. This general method essentially consists of a variety of ways in which you can coach, reinstruct, and simplify material for students who find the class material too complex or too difficult. Some instruction and simplification methods include:

1. Have the student follow one behavioral step, rather than a series of steps.
2. Have the student play a passive (coactor or nonspeaking) role in the role play prior to playing the role of the main actor.
3. Cut the role play short.
4. Instruct the student in what to say in the role play (either prior to the role play or by coaching during the role play).
5. Reinforce the student for improvement over prior performance rather than having him or her live up to standards set for other members.

Reduce threat. For students who find some aspect of the Structured Learning class threatening or anxiety producing, we recommend a series of methods to help the student calm down sufficiently so that he or she can attend to the task at hand. Some threat-reduction methods include:

1. Have one of the trainers model a particular task before asking the threatened student to try the task.
2. Reassure that student with remarks such as "Take your time," "I know it's hard," or "Give it a try and I'll help you through it."
3. Clarify any aspects of the student's task which are still unclear.

Elicit responses. This set of methods is called for in cases where the group is being unresponsive to your efforts to get students involved. Some elicitation methods include:

1. Call for volunteers.
2. Introduce topics for discussion.
3. Ask a specific student, preferably someone who has shown signs of interest or attention (i.e., eye contact, gesture), to participate.

Terminate Responses. We urge you to take a direct stand in situations where students are engaging in behaviors which divert the attention of the group from the task at hand. Some termination methods include:

1. Interrupt ongoing behavior.
2. Extinguish through inattention to student behavior.
3. Cease interaction with resistive student and ask others to participate.
4. Urge student to get back on the correct topic.

It is sometimes the case that a particular student, despite all your efforts to foster participation, cannot function in a Structured Learning group in any meaningful way. As a last resort, we recommend that such a student be eliminated from the group. As is true of all training programs, Structured Learning is not the answer for every youngster, and some will not benefit from its procedures. We hope, however, that your skill and sensitivity to the students' difficulties from the very beginning will enable you to include even a resistive youngster in the Structured Learning classes.

RECOMMENDED READINGS

Buckley, N.K. & Walker, H.M. *Modifying classroom behavior*. Champaign, Ill.: Research Press, 1970.

Carter, R. *Help! These kids are driving me crazy*. Champaign, Ill.: Research Press, 1972.

Givner, A. & Graubard, P.S. *A handbook of behavior modification for the classroom*. New York: Holt, Rinehart & Winston, 1974.

Goldstein, A.P. *Structured Learning therapy: Toward a psychotherapy for the poor*. New York: Academic Press, 1973.

Goldstein, A.P., Sherman, M., Gershaw, N.J., Sprafkin, R.P., & Glick B. Training aggressive adolescents in prosocial behavior. *Journal of Youth and Adolescents*, 1978, **7**, 73–92.

Goldstein, A.P. & Sorcher, M. *Changing supervisor behavior*. New York: Pergamon Press, 1973.

Goldstein, A.P., Sprafkin, R.P., & Gershaw, N.J. *Skill training for community living: Applying structured learning therapy*. New York: Pergamon Press, 1976.

Guzzetta, R.A. Acquisition and transfer of empathy by the parents to early adolescents through Structured Learning training. *Journal of Counseling Psychology*, 1976, **23**, 449–453.

Homme, L. *How to use contingency contracting in the classroom*. Champaign, Ill.: Research Press, 1970.

Martin, R. & Lauridsen, D. *Developing student discipline and motivation*. Champaign, Ill.: Research Press, 1974.

O'Leary, D.K. & O'Leary, S.G. *Classroom management*. New York: Pergamon Press, 1972.

Rosenthal, N.R. A prescriptive approach for counselor training. *Journal of Counseling Psychology*, 1977, **24**, 231–237.

Sloane, H.N. *Classroom management*. New York: Wiley, 1976.

Sprafkin, R.P. The rebirth of moral treatment. *Professional Psychology*, 1977, May, 161–169.

Stumphauzer, J.S. *Behavior modification principles*. Kalamazoo: Behaviordelia, 1977.

Swift, M.S. & Spivack, G. *Alternative teaching strategies*. Champaign, Ill: Research Press, 1975.

Wenrich, W.W. *A primer of behavior modification*. Belmont, Calif.: Brooks/Cole, 1970.

ADDENDUM 1

Outline A

Outline of the Opening Session
A. Introductions.
    1. Trainers introduce themselves
    2. Trainers invite students to introduce themselves. During this time trainers can ask for some additional information as a way of breaking the ice.
    Examples:—"How about if we go around the group, and each person say his/her name and one thing he/she likes (and one thing he/she dislikes) about school."
    —"Why don't you tell us your name and one activity you like outside of school."
B. Overview of Structured Learning.
    1. Trainers explain that the purpose of the group is to teach useful skills for dealing with people, dealing with feelings, dealing with anger, handling stressful situations more effectively, learning planning skills, and generally feeling more comfortable in different situations.
    Examples:—"In this class, we'll be teaching you some ways to get along better with parents, teachers and friends."
    —"We'll be looking at some ways to help you stay out of trouble."
    —"We'll be practicing some ways to express yourselves better to adults and others who don't seem to understand you."
    —Name some skills that will be useful. (Expressing anger in a way that doesn't wind up with you sitting in the principal's office, etc.)
    2. Trainers describe specific procedures for learning the skills, indicating that the method is the same as that for learning anything new (same way as you learn a sport, learn to drive a car, etc.).
    Examples:—a. Show (modeling): "We'll show you the way to do it."
    —b. Try (role playing): "You'll practice it, rehearse for
    — when you'll actually use the skill."
    —c. Discuss (feedback): "We'll all tell you what you did well and what you could use some improvement on."
    —d. Practice (transfer): "You'll try it during the week."
    3. Trainers introduce the idea of breaking a skill down into steps, as a way to make learning easier.

Examples:—"What are the steps in learning volleyball?"
  —"What do you do first? Second? Etc.?"
  —"What are the different things you need to know how to do in in order to play a musical instrument?"
  —Ask class to give steps for mastering some activity.
  —"What are the steps or parts that make up listening?"

C. Trainers discuss with group other rules and procedures.
  1. As the issues come up in the group, offer reassurance about embarrassment, fear of performing, safety of group, confidentiality, and any other issues of concern.
  2. Trainers describe group rules regarding attendance, lateness, group size, time, and place of meetings.

D. With some groups whose members have short attention spans, it may be necessary to modify or shorten the introduction. Some alternative methods include:
  1. Brief statement of procedures.
  2. Minimal description of procedures (e.g., show, try, discuss, practice description above) and then get right into learning by doing (begin modeling and role playing very quickly).
  3. Promise material reinforcements for cooperation in procedures. This may be done in several ways. One way is to assign a certain number of points a youngster needs to earn in order to get candy or other rewards at the end of the group. Youngsters are then told what behaviors will earn them points. Some behaviors which might earn points are: answering questions, paying attention, volunteering to role-play, following behavioral steps, etc. A tally of points for each student is kept up on the chalkboard. Rewards might also be offered without the point qualification, and simply distributed when the group is over (see Recommended Readings for references to implementing and monitoring token economies).

E. Trainers proceed to first skill, following Outline B which will be used for all succeeding sessions.

Outline B

Outline of a Typical Structured Learning Session
A. Trainer presents overview of the skill.
  1. Introduce skill briefly prior to showing modeling display.
  2. Ask questions which will help students define the skill in their own language.
  Examples:—"Who know what _____ is?"
    —"What does _____ mean to you?"
    —"Who can define _____ ?"

3. Postpone lengthier discussion until after viewing the modeling display. If students want to engage in further discussion, you might say: "Let's wait until after we've seen some examples of people using the skill before we talk about it in more detail."

4. Make a statement about what will follow the vignettes.

Examples:—"After we see the examples, we will talk about times when you've had to _____, and times when you may have to do it in the future."

5. Distribute Skill Cards, asking a student to read the behavioral steps aloud.

6. Ask students to follow each step in the modeling display as the step is depicted.

B. Trainer presents modeling display.

1. Trainer may opt to play only a portion of the audiovisual modeling display in any given session.

2. We recommend that each exposure to a skill (since a group may spend several sessions on the same skill) include at least the introduction and two or three modeling vignettes.

C. Trainer invites discussion of skill which has been modeled.

1. Invite comments on how a situation on the tape may remind students of situations involving skill usage in their own lives.

Examples:—"Did any of the situations you just saw remind you of times when you have had to _____ ?"

2. Ask questions which encourage students to talk about skill usage and problems involving skill usage.

Examples:—"What do you do in situations where you have to _____ ?"
—"Have you ever had to _____ ?"

D. Trainer organizes role play.

1. Ask a student who has volunteered a situation to elaborate on his/her remarks, obtaining details on where, when, and with whom the skill might be useful in the future.

2. Designate this student as a main actor, and ask him/her to choose a coactor (someone who reminds the main actor of the person with whom the skill will be used in the real-life situation).

Examples:—"What does _____ look like?"
—"Who in the class reminds you of _____ in some way?"

3. Get additional information from the main actor, if necessary, and set the stage for the role playing (including props, furniture arrangement, etc.).

Examples:—"Where might you be talking to _____ ?"
—"How is it furnished?"
—"Would you be standing or sitting?"

—"What time of day will it be?"

—"Where is _____ coming from?" etc.

4. Just prior to role playing, give each group member some final instructions as to his/her part.

Examples:—To the main actor: "Try to follow all of the steps as best you can."

—To the coactor: "Try to play the part of _____ as best you can. Say and do what you think _____ would do."

—To the other students in the group. "Watch how well _____ follows the steps so that we can talk about it after the role play."

E. Trainer instructs the role players to begin.

1. One trainer (or student helper) should stand at the chalkboard and point to each step as it is enacted.

2. The other trainer should be positioned near the actors to provide whatever coaching or prompting is needed by the main actor or coactor.

3. In the event that the role play strays markedly from the behavioral steps or otherwise departs from the theme, stop the scene, provide needed instruction, and begin again.

F. Trainer invites feedback following role play.

1. Ask the main actor to wait until he/she has heard everyone's comments before talking.

2. Ask coactor: "In role of _____ , how did _____ make you feel? What were your reactions to him/her?"

3. Ask observing students: "How well were the behavioral steps followed?"

"What specific things did you like or dislike?"

"In what ways did the coactor do a good job?"

4. The trainers comment on the following of the behavioral steps, provide social reward, point out what was done well, and comment on what else might be done to make the enactment even better.

5. Ask main actor: "Now that you have heard everyone's comments, how do you feel about the job you did?"

"How do you think that following the steps worked out?"

G. Trainer helps role player to plan homework.

1. Ask the main actor how, when, and with whom he/she might attempt the behavioral steps prior to the next class meeting.

2. As appropriate, the Homework Report forms may be used to get a written commitment from the main actor to try out his/her new skill, and report back to the group at the next meeting.

3. Students who have not had a chance to role-play during a par-

ticular class may also be assigned homework in the form of looking for situations relevant to the skill which they might role-play during the next class meeting.

ADDENDUM 2

Homework Report 1

Name _____ Date _____
Group Leaders _____

FILL IN DURING THIS CLASS
1. What skill will you use?

2. What are the steps for the skill?

3. Where will you try the skill?

4. With whom will you try the skill?

5. When will you try the skill?

FILL IN AFTER DOING YOUR HOMEWORK
1. What happened when you did the homework?

2. Which steps did you really follow?

3. How good a job did you do in using the skill? (Circle one)
   Excellent   Good   Fair   Poor
4. What do you think should be your next homework assignment?

Homework Report 2

(Advanced)
Name _____ Date _____
Group Leader _____

FILL IN BEFORE DOING YOUR HOMEWORK
1. What skill will you use?

2. What are the steps for the skill?

3. Where will you try the skill?

4. With whom will you try the skill?

5. When will you try the skill?

6. If you do an excellent job, will you reward yourself? (What will you say to yourself, and what will you do for yourself?)

7. If you do a good job, how will you reward yourself? (What will you say to yourself, and what will you do for yourself?)

8. If you do a fair job, how will you reward yourself? (What will you say to yourself, and what will you do for yourself?

FILL IN AFTER DOING YOUR HOMEWORK
1. What happened when you did the homework?

2. Which steps did you really follow?

3. How good a job did you do in using the skill? (Circle one)
Excellent   Good   Fair   Poor
4. How did you reward yourself?

5. What do you think should be your next homework assignment?

Skill Checklist

Name: _____
Class: _____
Listed below you will find a number of skills that youngsters are more or less proficient in using. This checklist will help you evaluate how well each youngster uses the various skills. You can then use this information in grouping students into Structured Learning classes. The information can also be used to decide which skills to teach to a given group of youngsters. For each youngster, rate his/her use of each skill, based on your observations of the individual's behavior in various situations.
Circle 1, if the youngster is never good at using the skill
Circle 2, if the youngster is seldom good at using the skill.
Circle 3, if the youngster is sometimes good at using the skill.
Circle 4, if the youngster is often good at using the skill.
Circle 5, if the youngster is always good at using the skill.
Do not rate those skills for which you have no information on the youngster's ability.
1. Listening: Does the student pay attention to someone who is talking and make an effort to understand what is being said?   1 2 3 4 5
2. Starting a conversation: Does the student talk to others about light topics and then lead into more serious topics?   1 2 3 4 5

3. Having a conversation: Does the student talk to others about things of interest to both of them?   1 2 3 4 5

4. Asking a question: Does the student decide what information is needed and ask the right person for that information?   1 2 3 4 5

5. Saying thank you: Does the student let others know that he/she is grateful for favors, etc.?   1 2 3 4 5

6. Introducing yourself: Does the student become acquainted with new people on his/her own initiative?   1 2 3 4 5

7. Introducing other people: Does the student help others become acquainted with one another?   1 2 3 4 5

8. Giving a compliment: Does the student tell others that he/she likes something about them or their activities?   1 2 3 4 5

9. Asking for help: Does the student request assistance when he/she is having difficulty?   1 2 3 4 5

10. Joining in: Does the student decide on the best way to become part of an ongoing activity or group?   1 2 3 4 5

11. Giving instructions: Does the student clearly explain to others how they are to do a specific task?   1 2 3 4 5

12. Following instructions: Does the student pay attention to instructions, give his/her reactions, and carry the instructions out adequately.   1 2 3 4 5

13. Apologizing: Does the student tell others that he/she is sorry after doing something wrong?   1 2 3 4 5

14. Convincing others: Does the student attempt to persuade others that his/her ideas are better and will be more useful than those of the other person?   1 2 3 4 5

15. Knowing your feelings: Does the student try to recognize which emotions he/she is feeling?   1 2 3 4 5

16. Expressing your feelings: Does the student let others know which emotions he/she is feeling?   1 2 3 4 5

17. Understanding the feelings of others: Do the others know which emotions he/she is feeling?   1 2 3 4 5

18. Dealing with someone else's anger: Does the student try to understand other people's angry feelings?   1 2 3 4 5

19. Expressing affection: Does the student let others know that he/she cares about them?   1 2 3 4 5

20. Dealing with fear: Does the student figure out why he/she is afraid and do something to reduce the fear?   1 2 3 4 5

21. Rewarding yourself: Does the student say and do nice things for him/herself when the reward is deserved?   1 2 3 4 5

22. Asking permission: Does the student figure out when

permission is needed to do something, and then ask
the right person for permission? 1 2 3 4 5

23. Sharing something: Does the student offer to share
what he/she has with others who might appreciate
it? 1 2 3 4 5

24. Helping others: Does the student give assistance to
others who might need or want help? 1 2 3 4 5

25. Negotiating: Does the student arrive at a plan which
satisfies both the student and others who have taken
different positions? 1 2 3 4 5

26. Using self-control: Does the student control his/her
temper so that things do not get out of hand? 1 2 3 4 5

27. Standing up for your rights: Does the student assert
his/her rights by letting people know where he/she
stands on an issue? 1 2 3 4 5

28. Responding to teasing: Does the student deal with
being teased by others in ways that allow the student
to remain in control of him/herself? 1 2 3 4 5

29. Avoiding trouble when with others: Does the student
stay out of situations that might get him/her into
trouble? 1 2 3 4 5

30. Keeping out of fights: Does the student figure out
ways other than fighting to handle difficult situations? 1 2 3 4 5

31. Making a complaint: Does the student tell others when
they are responsible for creating a particular problem
for the student, and then attempt to find a solution
for the problem? 1 2 3 4 5

32. Answering a complaint: Does the student try to arrive
at a fair solution to someone's justified complaint? 1 2 3 4 5

33. Sportsmanship after the game: Does the student express an honest compliment to others about how they
played a game? 1 2 3 4 5

34. Dealing with embarrassment: Does the student do
things which help him/her to feel less embarrassed or
self-conscious? 1 2 3 4 5

35. Dealing with being left out: Does the student decide
whether he/she has been left out of some activity, and
then do things to feel better about the situation? 1 2 3 4 5

36. Standing up for a friend: Does the student let other
people know when a friend has not been treated fairly? 1 2 3 4 5

37. Responding to persuasion: Does the student carefully
consider the position of another person, comparing it
to his/her own, before deciding what to do? 1 2 3 4 5

38. Responding to failure: Does the student figure out the reason for failing in a particular situation, and what he/she can do about it, in order to be more successful in the future?   1 2 3 4 5

39. Dealing with confusing messages: Does the student recognize and deal with the confusion which results when others tell him/her one thing, but say or do things which indicate that they mean something else?   1 2 3 4 5

40. Dealing with an accusation: Does the student figure out what he/she has been accused of and why, and then decide on the best way to deal with the person who made the accusation?   1 2 3 4 5

41. Getting ready for a difficult conversation: Does the student plan on the best way to present his/her point of view prior to a stressful conversation?   1 2 3 4 5

42. Dealing with group pressure: Does the student decide what he/she wants to do when others want the student to do something else?   1 2 3 4 5

43. Deciding on something to do: Does the student deal with feeling bored by starting an interesting activity?   1 2 3 4 5

44. Deciding what caused a problem: Does the student find out whether an event was caused by something that was within his/her control?   1 2 3 4 5

45. Setting a goal: Does the student realistically decide on what he/she can accomplish prior to starting on a task?   1 2 3 4 5

46. Deciding on your abilities: Does the student realistically figure out how well he/she might do at a particular task?   1 2 3 4 5

47. Gathering information: Does the student decide what he/she needs to know and how to get that information?   1 2 3 4 5

48. Arranging problems by importance: Does the student decide realistically which of a number of problems is most important and should be dealt with first?   1 2 3 4 5

49. Making a decision: Does the student consider possibilities and make choices which he/she feels will be best?   1 2 3 4 5

50. Concentrating on a task: Does the student make those preparations which will help him/her get a job done?   1 2 3 4 5

SKILL TRAINING GROUPING CHART

Instructions: Write in ratings (from Skill Checklist) and the date skill was covered. Ratings of 1 and 2 generally indicate a skill deficit. For selection purposes, students having low ratings on a number of skills within a skill group should be put together in the same class.

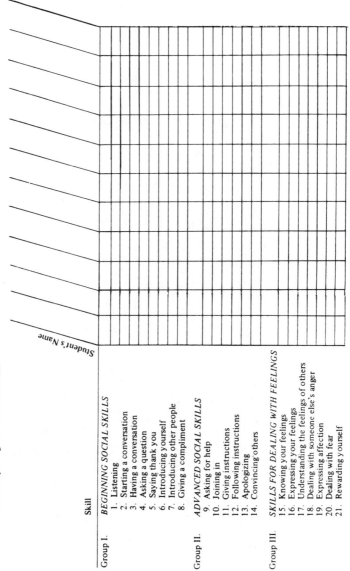

Student's Name

Skill

Group I. *BEGINNING SOCIAL SKILLS*
1. Listening
2. Starting a conversation
3. Having a conversation
4. Asking a question
5. Saying thank you
6. Introducing yourself
7. Introducing other people
8. Giving a compliment

Group II. *ADVANCED SOCIAL SKILLS*
9. Asking for help
10. Joining in
11. Giving instructions
12. Following instructions
13. Apologizing
14. Convincing others

Group III. *SKILLS FOR DEALING WITH FEELINGS*
15. Knowing your feelings
16. Expressing your feelings
17. Understanding the feelings of others
18. Dealing with someone else's anger
19. Expressing affection
20. Dealing with fear
21. Rewarding yourself

	Student's Name

Skill

Group IV. *SKILL ALTERNATIVES TO AGGRESSION*
22. Asking permission
23. Sharing something
24. Helping others
25. Negotiating
26. Using self-control
27. Standing up for your rights
28. Responding to teasing
29. Avoiding trouble with others
30. Keeping out of fights

Group V. *SKILLS FOR DEALING WITH STRESS*
31. Making a complaint
32. Answering a complaint
33. Sportsmanship after the game
34. Dealing with embarrassment
35. Dealing with being left out
36. Standing up for a friend
37. Responding to persuasion
38. Responding to failure
39. Dealing with confusing messages
40. Dealing with an accusation
41. Getting ready for a difficult conversation
42. Dealing with group pressure

Group VI. *PLANNING SKILLS*
43. Deciding on something to do
44. Deciding what caused a problem
45. Setting a goal
46. Deciding on your abilities
47. Gathering information
48. Arranging problems by importance
49. Making a decision
50. Concentrating on a task

186

SKILL TRAINING CLASS MASTERY RECORD

SKILL: _____   DATE: _____

Student's Name	Role play participation		Feedback participation	Homework		Rating of skill use in role play
	Main actor	Co-actor		Assigned	Completed	(assign one point for each behavioral step performed appropriately)
						Poor 1 — Fair 2 — Adequate 3 — Good 4 — Excellent 5

Behavioral Objectives: Participating appropriately in role playing as a main actor and completing assigned homework may serve as evidence of accomplishing the behavioral objective of mastering each skill.

Examples of Behavioral Steps

Skill 1. LISTENING

1. Look at the person who is talking.
2. Think about what he/she is saying.
3. Wait for your turn to talk.
4. Say what you want to say.

Skill 25. NEGOTIATING

1. Decide if you and the other person are having a difference of opinion.
2. Tell the other person what you think about the problem.
3. Ask the other person what he/she thinks about the problem.
4. Listen openly to his/her answer.
5. Think about why the other person might feel this way.
6. Suggest a compromise.

Appendix C
Structured Learning Manual for Police

Arnold P. Goldstein,
Syracuse University

Lieutenant Philip J. Monti,
Syracuse Police Department

Chief Thomas J. Sardino,
Syracuse Police Department

Deputy Chief Donald Green,
Syracuse Police Department

CONTENTS

INTRODUCTION

Surveys, observations, and analyses in several police departments across the United States have revealed that only about 20 percent of the typical officer's time is spent identifying and apprehending criminals or in other law enforcement and crime control activities. The average officer is involved in service çalls requiring primarily social regulation, or what has been called order maintenance, a full 80 percent of his time. While order maintenance calls may take many forms, the main concern of this manual is with those calls involving crisis intervention. These involve family fights, mentally disturbed or intoxicated citizens, suicide attempts, and accident victims. Such crisis calls have certain important similarities. First, one or more highly emotional citizens are likely to be involved in each such call, though the particular emotion being expressed will vary according to the type of crisis. Aggressive feelings are usually the mark of family disputes; anxiety or hysteria is typically present in suicide and accident crises; confusion and sometimes agitation are often the main features of mentally disturbed or intoxicated citizens. Because of their highly emotional nature, a second similarity of most crisis calls is high levels of unpredictable danger in the form of threats to the responding officer's safety. Family disputes and similar disturbance calls are particularly dangerous, accounting for 103 of the 786 police killed in the United States during 1963 to 1973. Forty percent of all police injuries also occur on these types of crisis intervention calls. The unpredictability of the sources of threat on these calls seems to be a major reason for their dangerous nature. We will focus on this problem in the first section of this manual, as a means of giving the police officer (to whom this manual is addressed) information which may reduce the unpredictability of such threats to his safety, prepare him better in procedures for spotting potential sources of danger, and thus, it is hoped, reduce the possibility of injury or death resulting from crisis intervention activities.

Once you have taken initial steps to protect your safety, you are faced with the task of dealing with the crisis situation effectively. To do so, your next job will be to calm the highly emotional citizens involved in the crisis. The second section of this manual provides you with several procedures for quieting highly emotional citizens, and also offers guidelines to help you decide which calming procedures to use with which types of citizens.

After quieting the scene, you will be able to proceed to gather the information needed in order to decide upon and to take appropriate action. Thus, the third section of this manual describes several information-gathering procedures and again emphasizes that different procedures will best be used with different citizens. The final section of this manual outlines several courses of action you may choose to take in order to resolve the crisis situation.

Thus, proceeding in order of occurrence, this manual provides very specific information to aid you in dealing effectively with crisis intervention calls by describing procedures for:

1. Observing and protecting against threats to your safety.
2. Calming the crisis situation.
3. Gathering relevant information.
4. Taking appropriate action.

We urge you to learn these procedures well. They will help protect your safety. Road experience, of course, is a key ingredient in any officer's learning to perform in a manner which keeps threats to his safety as low as possible. But do not depend on road experience alone. The majority of the 103 officers killed on such calls had five or more years of road experience! These procedures will help you handle the crisis call in an effective and flexible manner. We stress flexibility because no single procedure will work well in all or usually even in most crisis situations. To be truly effective, you will have to (1) develop skill in using several crisis intervention procedures, and (2) know when to employ each procedure. Finally, your effective use of these crisis interventions will also reduce callbacks, increase community goodwill toward your police department, and add to your own sense of competence and professionalism.

OBSERVING AND PROTECTING AGAINST THREATS TO YOUR SAFETY

Because of the overexcited, highly emotional state of the citizens involved and the unpredictability of the threats to your safety which may be present, crisis intervention is very dangerous police business. As noted earlier, crisis intervention disturbance calls are a major source of police deaths and injuries. They must be handled with great care, and must be seen as anything but "routine" calls. Your safety, your health, and your life may depend on it. Since the most gentle-appearing citizens can become abusive under certain circumstances, since the most harmless-appearing objects can be used as weapons, and since no officer can prevent all threats to his safety and still function effectively, there will always remain some danger in your handling of crisis calls. But such danger can be substantially reduced. This can be done by steps you yourself can take. It has been shown that threats to your safety will be reduced if you are adequately prepared in advance for the crisis situation in which you are intervening. After radio dispatch, but while still in your patrol car on the way to the crisis scene, you should:

1. Consider your prior experience on similar calls.
2. Anticipate that the unexpected may actually happen.
3. Form a tentative plan of action.

You are urged, first of all, to consider your prior experience on similar calls so that all the relevant past events that have actually occurred to you can be recalled and reviewed by you. You should think over not only how crises of the same type as the present call usually unfold, and how you usually have handled them, but also recall and review unusual past calls of this type. They may occur again this way, and if you are prepared, your safety is increased. Rehearse in your imagination the various ways (usual and unusual) in which crises like this have developed and specifically what you will do in each instance. As you think through these several alternatives, place particular emphasis on threats to your safety. What objects have been used against you as weapons in the past? What types of people have abused or attacked you when you didn't expect it? What did you fail to observe, scan, do, or have someone else do in the past which put you in danger?

Once you have thoroughly reviewed your past experience on similar calls, and used it in this preparedness-increasing way, we urge you to imagine threats to your safety which might occur even though they never have before. That is, anticipate that the unexpected might actually happen. The policeman's enemy here is the false security caused by routine. A salesman can approach 50 customers the same way. Forty-nine times they make a purchase, but the fiftieth may refuse. Since the salesman is so generally effective, he ignores this fiftieth customer and goes on using the same approach in the future. A police officer doesn't have the same luxury. His handling of 49 family fight calls can all proceed well, and cause no physical harm to the officer. If the officer is not wary on the fiftieth, not alert and prepared for both expected and unexpected dangers, he may lose not a sale, but his life. It is a hard task to get "psyched up" call after call, but each is a real or potential threat to your safety. Each must be preceded by a thorough review in your thinking of possible dangers, both from what has actually happened to you on earlier calls, and from what you imagine could happen.

The usefulness of preparation by these types of rehearsal will be increased if you are thoroughly familiar with your patrol area and the people who reside in it. Knowing who does or does not belong in a given residence, who works in a certain store, or ways in and out of a given business establishment may prove to be very valuable safety information if crisis intervention at such places proves necessary. Clearly, therefore, it is worth your effort to get to know the people and places which make up your patrol area before need arises.

Response time for the average call is usually rather brief. With all that you must do just to drive safely but quickly to the crisis scene in this short time, you have a lot already occupying your thinking. We have tried to make you even busier, by what we described above as rehearsal in your imagination of how the scene might be and how the crisis and its threats to your safety may develop. There is one final aspect of your in-the-car responsibility to your own safety which we wish to discuss. The emphasis up to this point has been upon what the citizen may do to you, and how you might prepare yourself to respond. But only part of the danger to responding officers is citizen caused. Serious injury or death may result from events or chains of behaviors which officers begin. You may, in other words, sometimes be a serious threat to your own safety. Most of our emphasis thus far has been on the danger to officers of being unprepared when responding to crisis intervention calls. An equally serious problem (to his own safety) is often the officer who is too prepared. Notice that earlier we described the final preparation step (in the car) as "Form a tentative plan of action." We stressed "tentative" because although preparedness is very desirable, the officer who is "sure" in his own mind about what will happen can often cause it to happen. This is sometimes called a "self-fulfilling prophecy." The officer who, after considering all past experiences and all possible relevant crises, decides that the citizens at the crisis scene are almost certain to attack him, may approach the citizen so belligerently or aggressively that he provokes the very attack he was expecting. Be prepared, but be open to the possibility that what you have decided probably will happen still has some chance of not happening. Form a tentative plan of action, and begin acting on it, but don't finalize it until you observe the actual crisis and gather all relevant information. A tenth repeat call to a family having a dispute which on the nine earlier occasions ended with the disputants quieting down, may unexpectedly turn violent and cause you serious injury.

Remember, the steps to follow on the way to a crisis call are:
1. Consider your prior experience on similar calls.
2. Anticipate that the unexpected may actually happen.
3. Form a tentative plan of action.

CALMING THE SITUATION

Step 1. Observe and Neutralize Threats to Your Safety

You have now arrived at the scene of the crisis call. If your preparation on the way has been adequate, you arrive with both a tentative plan of action in mind, and some specific ideas about threats to your safety which may be present. Your first step on arrival, therefore, should be to observe and neutralize possible threats to your safety. We mean by this not only the removal of obvious weapons such as guns and knives, but also the removal or neutralization of heavy and throwable objects (ashtrays, folding chairs, etc.), scissors, kitchen utensils, boiling water (in a pot on the stove, or in a coffee cup), and the like. We would also recommend routine and immediate separation of disputants, placing yourself away from windows and staircases, avoiding turning your back on any of the disputants, and both knowing where your partner is and if possible actually having him in view even when each of you is with a different disputant in a different room.

You should also take what steps you can to minimize threats to your safety which are caused by things you do or fail to do. At times it may be desirable to cruise past the crisis scene for a quick scan of places and people before returning there to park. If a disturbance is in progress, do not park your car immediately in front of the location of the crisis. While parking away from the scene may make you harder to find by other responding personnel, and also make it a bit harder for you to get to your radio and equipment, these disadvantages are outweighed by the one main advantage of such parking—the disputants won't see you arrive. On all types of disturbance calls, your safety is increased if you surprise the disputants, rather than if they see you first and possibly prepare to attack you.

Wherever you park, position your car so that it won't get boxed in. Secure your car, so that it is difficult for anyone not authorized by you to get at your equipment or anything else in the car which may be used as a weapon. A secure car will also increase the chances that you will have radio access to assistance if you need it. As you arrive, while still in the car, look over the crisis scene for anything you can learn about the nature and scope of the disturbance. Bicycles on a lawn, people sitting or standing on a porch, a car with its motor running, the number of rooms in the house with their lights on, and the general noise level are among the many things you may observe which can give you clues regarding how many people are at the crisis scene, their ages, and their possible emotional state.

Approach the scene quietly, and apart from your partner if you have one. Do not stand directly in front of the door, as disputants may shoot through it or, as has happened with glass doors, throw something through it. Stand to the side of the doorway and, if it is a door which opens toward you, be sure to stand to the side away from the hinges so that the door can't be pushed into you. Be ready to scan the room inside for threats to your safety as soon as the door is opened. Be prepared to enter, but be sure not to place your arm, leg, or nightstick into a partially opened door as it may be quickly shut on you thus holding you almost defenseless. Upon entering the apartment or house, visually "frisk" everyone; determine who is in the apartment and where; get and keep everyone in sight; look for and remove all actual or potential weapons; see that disputants are separated; and be sure that you avoid standing in places in which you are vulnerable to attack or injury. In carrying out these steps, remember that it is not only adult males who may attack you. Adult females, the elderly, and adolescents may all possess weapons, or may otherwise initiate aggressive behavior toward you.

While using these methods to neutralize threats to your safety, do not overlook your own gun. A high percentage of the 103 officers mentioned earlier who were killed on disturbance calls were killed by their own service revolvers. Finally, unless you must physically restrain a citizen, try to avoid crowding, threatening, grabbing, or otherwise touching an already hostile citizen as it may provoke him to even more violent behavior. At times you will be able to be aware enough of citizens' nonverbal behavior to spot violence just before it occurs, i.e., after the fuse is lit but before the explosion. Signs of impending violence often include a crouched torso, clenched fists, grinding teeth, dilated pupils, flared nostrils, flushed cheeks.

Step 2. Create a First Impression of Nonhostile Authority

Once you feel you have made a good beginning at protecting your own physical safety and the safety of the citizens involved, you may move to the second step in calming the situation. Keep in mind, however, that you may be threatened with danger at any time during the crisis call, so remain vigilant for unpredicted citizen violence throughout all phases of the call. The second step in calming the situation is to create a first impression of nonhostile authority. How the citizen reacts to you will, of course, be determined by his personality, by his history with other police officers, and by the crisis itself. But your behavior, especially your first impression behavior, will have a lot to do with how aggressively the citizen behaves and how cooperative he is with your efforts to calm the situation and resolve the crisis. We therefore recommend that you behave as a nonhostile authority in the initial phases of your dealing with the citizen in crisis by taking charge and instructing the citizen in what you want him to do in a firm, fair, even, and direct manner. In doing so, it is important to avoid being either too soft or too harsh. The officer who asks the citizen to do such and such too gently will often fail to achieve his purpose because he has neither captured the citizen's attention to a sufficient degree nor made the citizen feel sufficiently secure or reassured by the officer's presence. The officer who opens his arrival at a crisis call by being too harsh, by leaning too hard on the citizens involved, may also fail to achieve his purposes of calming the scene and resolving the crisis. In fact, just the opposite may occur. The disturbance level may actually increase, and threats to his safety may actually become more possible.

Step 3. Calm the Emotional Citizen

Whether involved directly or as just observers, the citizens present at a crisis scene are quite likely to be in a highly emotional state. Which particular emotion is being shown will depend partly on the citizen and partly on whether the crisis is a family fight, rape, accident, attempted suicide, assault, burglary, or an episode of mental disturbance or intoxication. Whether the persons involved are highly aggressive, anxious, confused, or hysterical, it is nonetheless the job of the officer first to calm the emotional citizen before he will be able to gather the information he needs in order to carry out proper police procedures and bring the crisis to an appropriate conclusion.

We have stressed elsewhere that the effective police officer is a flexible police officer. He does not try to use a single approach in all situations but instead varies his behavior depending upon the citizen and the nature of the crisis. In order to be flexible, he must know a variety of approaches well, and develop with experience the knowledge of which one to apply at which times. The material which follows is a brief description of the several procedures which effective officers have actually used successfully to calm citizen emotions in crisis situations.

1. Show understanding of the citizen's feelings. By his words, tone of voice, facial expression, and gestures, the officer makes it clear to the citizen that he accurately understands what the citizen is feeling and how strongly he is feeling it. For example, "You're really feeling very angry and upset at him," or "It can be awfully frightening when something like this happens," or "I understand that you're feeling very sad and alone after a loss like this." Note below, the officer maintains his impartiality and his professional role by avoiding taking sides. He says, "You're really feeling very angry and upset at him," and not, "You've got every right to feel angry and upset at him."

2. Modeling. By his words, tone of voice, facial expression, and gestures, the officer makes it clear to the citizen that he, the officer, is responding calmly to the crisis situation. His calmness and appearance of control can serve as a model for the citizen. By removing his hat, sitting down, speaking at a normal conversational rate and level, the officer communicates that *he* feels no need to be upset, angry, or anxious. Since we are all often ready to imitate people in authority, a demonstration of calmness by the officer will frequently have a calming effect on highly emotional citizens.

3. Reassurance. In using modeling to calm the situation, the officer's own behavior serves as an example which we hope the citizen will imitate. Use of reassurance takes matters a step further because the officer not only behaves in a calm manner but, in addition, gives the citizen reasons why he too should feel calmer. For example, reassurance is often delivered by such sentences as "It will be OK," "I've handled many like this," "The doctor will know how to handle this," "We've got him under control." Reassurance will be a particularly effective calming procedure if the officer has done a good initial job of establishing a first impression of himself as a nonhostile authority figure.

4. Encourage talking. It is very difficult for a citizen to continue yelling, screaming, crying, fighting, or behaving in a highly emotional manner while at the same time trying to answer a series of questions put to him by the officer. Thus, encouraging the citizen to talk is often an effective means for calming him down. Sometimes it will prove useful to encourage talking about the crisis itself (Encourage talking: Ventilation). Here, the officer asks the citizen to begin at the beginning; asks numerous investigative questions regarding exactly who did what, where, in what sequence, and at what times; includes several open-ended questions; and takes notes at a deliberate pace in order to slow down the citizen's rate of talking.

Some citizens, however, will remain upset when encouraged to talk about the crisis because it is the same crisis which upset them in the first place which they are now describing to the officer. When this occurs, or as a substitute procedure, it is often useful to encourage the citizen to talk about matters other than the crisis (Encourage talking: Diversion). In essence, this procedure is an attempt to divert the attention of the citizen away from the crisis and his feelings about it. Here the officer seeks "background information" which he claims he needs for his formal report, such as the names of the citizens involved, their addresses, ages, phone, occupations, legal relationship, and so forth.

5. Distraction. At times, an effective means for calming emotional citizens will be to divert their attention from the crisis in ways other than by asking for background information. Distraction procedures, however, are likely to have a rather temporary effect. Thus, the officer must be prepared to follow them with use of other calming procedures if necessary. Distraction may be accomplished by:

a. Asking a favor, e.g., "May I have a glass of water?"
b. Asking a question totally irrelevant to the crisis situation, e.g., "Can you tell me where you got that (household item)?"
c. Asking a question relevant to the crisis situation, but opposite to what the citizen is likely to expect, e.g., "Would you really prefer to be arrested?"
d. Offering an observation totally irrelevant to the crisis situation, e.g., "I've got the same brand of TV, but we've been having trouble with it lately."
e. Giving a suggestion or command which tells the citizen to continue exactly what he expects you to try to stop, e.g., "Please yell louder."

6. Use of humor. There will be citizens with whom the officer may effectively use humor as a calming procedure. Humor can put the crisis in more accurate and less serious perspective, it can communicate to the citizen that the officer is not overly upset by the crisis (modeling), and it can often cool tempers off in a crisis of a highly aggressive nature.

The first six methods we have presented for calming crisis situations may all be considered "conversational" methods. By showing understanding, modeling, reassuring, encouraging talking, or using distraction or humor, the officer seeks to calm the emotional citizen by words and deeds designed to have a quieting effect. We recommend that one or more of these first six calming methods be used initially by the officer in crisis situations unless, of course, physical dangers to himself or to other citizens are apparent. When these converstional methods fail, we recommend use (in the order presented below) of two assertive methods for calming citizens in crisis.

7. Repetition and outshouting. When individuals are very angry, very anxious, very depressed, or very confused, they are tuned into their own feelings but often are unresponsive and even unaware of the feelings, communications, and sometimes even the presence of others. The officer may have to repeat himself several times to "get through" to the citizen. When the citizen's emotion is anger and an altercation is still in progress, the officer may have to outshout the citizen to be heard. This display of authority, or similar steps such as slamming a clipboard loudly, will often yield an immediate quieting effect.

8. Physical restraint. When conversation calming methods fail, when repetition and outshouting prove not to be assertive enough, or where considerations of physical danger demand it, the officer must physically restrain and subdue the highly aggressive citizen. You are urged to use just enough force to accomplish this goal, to avoid excessive force. While subduing one disputant, remain aware of the other one. In family disputes, for example, it is not unusual for a complainant wife to turn on the officer and try to resist her husband's arrest even though she was the one who called the police in the first place.

There will be crises in which calming the citizen is best handled by means other than the conversational or assertive methods described above.

9. Use of trusted others. Circumstances may occur in crisis situations which make it appropriate for the officer to ask someone else either to assist in or to take full responsibility for calming the emotional citizen. This someone else may be a fellow officer, but will often be a trusted friend, relative, or neighbor of the emotional citizen. Such use of trusted others as calming sources may prove necessary when the officer is too busy with danger or threat aspects of the crisis, when there are too many highly emotional citizens involved in the crisis for him to handle alone (or with his partner), when the citizen is too fearful of police, when the citizen speaks only a foreign language, and when conversational and assertive methods have not succeeded.

10. Temporarily ignore. We have described a number of calming procedures and suggested some broad guidelines for the rough order in which they ought to be used. There are times, however, when the effective officer will use none of these procedures but decide instead to deal with the emotional citizen by temporarily ignoring him. Depending upon threats to officer or citizen safety, and upon emergency aspects of the crisis itself, the officer may have to devote priority attention to matters other than the citizen's feelings. The bleeding accident victim must be given first aid while his hysterical spouse's behavior is ignored for the time being, the disputants in a bar-room disturbance must be separated and restrained before the officer can attend to the distress of the bar owner, and burglarized premises may have to be secured before the anxious and upset tenant can be attended to by the officer.

This section has presented several alternative methods for calming the anger, anxiety, hysteria, or confusion of highly emotional citizens in crisis situations. While we have provided a general idea regarding the order in which we recommend that these calming procedures be used, it is not possible to provide you with more specific rules for matching procedures to specific emotions or specific crises. For one officer, modeling may be very effective in calming participants in certain family fights, in other such fights he may have to resort to physical restraint. A second officer may be excellent at reassuring accident victims, while a third may be more effective with other techniques in similar cases. Which procedures, in which crises, with which citizens will work most effectively for you is a matter you will have to determine from your own experience. This manual simply asks that you not expect one or two procedures to work in all situations, and that you try to be flexible and work out your best match by trying different calming procedures with different types of crises and citizens.

Remember, the steps for calming the situation are:
1. Observe and neutralize threats to your safety.
2. Create a first impression of nonhostile authority.
3. Calm the emotional citizen.

GATHERING RELEVANT INFORMATION

Step 1. Explain To the Citizen What You Want Him to Discuss with You and Why

You have calmed the crisis situation in order that the citizens involved will be more accurate and reliable sources for the information you need in order to take appropriate action.[1] Your information gathering, of course, began with with your radio call and was supplemented by your observation of people and events as you sought to calm the situation. Now that the citizens are relatively calmer, however, your main information-gathering activity must begin. The first step in doing so is to explain to the citizen what you want him to discuss with you and why. The purpose of the interview you are about to conduct should be carefully explained in detail to the citizen so that his expectations regarding the types of information you want are accurate and his cooperation in providing it is maximized. Once the stage is correctly set, that is, once you have successfully begun to calm the citizen, his expectancies for the interview are made clear, and his cooperation maximized, the interview can begin.

Step 2. Interview the Citizen so as to Get Details of the Crisis as Clearly as Possible

While it is obviously true that the main purpose of the officer's interview of citizens at a crisis scene is to gather relevant information, we wish to mention briefly two other important goals which may be accomplished at the same time. If the interview is conducted in a highly professional manner, with the officer providing the citizens with an impression of a skilled, aware, sensitive, and purposeful interview, the interviewing officer will not only obtain maximal amounts of accurate information from the citizens, but he will also: (1) give information about himself and his skills which will maintain the level of emotional calm he built earlier, and (2) build goodwill for himself and the police department he represents.

In our earlier discussion of calming the situation, we mentioned several calming procedures and explained that the choice of procedure to be used at any given time would depend on the particular citizen involved, and the nature and level of his emotional state. In general, we recommended that the officer first use one or more of the conversational calming methods and then, if necessary, shift to more assertive procedures. We wish to make a number of similar recommendations about the several interviewing procedures we will describe. As was true of calming procedures, different interviewing methods are best used for different citizens. Which ones to use at which times will have to be partly decided by each individual officer's own experiences in crisis situations. We can, however, provide general guidelines.

---

1. Many crisis calls will proceed with successful calming of the citizen involved, followed by your gathering relevant information. In many other crises, however, your use of calming procedures will have to continue throughout the entire call, and sometimes even be continued further by a neighbor or relative after you leave.

Described below are three sets of interviewing procedures. The procedures are presented in order of increasing directiveness on the part of the interviewer (officer). Thus, Open-ended questions and Listening (procedures 1 and 2) require much less officer directiveness and assertiveness than, for example, do Confrontation and Demanding (procedures 9 and 10). In general, we recommend that the officer begin his interview with the least directive procedures, and make use of increasingly directive procedures as circumstances warrant. While low directiveness procedures will be all that prove necessary in many crisis situations, the very angry, very anxious, or highly confused citizen will require forceful interview procedures before accurate information can be obtained from him. The specific procedures are:

Procedures for Interviewing Citizens in Crisis
Nondirective procedures
1. Open-ended questions
2. Listening
3. Closed-ended questions
4. Restatement of content (paraphrasing)
5. Reflection of feeling

Moderately directive procedures
6. Selective inattention and use of silence
7. Encouragement and use of specific and simplified invitations
8. Self-disclosure and use of immediacy

Highly Directive Procedures
9. Confrontation
10. Demanding

We now wish to describe each of these procedures in greater detail.

1. *Open-ended questions.* Questions which give the citizen the freedom and opportunity to give an answer of considerable length, an answer shaped mostly by the citizen's wishes and not the officer's, are open-ended questions. Examples of such questions in a crisis context include: "What happened here?"; "What do you mean by nagging?"; "Why do you describe him as crazy?" These are usually questions which begin with "what," "why," or "how."

2. *Listening.* How well the citizen feels the officer is listening to him will clearly influence how open and detailed the citizen's statement is. That you are listening is communicated to the citizen by both what you do and what you avoid doing. The skilled listener maintains eye contact, shows by his posture and gestures that he is paying attention, and makes occasional comments to the citizen which also show interest and attention, e.g., "I see what

you mean," "I can understand that." The skilled listener also avoids trying to interview more than one citizen at a time, remembers to make reuse of calming procedures as often as necessary, and physically separates disputants so that they will not distract one another.

3. *Closed-ended questions.* Questions which can be answered with yes or no or with brief, factual replies are closed-ended questions. They are questions which usually begin with "do," "is," or "are." Such questions are a necessary and valuable part of the officer's interview, and only present a problem when used where open-ended questions would be preferable. That is, closed-ended questions may be inefficient (when the officer has to ask a great many of them instead of a few open-ended questions) or leading (when they suggest answers to the citizens, a fault less usually true of open-ended questions).

4. *Restatement of content (paraphrasing).* Use of this procedure serves to show the citizen you are "with him" and thus are paying attention, and also encourages him to go on and provide further details. The procedure consists of saying back to the citizen, in words somewhat different from his own if possible (i.e., paraphrasing), the essence of what he has already said to you. Examples of restatement of content include: "So you want your husband home tonight even though he hit you"; "You're saying you did everything you were supposed to: paid the rent, didn't make too much noise, and so on." You will find that perhaps your most effective use of restatement of content, as far as getting the citizen to provide you with more details on a given topic is concerned, will involve restating a single word, the word most central to the topic you want elaborated by the citizen. Such words, often presented as a one-word question, include "fight?" after a citizen states, "We fight every day," and you wish to learn more about their past; "never?" after the same complainant spouse states, "He's never been a good husband," and you'd like to know more about any positive strengths in their relationship; and "hopeless?" when you wish to learn about any optimistic thoughts after an attempted suicide in which the citizen describes his world as "all black, hopeless, and terrible."

5. *Reflection of feeling.* Whereas restatement of content stresses saying back to the citizen one or more of the facts in his statement, this procedure focuses on expressing to the citizen an understanding of his main feelings. To reflect a citizen's feelings accurately, the officer must pay attention both to what the citizen is saying and how he is saying it. The complainant spouse noted above, who tells the officer, "We fight every day. He's never been a good husband," might be told, "You really seem to feel very angry at him, and not very hopeful that things will change." The suicidal citizen might have his feelings reflected with an officer statement such as "Everything seems just awful to you, nothing's even slightly hopeful." The point about reflection of feeling is that when people feel that you understand their appar-

ent or even somewhat hidden feelings, they are much more likely to continue
to provide you with information.

6. *Selective inattention and use of silence.* An excited citizen will often
provide the officer with details of a crisis which are either irrelevant to what
the officer needs in order to take appropriate action or, if relevant, in excess
of what is needed. That is, in contrast to the reluctant, resistive, or too silent
citizen, one may be faced with a disputant, a victim, or a relative who talks
too much, and who is difficult to divert back to the task at hand. Simply
failing to pay attention to irrelevant or excessive citizen statements will often
be an effective means of stemming the flow. Thus, in a manner opposite to
our earlier listening instructions, here the officer should respond to unwanted
and excessive statements by not maintaining eye contact, not providing posture and gestures which signify paying attention, and not making statements
which show understanding.

7. *Encouragement and use of specific and simplified invitations.* People
under stress often become quite confused and disorganized in their thinking
and speech. Simple officer questions like "What happened here?" may yield
agitated and erroneous answers from such citizens. Under these circumstances it will be the officer's task to simplify matters for the citizen, and to
make questioning very concrete and stepwise. "Encouragement and use of
specific and simplified invitations" means the officer often must be a patient
questioner, restater, or reflector who sets up and asks a simplified series of
questions, praises the citizen not only for answers but even for trying to
answer, asks only one question at a time, and builds his interview with one
question or statement logically following the other. In this manner, especially when combined with appropriate calming techniques, the citizen is likely
to become less confused and agitated and more accurate and detailed in his
statement.

8. *Self-disclosure and use of immediacy.* People tend to be more open with
those who are open with them. We tend to be more disclosing about our own
thoughts, feelings, ideas, and backgrounds when others first reveal such
information to us. There will be crisis situations in which self-disclosure by
the responding officer will prove to be a useful interviewing procedure. We
wish to stress, however, that there is an important difference between private
self-disclosure and public self-disclosure. Private self-disclosure would include information about any fighting or arguing the officer has done with his
own wife, any feelings of depression the officer himself has experienced, any
fears the officer has about being assaulted. Such private self-disclosure is not
a useful or appropriate interviewing procedure. It will tend to diminish the
officer in the eyes of the citizen, and fail to increase citizen self-disclosure.
Public self-disclosure, in contrast, does involve the officer's revealing information about himself, but not what we have described above as private infor-

mation. Thus, the self-disclosing officer may usefully reveal public experiences he has had which are relevant to the crisis interview, places he has been, types of people he has dealt with, and the like. This moderately directive interview procedure also involves "use of immediacy," a term referring to the disclosure-increasing effects on the citizen of positive officer comments about the immediate relationship formed by the officer and the citizen. Comments by the officer such as "I can see just from what you've said so far that you're really trying hard," or "You make me feel you can be trusted, so maybe you impress other people the same way," are examples of use of immediacy. As we cautioned earlier, remember to avoid the appearance of taking sides when making statements like these.

9. *Confrontation.* Confrontation, as an interviewing procedure, is the directive pointing out to a citizen any discrepancies between either (a) two things he has said, or (b) something he has said and the quite different way in which he said it. An example of the first, a content-content discrepancy, would be, "You said he started it all, but you also said what sounded like he was just minding his own business when you went over to him." The second, a content-feeling discrepancy, is illustrated by, "You told me you want him out of here tonight and you don't care how, but now you're really getting angry at me for arresting him."

10. *Demanding.* The several methods described thus far may all prove unsuccessful if the citizen is very hostile, resistive, or indifferent to your interviewing efforts. Both nondirective and moderately directive procedures may simply prove inadequate for some citizens, and greater interviewer directiveness may be required. It is here that the officer's earlier success in creating a first impression of nonhostile authority will pay off. Demanding requires forthright and firm instructing of the citizen in what he is to tell you, and tell you now! It is a no nonsense, businesslike (but not hostile) stance by the interviewing officer, one in which the officer insists, rather than asks, tells rather than requests.

The resistant citizen. There will be citizens you will meet on crisis calls who, in spite of your skilled use of the interviewing procedures described above—including Demanding—remain reluctant or resistant to providing you with the information you need to form a sound plan of action. They may be too angry, too frightened, or too confused. When this occurs, we suggest that you once again make use of one or more of the procedures described earlier in this manual for calming the highly emotional citizen. Specifically, the reluctant or resistant citizen is likely to become a more cooperative interviewee if the officer:

1. Shows understanding,
2. Provides reassurance,

3. Offers encouragement,
4. Patiently repeats, and/or
5. Uses humor.

In addition to use of these calming procedures, a number of officers have effectively reduced citizen resistance to providing information by (a) restating their questions in a briefer and clearer manner, (b) praising the citizen and showing appreciation for whatever partial or incomplete information the citizen has revealed, and (c) carefully prompting the citizen to provide answers by, in a sense, giving him several possible answers from which to choose. (In using prompting procedures, the officer must be careful to avoid self-fulfilling prophecies. That is, he should give the citizen as complete a range of answers as possible from which to choose. Otherwise, the officer runs the serious danger of putting his own words in the citizen's mouth, and thus getting answers which merely serve to fulfill the officer's expectancies, not provide accurate information about the crisis.)

Step 3. Show That You Understand the Citizen's Statements and Give Accurate Answers to His Questions

The citizen being interviewed will be most likely to continue providing the information being sought by the officer if the officer shows the citizen in a variety of ways that he is understood. These include certain of the methods described earlier (Restatement of content; Reflection of feeling), direct statements to the citizen, e.g., "I understand what you mean," and other officer statements which show the citizen you are "staying with him." Giving accurate answers is one example of such statements. Giving clear, patient, and accurate answers to citizen questions will also make your eventual task of taking appropriate action easier, as the informed citizen is more likely to be a cooperative source in deciding upon and carrying out crisis resolving solutions.

Step 4. Review Your Plan of Action if Appropriate

Recall that the effective officer forms a tentative plan of action while still in his patrol car on his way to the crisis scene. His observations at the scene, the events which occur as he calms the citizens present, and the facts and impressions he gathers from his interviews of them, all provide him with information necessary to revise his plan and to finalize it so that he can act upon it. By "finalize" it, we mean (1) decide in his own thinking that the plan is a wise one; (2) check it out with his partner if possible; and (3) plan on how to present it to the citizens involved.

In summary, in gathering relevant information, you should:
1. Explain to the citizen what you want him to discuss with you and why.

2. Interview the citizen so as to get details of the crisis as clearly as possible.
3. Show that you understand the citizen's statements and give accurate answers to his questions.
4. Revise your plan of action if appropriate.

TAKING APPROPRIATE ACTION

You have quieted the citizens involved in the crisis call and obtained from them the information you need to decide upon and to begin appropriate action. The steps we recommend that you follow in taking appropriate action are:
1. Carefully explain your plan of action to the citizen.
2. Check that the citizen understands and agrees with your plan of action.
3. Carry out your plan of action.

Steps 1 and 2 seem to require no further explanation. Step 3, however, can take many forms and thus will be the main topic of this section. We emphasized earlier that the effective, professional policeman is a flexible policeman, skilled in a variety of actions which he can apply depending on what is appropriate in a given crisis. There are crisis situations, of course, in which the officer has no choice of action. For example, the very aggressive, abusive, and potentially dangerous citizen who successfully resists your best efforts to calm him down will make your plan of action necessarily one in which you subdue, restrain, and probably arrest him. In most crisis situations, however, you will have a choice regarding which action plan to follow. We provide below some broad guidelines that can help you choose which plan is most likely to succeed in which situations, but this decision will also have to grow from your own crisis experience on patrol. What works best in each crisis situation will vary to some extent from officer to officer, from citizen to citizen, and from crisis to crisis. Deciding on the best approach for any given officer-citizen-crisis set is a continuing challenge to the professional police officer.

There are five courses of action an officer might follow in a crisis situation: mediate, negotiate, counsel, refer, and arbitrate. We wish now to consider each of these alternatives.

Mediation

Teachers, psychologists, psychiatrists, and other professionals who are concerned with helping people solve problems all seem to agree that the most lasting and effective solutions are those that the citizens involved come up with themselves. The officer's goal in mediation is to assist the citizen in solving his own crisis problem, not to solve it for him. Rather than give possible answers or solutions, the mediating officer helps the citizen express what he himself thinks will work. In a husband-wife dispute being dealt with by two officers, each officer would, first separately and then with husband and wife together, encourage, assist, elicit, urge, and so forth to help the two citizens first suggest solutions and then give and take to each other so that they come to an agreement of their own making regarding how the crisis may be dealt with best. The agreement may be not to spend certain monies for liquor again, for the husband to spend the night at a friend's house, to call a given agency in the morning, or something else. The important feature of the solution, however, is that it was arrived at by the citizens, with the officer serving in the role of go-between or mediator.

A report describing a Florida Crisis Intervention Seminar (Office of the Sheriff, Crisis Intervention Seminar, Jacksonville, Florida, 1975) suggests a number of useful guidelines for conducting mediation:

a. If possible, use mediation as your first approach to crisis intervention.
b. Inform the citizens that you cannot solve their problems, that they must do so themselves.
c. Avoid suggesting solutions.
d. Elicit suggestions from the citizens as to how their problem can be solved.
e. Check each proposal with the other disputant, until there is acceptance or compromise.
f. Avoid criticizing the citizen's solutions even if you don't agree with them.
g. Offer encouragement for them to follow through.

Negotiation

You will recall that when we described calming procedures and later, interviewing procedures, we began with the least directive approaches and went on to describe increasingly forceful, directive police interventions. We wish to follow a similar sequence here, as we describe alternative action plans. In mediation, the officer is least directive, serving as an encourager and go-between. When this method is either tried and fails, or not tried in the first place because the citizens were in one way or another not ready or able to suggest their own crisis solutions, the officer must become somewhat more directive. In negotiation, the officers do suggest solutions, compromises, or other ways of dealing effectively with the crisis. As in mediation, the officers also help the disputants bargain, and remain neutral as they aid in this give and take.

In a husband-wife dispute, for example, one officer might suggest a solution to the husband, the other officer might do so (separately) to the wife. When the two disputants and the two officers then come together to reach a joint solution, the officers can see to it that husband and wife negotiate (with the two officers continuing to help) according to rules shown elsewhere[2] to be effective steps in successful negotiation:

a. State your position.
b. State your understanding of the other person's position.
c. Ask if the other person agrees with your statement of his position.
d. Listen openly (not defensively) to his response.
e. Propose a compromise.

Counseling

We mentioned above that when serving as a negotiator, the officer does suggest crisis solutions to the citizens involved. When providing counseling, the officer becomes even more directive. He may not only offer suggestions and advice, but he may help the citizens express and understand both their own and other disputants' feelings, wishes, expectations, and other less obvious aspects of the crisis. The skilled counselor pays attention, listens carefully, shows interest, observes nonverbal behavior, helps citizens express themselves, and in general makes use of many of the procedures described earlier in connection with calming and interviewing procedures. The most useful of these procedures for counseling purposes are showing understanding, restatement of content, and reflection of feeling.

Counseling citizens in crisis takes time. Often it will pay the officer to invest this extra time on a crisis call, because it both helps resolve the crisis and decreases the likelihood of callbacks. But the problems of people in crisis are often very longstanding ones. The marital fight, the depressed suicidal person, the drunken citizen all often have long histories of their given problem, and thus the problem can't be resolved in a one-shot counseling meeting held under crisis stresses. Thus, the officer-as-counselor will often be doing his job as counselor very well not by resolving the crisis situation, but by opening a door to it, by helping the citizens acknowledge to themselves that a problem exists, and by getting them to agree to do something constructive about it. This "something" will often involve the citizen making use of certain agencies or professional persons in the community. Since the citizen very often does not know about these helping sources, the officer may do him a great service by skillfully making an appropriate referral, which is the next action plan we describe.

---

2. Goldstein, A.P., Sprafkin, R.P. & Gershaw, N.J., *Skill training for community living* (New York: Pergamon Press, 1976).

Referral

The officer's first task in skillfully referring a citizen for further crisis intervention and problem solution is the counseling activity described above. That is, before he can expect referral advice to be followed, the officer must help the citizen realize that there is a problem which can be helped, and must motivate the citizen to want that help.

The referral will not be a skillful one if the only basis for it is a listing of referral agency phone numbers for the community. The officer is not able adequately to describe the full range of services offered by each agency, to answer citizen questions about each agency, or even to have a complete enough idea about which agency to recommend at which times unless he is quite familiar with each agency. You are urged to visit these agencies and learn more about their nature and functioning. Personnel at each agency will usually welcome such visits. You are also urged not to limit yourself to the most frequently used agencies. Gradually, you should learn about other sources of help in your community for citizens in crisis. Many such sources usually exist.

The following guidelines will be of assistance to you in making a successful referral:

1. Let the citizen know that you understand his crisis problem and his feelings about it.
2. Tell the citizen that the chances are good that the agency to which you would like to refer him can be of help to him regarding the crisis problem.
3. Give the citizen the appropriate referral information, in writing, and make sure he understands it.
4. Deal with any citizen resistance to the referral, e.g., most agencies take people at all salary levels.
5. If possible, have the citizen call the agency while you are still present.
6. If the citizen is too upset or otherwise unable to call the appropriate agency, get his permission to make the call on his behalf, and do so.
7. If circumstances make it inappropriate for either you or the citizen to telephone the agency at the time of your crisis call, obtain a commitment from the citizen (or other person at the crisis scene) that the agency will be contacted at the earliest possible time.

Arbitration

You have tried to help the citizens in crisis solve their own problems (mediation); you have suggested solutions and tried to help them reach a compromise (negotiation); you have tried to help them understand both the problem and what underlies the problem better (counseling); or you have steered them to the appropriate source other than yourself for such help (referral).

When all of these alternatives either fail or are simply inappropriate because one or more of the citizens involved remains highly emotional or aggressive, you may have to impose a solution directly. Such arbitration is clearly not the best means for lasting results. Of the methods examined here, it results in the highest number of return calls, is probably the most dangerous of the five action approaches, and thus should be used only when unavoidable.

In arbitration, the following steps are recommended:
1. Consider the strengths and weaknesses of possible solutions to the citizen's problem.
2. Try to be aware of your own biases and prejudices, and take account of their effect in your consideration of solutions.
3. Choose the solution you feel is best and, if possible, discuss this choice with your partner.
4. Make a final decision and tell the citizen to act upon it.

In summary of this section, when taking appropriate action, you should:
1. Carefully explain your plan of action to the citizen.
2. Check that the citizen understands and agrees with your plan of action.
3. Carry out your plan of action.

CONCLUSION

We have described in this manual a series of steps we recommend you try to follow when responding to crisis calls. Success in performing these steps will result in a decrease in threats to your safety, reduced citizen emotionalism, more accurate information gathering, and finally, more professional resolution of the crisis. For reference and review purposes, the steps are:

Steps in Crisis Intervention

I.   Observing and Protecting against Threats to your Safety
    1. Consider your prior experience on similar calls.
    2. Anticipte that the unexpected may actually happen.
    3. Form a tentative plan of action.
II. Calming the Situation
    1. Observe and neutralize threats to your safety.
    2. Create a first impression of nonhostile authority.
    3. Calm the emotional citizen.
III. Gathering Relevant Information
    1. Explain to the citizen what you want him to discuss with you and why.
    2. Interview the citizen so as to get details of the crisis as clearly as possible.

3. Show that you understand the citizen's statements and give accurate answers to his questions.
4. Revise your plan of action if appropriate.

IV. Taking Appropriate Action
   1. Carefully explain your plan of action to the citizen.
   2. Check that the citizen understands and agrees with your plan of action.
   3. Carry out your plan of action.

Appendix D
Hostage Negotiation Procedures

I. SAFETY

1. *Sufficient Personnel.* Make certain sufficient personnel are both trained in hostage management strategy and tactics and available in adequate numbers for a hostage situation.
2. *Chain of Command.* The hostage management area, inner and outer perimeter personnel, firepower, communications, and related resources must be controlled and coordinated by a single source.
3. *Media Cooperation.* Influence media, if possible, so that no mention is made of tactical plans and resources.
4. *Communication.* Maintain communication among responding personnel.
5. *Identification of Personnel.* All inner perimeter personnel must be readily identifiable. Police and nonpolice (e.g., "Outside" negotiation advisors) personnel should wear clothing whose colors, markings, or other characteristics clearly identify them as law enforcement personnel. The hostage management situation may deteriorate suddenly, as when a hostage is unexpectedly killed, and rapid, substantial firepower may quickly be put into use. Under such circumstances, in which firepower must be used with rapid judgment and acute perception, especially clear identification of inner perimeter personnel is obviously highly desirable.
6. *Negotiator Position.* The negotiator should be physically near the perpetrator, but secure enough that he won't become a hostage himself. Where and how the negotiator is positioned should reflect both concern with his personal safety and the importance of his establishing rapport with the perpetrator. He should not be face to face with the perpetrator, but should be close enough that he can communicate if possible directly by voice without aid of bullhorn or similar equipment. This may mean communication through a closed door or around a corner. This physical arrangement will often not be possible, in which case telephone communication is the desirable alternative.
7. *Hostage Identification.* Make sure there *is* a hostage. By use of binoculars, telephone, or other means, verify that hostages exist. If possible,

ascertain their number and identity. If possible, seek opportunity actually to see the hostages. When you are able to do so, remember prominent physical characteristics of hostages and communicate these descriptions to all inner-perimeter personnel. Such communication minimizes chances of confusion of hostages and perpetrators by responding personnel. In doing so, remember not to rely on clothing, glasses, or similar items in your description of hostages, as such items are easily switched by perpetrators.

8. *Perpetrator Requests for Others.* Do not fulfill perpetrator requests to bring relatives or friends to the scene. The presence of the perpetrator's relatives or friends adds unpredictable elements to a situation you are trying to control and make at least moderately predictable. Such friends and relatives may be employed as allies by the perpetrator, or he may use them as additional hostages, or his purpose in seeking their presence may be as an audience in front of which he may enact violent and sometimes suicidal acts. In none of these examples is your ability to manage the resolution of the hostage incident successfully increased. Thus, the request should generally not be fulfilled. Your optimal way of dealing with the request will probably be to stall, to indicate you have to seek approval for it up the chain of command, etc., rather than to refuse outright.

9. *Avoid Show of Force.* Avoid a show of force, especially when a single perpetrator is involved. A visible display of S.W.A.T., Special Reaction Team, or similar groups of highly armed and numerous personnel may provide the spark which ignites the short fuse of violence in the unstable perpetrator. That is, a massing of visible firepower may result in exactly the opposite of the deterrent effect intended. Whether due to fear, enhanced chance for glory, or as a play-to-the-audience effect, a show of force may lead to killing of hostages. Some authorities have suggested that a show of force is a useful hostage management technique in prison settings, as a means of acting before the group consolidates, and when several perpetrators—especially political terrorists—are involved, as the show of force may weaken the commitment of one or more of the perpetrators.

10. *Nonnegotiables.* Do not negotiate for new weapons, alcohol, narcotics or other items likely to increase the threat to hostage or negotiator safety. Such items will at times be included among perpetrator demands. Like requests for the presence of relatives or other people who may become additional hostages, requests for weapons or other danger-increasing items are best dealt with by stalling, appealing to chain of command delays, and using several other negotiation techniques described later in this appendix.

11. *Avoid Shifts of Location.* If at all possible, avoid movement of the perpetrator and hostages to another location. The perpetrator at a hostage scene may demand that he and his hostages be moved elsewhere. Most often this demand will be for purposes of escape, e.g., demands to be taken to an airport and a readied plane. Sometimes the demand is to a place where certain other people reside, e.g., mother, wife, girlfriend. Other movement demands are sometimes made. In all instances, agreeing with such demands is to be avoided if at all possible. Movement of perpetrator and hostage severely diminishes the control you have established at the hostage scene. New people, new resources for the perpetrator, and new unfavorable turns of events may all enter the scene if you permit it to shift at the demand of the perpetrator.

12. *Safety Instructions for Hostages.* If it is possible to communicate by any direct means with the hostages, provide them with the following suggestions designed to increase their safety:
    1. Stay as calm and alert as possible.
    2. Do not try to fight with perpetrators, avoid provoking them.
    3. Try to build a positive relationship with the perpetrator.
    4. Try to be as real a person to perpetrators as possible (share thoughts on your hopes, plans, family, problems).
    5. Follow perpetrator instructions to the extent possible.
    6. Avoid political discussions.
    7. Eat food offered you.
    8. Be aware that many of the effects of drugs are psychological.
    9. Stay face-to-face with armed perpetrators.

II. INFORMATION TO BE OBTAINED

1. *Information about the Perpetrator.* Relevant information about the perpetrator should be gathered as completely and rapidly as possible. To help the negotiator determine both the tone and content of his statements to the perpetrator, the following information about the perpetrator will be valuable:
    1. Characteristics: names, number, age, sex, size, physical condition.
    2. Background: race, ethnic group, politics.
    3. Personality: degree of rationality, tolerance for ambiguity, aggression potential.
    4. Prior crimes and police record.
    5. Specific details of present crime.
    6. Purpose of hostage act: criminal, terrorist, mentally disturbed.
    7. Intelligence.

8. Emotional state.
9. Any at-the-scene behavior.
10. Stated reasons for hostage taking (motivation and plans).
11. Nature and amount of arms.
12. Specialized skills.
13. Special affiliations.
14. Unusual habits.

2. *Information about the Hostages.* Relevant information about the hostages should be gathered as completely and rapidly as possible. To help the negotiator determine both the tone and content of his statements to the perpetrator, the following information about the hostages will be valuable:

1. Characteristics: number, age, sex, size.
2. Background: race, ethnic group.
3. Aggression potential.
4. Intelligence.
5. Emotional state.
6. Medical problems or special requirements.

3. *Information about the Hostage Site.* Ascertain the following about the hostage site:

1. Safe observation positions.
2. Escape routes.
3. Safest approach routes.
4. Any telephone present.
5. Amount of space, number of rooms, ventilation.
6. Food, water.
7. Method required for effective gassing.

III. THE NEGOTIATOR

1. *Optimal Negotiator Characteristics*:
1. Interpersonal sensitivity.
2. Cognitive complexity.
3. Tolerance for ambiguity.
4. Positive self-concept.
5. Low authoritarianism.
6. Interviewing experience.
7. Past experience in stressful situations.
8. Verbal skills.
9. Flexibility, especially under pressure.
10. Work history with many different types of perpetrators.
11. Belief in the power of verbal persuasion.

12. Conciliation, compromise, bargaining skills.
13. Mature appearance.
14. Apparent rank of Patrolman[1] (even a Sergeant may be seen as a final decision maker).
15. Good physical condition.
16. Familiarity with the ideology of perpetrator if a terrorist is involved.
2. *Undesirable Negotiator Characteristics*:
   1. Strong belief in physical force, power, and toughness.
   2. Over-conformity and formality.
   3. Difficulty expressing personal feelings.
   4. Machismo orientation.
   5. High authoritarianism.
   6. Rigidity or inflexibility.
   7. Poor verbal skills.
   8. Tendency to project own feelings on others.
   9. Tendency to avoid introspection.
   10. Nonvaried work history.
   11. Poor bargaining skills.
   12. Immature appearance.
   13. Poor physical condition.
   14. Unfamiliarity with ideology of perpetrator.
3. *Negotiator Styles*.

Table D.1. Negotiator Styles and Strategies.

Negotiator	Win-Lose Battler	Equalizer	Soft Bargainer
Apparent Negotiating Strategies	Forcing	Problem-Solving Compromise	Giving In

An equalizer negotiator style, in which problem solving and compromise are the negotiating strategies preferred, is the negotiator style to be recommended for hostage situations. Unsatisfactory negotiating outcomes are much more likely when the negotiator's preferred style of operation is too forceful (the win-lose battler) or too gentle (the soft bargainer).

---

1. To insure perpetrator is aware that all decisions must be approved at other command levels.

IV. NEGOTIATING STRATEGIES

1. *Initial Strategy.* At the outset, contain and stabilize are your two goals. Avoid all precipitous acts. Your initial negotiating strategy should seek to increase the predictability of the hostage scene and your control over it. Calming the agitated perpetrator and building rapport with him, are your initial tactical goals. Precipitous acts, e.g., sudden and obvious movement of large numbers of men and equipment toward the perpetrator, will work opposite to your contain and stabilize purpose. Your ability to control the scene and begin implementing your negotiations will, of course, depend a great deal on your pre-event planning, negotiator training, and command efficiency at the scene.

2. *Establish a Problem-Solving Climate.* Establish a problem-solving negotiation climate. In all possible ways, communicate to the perpetrator your awareness that a problem exists, your desire to understand the problem and, in all reasonable ways possible, your willingness to help solve the problem. Establishing a problem-solving climate will mean trying to lead the perpetrator to believe you and he are working together in seeking problem solutions acceptable to both of you. Success in establishing this climate will mean considerable use of "we" and "us" (and not "you" versus "me"), considerable (and time-consuming) exploration of alternative problem solutions, and the likelihood of further development of negotiator-perpetrator rapport beyond that established by procedures described later. As other authorities have suggested, try to establish a climate in which you are both focusing upon defeating the problem, not each other. We agree with Schlossberg (1974), whose overall negotiating strategy is:

> Our approach resembles crisis intervention therapy for suicidal people. You try to establish contact with the person, identify with him, find out his problem, and get him to look for another solution. . . . What we're looking for is time until his anxiety maybe abates and the negotiations appear to offer him an alternative course of action. (p. 43)

3. *Establish Climate of Compromise.* Seek to develop an atmosphere in which compromise is a major goal. In seeking to create a climate of compromise, the negotiator communicates a give-and-take attitude, a willingness to bargain, an openness to yield on certain matters while holding firm on others. Each side, he makes clear, can gain something. The "something" for the negotiator, of course, is the release of the hostages.

4. *Avoid Forcing Climate.* Minimize use of force or coercion. The negotiator using this strategy has also been described as the "win-lose battler." He is tough and rarely compromises. He will win some, but he will lose

some also—too many. An aggressive, unyielding negotiator approach will needlessly threaten the lives of hostages and should be actively avoided.

5. *Avoid Use of "Soft Bargainer" Climate.* Avoid use of a soft-bargainer negotiating strategy. Just as some negotiators can be too tough, others can be too gentle. The negotiator who is too concerned with perpetrator feelings, too concerned with being accepted and well liked, and too willing to yield to perpetrator demands will fail to bring the negotiations to a satisfactory conclusion.

6. *Strategy Varies with Perpetrator.* Use the negotiating strategy which your prenegotiating investigation reveals best fits the nature of the perpetrator involved. Optimal negotiator strategy and tactics will vary with the type

Table D.2. Negotiator Strategies and Types of Perpetrators.

Criminal (Instrumental Behavior)	Terrorist	Psychotic (Expressive Behavior)
Emphasize: Rational Techniques a. Problem-Solving b. Compromise		Emphasize: Emotional Techniques a. Reflection of feeling b. Restatement of content

of perpetrator. We call this "prescriptive negotiating." The criminal, who may take hostages to avoid capture after an unsuccessful robbery or other crime, has been described by several authorities as essentially rational and logical, and thus open to rational negotiating techniques. These include direct attempts at problem solving and compromise. The mentally disturbed perpetrator is usually less accessible to appeals to reason. He is much more unpredictable and often closed to logical problem solving. The negotiator with such perpetrators is well advised to focus on a more emotional negotiating strategy, in which he shows understanding, reflects perpetrator feelings, restates perpetrator content, and in other ways shows the perpetrator he is with him. The terrorist perpetrator presents a mixed picture in our view; he is "emotionally rational" and must be approached by means of joint rational and emotional negotiating techniques.

7. *Use of Force.* Use of force should be planned for, but implemented only as a last resort.

V. CALMING THE PERPETRATOR

1. *Show Understanding.* Attempt to calm the agitated perpetrator by showing understanding of his feelings. By your words, tone of voice (and, if

visible to the perpetrator) your facial expression and gestures, make it clear to the perpetrator that you accurately understand what he is feeling and how strongly he is feeling it. Some examples of calming attempts by showing understanding include, "You're really feeling very angry and upset at him," or "What you just said is something you seem to feel very positive about."

2. *Modeling.* Attempt to calm the agitated perpetrator by displaying your own calmness to him. By your words, tone of voice (and, if visible to the perpetrator) your facial expression and gestures, make it clear to the perpetrator that you, the negotiator, are responding in a calm and controlled manner to the hostage incident. You can speak at a normal conversational level, at a slow and deliberate rate, and if appropriate from a safety standpoint, you can sit down, remove your hat, and behave in a variety of other ways to demonstrate calmness and the fact that a show of police force is not imminent. Since we are all likely to imitate people in authority, the negotiator's calmness will often have a direct calming effect on the agitated or highly emotional perpetrator.

3. *Reassurance.* Attempt to calm the agitated perpetrator by reassuring him. In using modeling to calm the agitated perpetrator, the negotiator's own behavior serves as an example we hope the perpetrator will imitate. Use of reassurance takes the calming attempt a step further because the negotiator not only behaves calmly but, in addition, provides the perpetrator with reasons why he, too, should feel calmer. Examples of reassuring statements include: "We'll be able to work this out"; "I think we can deal with this a step at a time"; and "I'm really interested in solving this with you."

4. *Encourage Ventilation.* Attempt to calm the agitated perpetrator by encouraging him to talk. The negotiator is likely to be successful in calming a highly emotional perpetrator if he can be kept talking—about his demands, their background, complications, his hopes, and so forth. It is quite difficult to remain highly emotional and at the same time answer questions, present information at length, and otherwise respond to the negotiator. The negotiator's efforts at encouraging the perpetrator to ventilate will be aided by negotiator use of open-ended questions, good listening skills, and the other interviewing techniques described later in this appendix.

5. *Distraction.* Attempt to calm the agitated perpetrator by distracting him from the source of his concern. At times, an effective means for calming the agitated perpetrator will be to divert his attention temporarily away from the hostage negotiations. This can be done effectively by (1) asking a question totally irrelevant to the hostage situation; (2) asking a question which is relevant to the hostage situation, but opposite to what the perpetrator is likely to expect; (3) bringing up a topic of discussion which is irrelevant to the hostage situation; and (4) giving a suggestion which

tells the perpetrator to continue doing something that he expects you to want him to stop (or otherwise behave in a manner contrary to his expectancies about negotiators or police).

6. *Nonverbal Cues of Aggression.* Try to anticipate perpetrator violence by being sensitive to nonverbal cues of aggression. You may be able to anticipate likely increases in perpetrator violence by observation of such nonverbal cues as increases in the pace and loudness of his speech, increased restlessness, crouched torso, clenched fists, grinding teeth, dilated pupils, flared nostrils, and flushed cheeks.

7. *Avoid Provoking the Perpetrator.* Avoid any aggressive, offensive, or humiliating comments to the perpetrator; do not agree with him; avoid outright rejection of all his demands; avoid sudden surprises. All of these provocative actions have the potential, at best, of making your attempts at successful negotiation more difficult and, at worst, of increasing the chances of injury or death for the hostages.

VI. BUILDING RAPPORT

1. *Stall for Time.* Most authorities agree that time works for the police and against the perpetrator. As time progresses, relationships can develop. The development of the perpetrator-negotiator relationship means greater trust, greater likelihood that the negotiator's suggestions will be seriously considered, and greater likelihood of a negotiated surrender of hostages. The development of the perpetrator-hostage relationship means decreased likelihood that the perpetrator will kill or injure the hostages. As time passes, not only relationships develop. The dramatic level of the hostage scene may diminish. Perpetrators get tired, hungry, thirsty, and so forth— all opportunities for negotiation of demands that benefit police. Alert negotiators will often be able to take advantage of slips, errors, or luck that may occur during protracted negotiatons.

2. *Self-Disclosure.* Disclose information about yourself to the perpetrator, as it may help build rapport. People relate more quickly and more positively to others about whom they know something. To help build perpetrator trust in the negotiator, negotiator self-disclosure is encouraged. As it seems appropriate in the conversation (not forced), the negotiator may discuss his own feelings, interests, preferences, and even aspects of his professional and personal life. Negotiator self-disclosure, beyond its rapport-building effectiveness, will also prove useful as an information-eliciting technique, i.e., your self-disclosure is often likely to be reciprocated by perpetrator self-disclosure.

3. *Empathy.* Show high levels of empathy in your response to what the perpetrator says and does. One of the most effective means for building rapport with the perpetrator is to show him you are able to understand

his feelings and thinking, that you are able to step into his shoes for the moment and see the world as he sees it. In being highly empathic, the negotiator need not agree that the situation "really is" as the perpetrator sees it. The important quality of high empathy is that the negotiator communicates his accurate understanding of the perpetrator's views to the perpetrator. Two excellent techniques for communicating high levels of empathy are restatement of content (see section VII, no. 4) and reflection of feeling (see section VII, no. 5). In addition, the empathic negotiator will concentrate with intensity on what the perpetrator says and does, will use language that the perpetrator readily understands, and will at times help the perpetrator think thoughts and feelings that he (the perpetrator) only partly understands.

4. *Warmth.* Show high levels of warmth in your response to what the perpetrator says and does. Like empathy, showing high levels of warmth toward the perpetrator is a very effective means of encouraging trust and building rapport. The negotiator can show warmth in a variety of ways: by his tone of voice, his interest, his effort to understand the perpetrator, his concern that they reach a mutual solution, his own commitment to solution finding, and his holding out hope for at least long-term or eventual answers to the perpetrators' demands.

5. *Helping Save Face.* Help the perpetrator save face. When the perpetrator feels cornered, publicly defeated, or humiliated, he may respond with sudden violent behavior. If you suspect that such a situation has developed, it will be to your advantage to defuse the situation as rapidly as possible. In addition to the calming procedures described elsewhere in this appendix, you should (1) help the perpetrator retreat gracefully; (2) control the pace of perpetrator concession giving; and (3) provide the perpetrator with relevant, face-saving rationalizations. If appropriate, reassure the perpetrator that you will lead him from the hostage scene in such a manner that it will appear that he was overpowered and arrested by far superior firepower, rather than having meekly and quietly given up on his own.

6. *Don't Belittle Perpetrator.* Avoid "talking down" to the perpetrator. The perpetrator may in a sense be childlike—in his inability to control anger, his bullying use of threats to get what he wants, his emotional ups and downs, and his inability to seek what he wants in more mature and adult ways. But don't treat him like a child. If he feels you are not taking him seriously as an adult, the likelihood of his behaving in a violent manner may increase.

7. *Avoid Criticism, Threat, and Impatience.* Do not criticize, threaten or act impatiently toward the perpetrator. As noted earlier, time is on your side. A problem-solving climate works in your favor. If you rush decisions, criticize the perpetrator, or threaten him, you are working against your

own strategy. You will have ample opportunity to use threats and similar actions if your less directive negotiations fail.

VII. GATHERING INFORMATION

1. *Open-ended Questions.* Attempt to gather information from the perpetrator by use of open-ended questions. Open-ended questions are those which give the perpetrator a chance to give long answers. They are questions which usually begin with "what," "why," or "how." Examples of such questions, as they might occur in a hostage situation, include: "What happened here?"; "What do you mean by unfair?"; "How do you feel we can compromise?"
2. *Closed-ended Questions.* Attempt to gather information from the perpetrator by use of closed-ended questions. Questions which can be answered with "yes," "no," or a brief, factual reply are closed-ended questions. They usually begin with "do," "is," or "are." Such questions are a valuable part of the negotiator's information-gathering attempt, but must not be overused, particularly as substitutes when open-ended questioning would be more effective. Examples of closed-ended questions include: "Do you accept what I said?"; "Is that the medicine that you asked for?"; "Are you ready to surrender?"
3. *Listening.* Attempt to gather information from the perpetrator by use of good listening skills. How well the perpetrator feels the negotiator is listening to him will clearly affect how open and detailed the perpetrator will be. Good listening skills include both things you do and things you avoid doing. The skilled listener makes comments which show the perpetrator that he is interested in what he is saying and is paying attention, e.g., "I see what you mean," or "I can understand that." If safety considerations permit, and the negotiator has gone face to face with the perpetrator, the negotiator should also indicate his interest and attention by his gestures, posture, and eye contact. The skilled listener tries to avoid conversation with more than one person at a time and reuses calming techniques whenever necessary.
4. *Restatement of Content (Paraphrasing).* Attempt to gather information from the perpetrator by use of restatement of content. Restatement of content consists of saying back to the perpetrator, in words different from his own (i.e., paraphrasing), the essence of what he has already said to you. This information-gathering procedure, like good listening skills, shows your interest, attention, and understanding of what the perpetrator is saying, and is likely to keep him talking.
5. *Reflection of Feeling.* Attempt to gather information from the perpetrator by use of reflection of feeling. Whereas restatement of content emphasizes

paraphrasing to the perpetrator one or more of the facts in his statement, reflection of feeling focuses on expressing to the perpetrator an understanding of his main feelings. To reflect the perpetrator's feelings accurately, the negotiator must pay attention both to what the perpetrator is saying and how he is saying it (its strength, tone, inflection, pace, target, etc.). The main point about reflection of feeling is that when someone feels that you understand his apparent or even somewhat hidden feelings, he is more likely to continue to provide you with information.

6. *Discrepancy Confrontation.* Attempt to clarify information you receive from the perpetrator by pointing out discrepancies in what he has said. Discrepancy confrontation means pointing out to the perpetrator discrepancies either in two things he has said (content-content discrepancy), or between something he said and the way he seems to feel about it (content-feeling discrepancy).

7. *Nature of Demands.* Expect the perpetrator's demands to be presented to you as:[2]
   1. Not open to negotiation.
   2. All must be met, and in full.
   3. With a specific time limit.
   4. With a threat of specific consequences if all demands are not met, in full, within the specified time period.

VIII. PERSUADING THE PERPETRATOR

1. *Agree, in Part, with Perpetrator's Views.* Start your persuasion attempts by agreeing with part of the perpetrator's views. Presenting views which you believe are already held by the perpetrator early in your negotiations, gives some chance of decreasing part of his resistance to your later arguments.

2. *Deal with Smaller Issues First.* Try to build a climate of successful negotiation by dealing with smaller, easier to settle items first. Dealing first with more easily negotiated items, such as choice of communication channels, food, and medicine, will increase the chances that the perpetrator may be open to your views on more central issues, including hostage release. In some hostage situations, this suggestion can best be followed by taking a larger issue and breaking it into several smaller, more workable issues.

---

2. As the next section describes, the suggested negotiator opening response to demands presented in this manner is that the set of demands, as a package, is not acceptable, but that we are willing to negotiate some of them.

3. *State Conclusions.* Don't just give the perpetrator the facts with the hope that he'll change his mind in your direction. Tell him exactly and specifically what conclusions you believe the facts lead to.
4. *Promote Active Listening by the Perpetrator.* Encourage the perpetrator actively to imagine or "try on" the position you are trying to convince him of. Ask him, "What would it be like if . . . ?" or similar questions. Passive listening does not promote change in thinking, but active listening by the perpetrator will increase your chances of persuading him.
5. *Present Both Sides of the Argument (Yours and His).* Both sides of an issue should be presented by the negotiator. Presenting your understanding of the perpetrator's side of an argument will help convince him that you are taking him seriously, that you view his argument as having some objective basis, and it will give you the opportunity to try to refute it in comparison to your own views. Anticipating the perpetrator's arguments in this manner will increase your persuasiveness.
6. *Consider the Perpetrator's Motivations.* Slant your persuasive appeal to the needs and goals of the perpetrator. Respond to his sense of pride, feelings toward his loved ones, need for status, political views or other of his needs you have learned about or suspect from your background inquiries.
7. *Argue against Yourself.* Argue against one or more unimportant aspects of your own position. It will increase your credibility with the perpetrator if you argue against an (unimportant) aspect of your position, impress him with your fairness and open-mindedness, and put the burden on him to yield an aspect of his demands.
8. *Point out Similarities.* Point out to the perpetrator any perpetrator-negotiator similarities. People are more persuaded by others they perceive as similar to themselves. The negotiator should, therefore, subtly make sure the perpetrator is aware of negotiator-perpetrator similarities in background, ethnic group, race, or other salient characteristics.
9. *Request Delayed Compliance.* Request delayed compliance, especially on issues which you predict will be difficult for the perpetrator to yield on; follow your persuasive attempt with the suggestion that the perpetrator not make up his mind immediately, that he think it over, and, hopefully, accept your view at a later point. A side benefit of requests for delayed compliance are that they add further time to the negotiation process.
10. *Minimize Counter Arguments.* Minimize counter arguments; include in your persuasive attempts weakened versions of the arguments with which the perpetrator is likely to respond. This "co-opts" his response to some extent, and thus may increase the chances he will accept your position.
11. *Try to Persuade Gradually.* Seek to change the perpetrator's thinking and behavior a small step at a time. When you try to change too much

of the perpetrator's thinking or behavior at one time, a boomerang effect may result. Instead of agreeing with your view, his resistance may increase. You are likely to be a more effective negotiator if you attempt piecemeal changes in the perpetrator's thinking.

12. *Initiate Issues to Negotiate.* Introduce issues into the negotiations yourself so that you can give in on them later as a way of encouraging concessions from the perpetrator.

13. *Reward Perpetrator Yielding.* Reward the perpetrator for any statements or steps he makes toward successful resolution of the hostage situation.

14. *Use Factual Evidence.* Use clear, unambiguous, factual evidence to support your position. For those items on which you cannot compromise at all, try to provide the perpetrator with clear, unambiguous factual evidence in support of your firmness. The more powerful the evidence you provide, the more likely you are to convince the perpetrator that your position will not change.

15. *Avoid Audiences.* Avoid negotiating in front of others to the extent such "privacy" is possible. Your negotiating efforts are likely to be less complicated and, perhaps, more successful if audience effects are avoided. Face saving, unexpected pressures or interruptions, overreaction, increased irrationality, and heightened potential for violence are all increased if others can hear (and interfere with) your negotiations. Thus, seek to negotiate by direct or by telephone communication in a manner consistent with safety concerns. Avoid use of bullhorns and similar devices if possible.

16. *Avoid Challenging.* Do not challenge a perpetrator, or dare him to act. Leave room for the perpetrator to maneuver. If he feels his back is to the wall, there is a good chance he will strike out violently. Maintain the problem-solving climate we have described. Do not threaten the perpetrator, accuse him of bluffing, or otherwise put him on the spot in such a way that he feels he must "save face" by acting violently. If you do so, you may win the debating point but lose your hostages.

17. *Reduce Perpetrator Irrationality.* Try to decrease the level of perpetrator irrationality. The perpetrator will often be very anxious, frightened, angry, and emotionally unstable. All of these forces may result in irrational thinking patterns, patterns which will make your negotiating attempts more complicated and less likely to succeed. Any steps you can take to reduce perpetrator irrationality will simplify the negotiations, increase their predictability, and make a successful outcome more likely. The several calming procedures we have described elsewhere in this chapter will help decrease perpetrator irrationality. In addition, use suggestion, clarification, and concretization to help the perpetrator better understand his own intentions, expected gains, and likely costs. When the perpetrator presents issues in a global, intangible, irrational, or general manner, recast them in specific, tangible, rational terms.

18. *Demands which Benefit Police.* Agree with clear reluctance to any demands which in reality benefit the police position. There will on occasion be perpetrator demands which, in fact, are of strategic or tactical benefit to the police position, and not the perpetrator's. To obtain "points," as it were, for later barter on yet further issues to benefit the police position, negotiators should yield on these demands with obvious reluctance.

19. *Demands which Benefit Perpetrator.* Whenever possible, stall on demands which benefit the perpetrator. We do not want to strengthen the perpetrator's negotiating position. When agreeing to one of his demands would have this effect, e.g., making access to the hostages more difficult, the negotiator's optimal responses may be to stall. He should maintain the basic problem-solving climate of the negotiations by clearly showing his willingness to explore (at length) solutions alternative to that being demanded. While striving to avoid angering or increasing the volatility of the perpetrator, the negotiator must if at all possible, not yield to situation-worsening perpetrator demands.

20. *Offering Suggestions.* Offer only those suggestions you feel are clearly necessary, as any suggestions may speed up the time factor in ways not to your advantage.

21. *Keep Perpetrator's Hopes Alive.* Keep alive the perpetrator's hope of escape. The possibility of encouraging acts of desperation through negotiating mistakes must be kept in mind at all times. Such mistakes include any statements which lead the perpetrator to feel he has nothing to lose if he kills his hostages. Through joint problem solving, the perpetrator should be made to believe he will get some of the results he had in mind when he started the hostage situation. In addition, if at all possible, keep alive his hopes of escape until all hostages have been released.

22. *Perpetrator Escape.* Be open to the possibility that you may have to let the perpetrator escape in exchange for hostages. Your primary responsibility in a hostage incident is the safe release of the hostages. If this can be negotiated along with the perpetrator's surrender, all to the good. If a trade-off, hostages for perpetrator, is the best that can be accomplished, this solution should be accepted. The chance that the perpetrator will be captured later is high. In negotiating such an exchange, however, only accept it if more desirable outcomes have been persistently unobtainable.

Appendix E
Self-Instruction
Structured Learning

1. Behavioral description. The first procedure of Structured Learning is to describe the skill you wish to learn in behavioral terms, so that it might be learned rapidly and effectively. We have done this for 25 skills relevant to aggression. If you think of others you wish to learn, try to describe them to yourself behaviorally by breaking the skill down into its steps. You can sometimes do this in your own imagination, sometimes by discussing the skill with others, and sometimes by carefully and closely watching someone who is actually using the skill just as you would like to use it. Wherever the behavioral steps of the skill you wish to learn come from—our list or your efforts—study and memorize them as your first step in learning to use the skill when you really need it.

2. Behavioral rehearsal. Structured Learning requires you to train yourself actively so that effective and lasting learning may occur. You may be able to learn and use some skills simply by reading the skill's steps. But for most skills, passive reading of what to do probably won't be enough. Rehearsing the behavior is one excellent way for you to become actively involved in learning the skill.

Behavioral rehearsal allows you to practice a skill's steps in such a manner that you gradually become more and more skillful in using it in the real-life situations in which you need it. The key here is gradualness. It is important that you be certain to practice the skill in easier situations before moving on to more difficult situations. We suggest you use the following gradual sequence to practice the behavioral steps for the skill you have selected.

A. In imagination. Think about the various situations in which you'd like to use the target skill. Pick one and picture yourself in that setting. Imagine where it is, when you might be there, and who is likely to be there with you. Imagine yourself going through the behavioral steps in the correct order and with no errors. Let the entire sequence unfold as smoothly as you can. Imagine not only what you would think, say, or do, but also what the other people involved might say or do in response to you.

B. Openly, alone. Now go through the correct behavioral step sequence again, but this time say aloud what you might actually say and do in the real-life skill situation. Even if it feels a bit strange to do, try to make your words, expressions, gestures, and movements as real and as relevant as you can. Make it a true behavioral rehearsal. For reasons we will discuss below, in order to get feedback on your performance, we urge you in this step of rehearsal to use a mirror and, if available, a tape recorder.

C. *Openly, with someone you trust.* Let's assume your skill goal is "Expressing a complaint." Your intention is to develop this skill to a point at which you can express a justifiable complaint to, for example, a coworker who has frequently treated you unfairly. You have practiced the behavioral steps that make up "Expressing a complaint" both in your imagination, and aloud in front of a mirror, using a tape recorder. In the third stage of behavioral rehearsal, a second person becomes involved. This is your chance to go through the steps again, but this time, do it while looking someone else in the eyes, responding to their comebacks. In this first attempt with someone else, the other person should, if possible, be a person whom you trust and who will cooperate. First, describe the skill you want to practice and why you would like help. Give your helper all the details you can about the real-life situation in which you eventually want to use the skill, where, when, why, and with which real-life target person. Tell him all about the person to whom you want to express your complaint, the individual's name, appearance, characteristics, and most important, what response this target person is likely to have to you. Tell the person helping you to imitate the other person's behavior as closely as possible while you practice the skill. This is a rehearsal. It's designed to teach you a skill for use where, when, and with whom you really need it. The more realistic the rehearsal, the better your real-life skill behavior will be. It will often be useful to repeat this rehearsal a number of times, until you feel fully comfortable using your new skill behavior.

D. *Openly, with the real-life target person.* Your final stage is to use the skill with the actual people in the actual places, where it counts. In using your newly learned skill behaviors at work, at home, in social situations, and elsewhere, gradually work up to using them with your target people. If it is easier for you, take on a coworker before trying the skill with your boss. Try other skills out with people who are more cooperative before you deal with those who are less cooperative. Use the skill in less difficult situations before you tackle the really tough ones. Challenge yourself, but do it gradually!

3. Behavioral feedback. You have studied a skill and tried it out both alone and with one or more people. It's important now to determine how well you're doing. Are you carrying out the behavioral steps correctly? Are you doing them in the proper order? Could you do it better? Are you doing well in some situations but still having difficulty in others? Why aren't you getting the results you expected? Feedback on questions like these is crucial to your progress. With adequate feedback, you can eliminate errors and sharpen your skill performance. Without such feedback, your skill deficiency may remain unchanged. And without feedback, you may never understand why a particular situation doesn't turn out the way you'd like it to.

You can provide yourself with behavioral feedback during the first two rehearsal stages ("In imagination" and "Openly, alone"). Use your mirror and tape recorder to help you judge honestly whether the words, expressions, gestures, and movements of your rehearsal actually fit the skill's behavioral steps. When you shift to rehearsal with someone you trust, ask that person the same questions: Am I following the steps? How do I look and sound? Do I look natural and comfortable using the skill? Can you suggest anything I might improve upon?

There is another type of feedback your helper can give you, and it is very important feedback indeed. The behavioral steps that make up all of the skills are designed to be effective means for solving whatever problem is involved. The goal in designing the steps for "Expressing a complaint," for example, was not just to make you feel better (or to "get it out of your system"), but especially to maximize the chances that the person you confront will respond to you as you wish (an apology, correcting an error he or she has made, etc.). That is, often the most important feedback we can get is results. Did it work? Did I accomplish my goal in using the skill behavior? You can get approximate answers to such questions during the rehearsal process by asking the person helping you to react to your skill rehearsal just the way the actual target person would react. If you've set up the rehearsal well, you've told your helper a great deal about the target person and his or her typical reactions. Having your helper try to be that person, especially in reacting to your behavior, can often provide especially valuable feedback. In the example we have been using, if your helper feels your expression of a complaint would result in an apology, he or she should apologize. If your helper feels it would lead to counter-complaining toward you, he or she should do that. Urge your helper to provide you with whatever real-life reaction seems most likely. Only then can you evaluate your progress realistically, and prepare adequately for real-life encounters.

It is, of course, the feedback from the real-life people themselves that ultimately tests how adequate and competent your skill behavior has been. If, in general (there may always be exceptions), people in your world are responding to you as you would like, you're probably using your skills effectively. If, on the other hand, many of your skill trials yield unsatisfying or ineffective results, there's an excellent chance that you need to work more on developing those skills. Be quite sure, however, when evaluating any negative feedback or results you receive, to discover what caused the negative results. Were you using your skills ineffectively? Or was it the case that the other person was unreceptive, stubborn, or lacking in skills? It's true that there will be some times when even though you've done your best, others may not respond quite as you hoped they would. In general, however, using a skill effectively will most often lead to rewarding outcomes.

4. Behavioral transfer. If you identify the skills in which you are weak accurately and apply the first three procedures of Structured Learning, there's an excellent chance you will learn the skills that were your goal. Yet psychologists have shown repeatedly that a number of things can cause people to forget newly learned skills. They can usually use the skill when they first learn it but, all too often, the skill is gone a week or a month later. Sometimes skills disappear even more quickly, especially when you've rehearsed them successfully with a trusted friend but now have to try them with a stranger, your boss, or an angry spouse. In short, new skills are often fragile and therefore no skill training program is complete unless it includes procedures for making changes stick. In this section, which concerns transferring skill behavior from where you learned it to where you need it, we will present a number of possible ways you can minimize skill loss. Through the use of these techniques you can both increase the chances of holding on to what you've learned, and sharpen your skills even further.

A. Be sure your original learning of the skill is sufficient. Of the several reasons why you may forget a newly learned skill, not learning it well enough in the beginning is the easiest to correct. Usually, the main reason turns out to be not enough rehearsal or not enough feedback. You can increase the chances that your new skill will hold up over time, therefore, by (1) increasing the quantity of rehearsal before trying a skill in real-life settings, and (2) finding better sources of feedback about the quality of your skill use. When you do rehearse a skill, be sure to practice several times after you've used it well. Don't stop after only using the skill well once or twice. Keep going, even though you feel you've got it. Psychologists call this "overlearning," and it works!

B. Be sure your original learning of the skill is realistic enough. Psychologists have found that the more similar the practice situation is to the situation in which you really have to use the skill, the better you'll retain the skill. That is, sometimes a skill can be learned well but in a form that makes it difficult to transfer the skill to where you need it—on the job, at home, on a date, etc. In a case like this, you should consider such matters as (1) how realistic your original rehearsal of the skill was, and (2) with how many and how many different kinds of people you originally rehearsed the skill. You can make the learning situation more realistic by rehearsing the skill with people and in places most similar to the real-life people and places in which you need the skill. You can make the learning situation more varied by rehearsing the skill with several different people. The greater the variety of other people you practice the skill with, the greater the chances that some of these practice partners will be similar to the people with whom you'll need to use the skill in real life.

    C. Instruct yourself in ways that keep your skill use effective. Psychological research supports the idea that it is often useful to talk to yourself! This "self-instruction" research shows the benefits of coaching yourself, prompting yourself, guiding yourself, and encouraging yourself. So, to help make your skills stick, we urge you to:

1. Remind or prompt yourself sufficiently about the skill's behavioral steps when you're in a real-life situation in which you need the skill.
2. Say encouraging things to yourself—"You can do it!"—rather than dwelling on possible skill failure.
3. Note the similarities (and/or differences) between a past situation in which a skill worked well and a current situation in which you are less effective in using the skill. If there are similarities, perhaps you should use the skill in a similar manner; if there are differences, you may have to use the skill differently or combine it with other skills, or perhaps not even use it at all and replace it with another skill.
4. Point out to yourself the specific benefits that will probably accrue to you if you use the skill correctly, as well as the negative outcomes you're likely to avoid in this way.

    D. Maximize the chances that others will reward you if you use the skill correctly. If others praise, approve, agree, comply, or otherwise reward you, you're likely to keep using a skill. If they complain, disapprove, disagree, ignore, reject, or otherwise punish you, your skill behaviors are destined to fade away. There are steps you can take to maximize the chances that your correct use of the skill will be rewarded by others:

1. Say and do things that try to change what others expect of you. Instruct them; change their anticipations about how they expect you to behave; ask them to pay attention to the new things you are doing.
2. Ask other important people in your life to change their behavior so that it is compatible with or complements or rewards the skill behaviors you're using. Ask your spouse, for example, to use the skills that seem to go along with the skills you are trying to use. For example, ask him or her to respond with "Listening" or "Responding to your feelings" when you "Express affection" or "Express a complaint." You might even ask your boss to "Negotiate" with you when you are trying to "Negotiate" with him.
3. Go places, choose times, and select people who are likely to reward your effective skill use.
4. Avoid places, times, and people who are unlikely to reward effective skill use.

E. Provide yourself with sufficient and appropriate self-reward for using the skill correctly. You can also use self-rewards to keep what you have learned, and to avoid forgetting skill behaviors. Remember, rewards do not only come from others. You can and should reward yourself, both by what you say to yourself and by things you do for yourself. Self-reward, therefore, is a combination of saying something encouraging to yourself and doing something special for yourself. You should observe the following rules to be sure that your self-rewards have a maximum effect in helping you retain the skills you've learned:

1. Choose your rewards carefully. Be sure that the rewarding statement you make to yourself is clear and unambiguous—e.g., "I really handled that well." Be sure that the special thing you do for yourself isn't something you'd do any way. For example, don't reward yourself by buying something you already planned to buy. Don't go to a certain movie as a reward if you would have seen it even if you hadn't used a skill especially well. A second type of "doing for yourself" reward can be everyday things you got anyway, but that you're now denying yourself until you use the skill well. For example, save the special dessert or expensive cigar as a reward that you can present yourself for good progress.

2. Always reward yourself immediately after you use the skill well, or as soon as possible after. Don't delay in self-reward if at all possible. The greater the delay, the greater the chances that your self-reward will fail to serve its purpose of helping to make changes stick.

3. Be very careful to reward yourself only when you have used the skill well. Saying nice things to yourself and doing things for yourself should occur only when you've followed all the skill's behavioral steps. When you have followed some of them well, we suggest you provide yourself with verbal self-reward only, e.g., "Good try."

F. Minimize the chances that other skill deficiencies that you have not yet worked on are interfering. You may learn a number of the skills, and chances are that when you set out to use them in real life, you (wisely) try one skill at a time. Getting along effectively in the real world, however, often demands more. Often, a problem can't be solved or a relationship established unless you skillfully use a combination or a sequence of skills. For example, before you can effectively use the skill "Negotiating," you may first have to be equally effective in "Setting problem priorities" and "Making a decision." In general, before entering a real-life situation, it's frequently useful to consider the situation carefully. Ask yourself what skills this situation might demand of you. This type of planning for use of specific skill combinations or skill sequences can often prove quite valuable. There is no magic formula for figuring out which skills you'll need, or in what order you'll need them. Rather, success at planning skill sequences is usually a matter of thinking carefully about what you and the others involved in an actual situation are likely to do. Focus on the actual behavior that is likely to take place.

Work at it a bit and you'll find that even the most complex situation can be broken down into the skills that are likely to be needed. After doing this a while, there is a very good chance you'll become expert at this type of skill-use planning.

Example: Tom and Helen Burns fought over a lot more than just occasional visits from her parents. Disciplining their children, their tight budget, sex that somehow didn't work out, big things like their future and little things like which movie to see. One particularly frequent argument, at least twice a week in the months since Helen took a job, had to do with sharing household chores.

Tom would come home from work and hardly ever lift a finger. Sure he was tired, but he would plop down in front of the TV, and wait for the world to wait on him. Helen would come home from her job, have to fix dinner, take care of the children, clean up the kitchen, and whatever else needed doing. Sometimes Helen responded with a slow burn, saying nothing, but really fuming inside. Other times she'd yell and shout as loud as Tom ever did, demanding at the top of her voice that he get off his ass and help out.

Well, she was getting nowhere. Keeping quiet didn't work; blowing her top was no better. There had to be a middle course. There had to be a skill that she just wasn't using to fit this situation. Helen thought long and hard about the Structured Learning skills and decided that Giving Instructions was the middle course she was after. The steps in Giving Instructions are:

1. Define what needs to be done and who should do it;
2. Tell the other person what you want him or her to do, and why;
3. Tell the other person exactly how to do what you want him or her to do, and why;
4. Ask for his or her reaction; and
5. Consider his or her reactions and change your directions if appropriate.

Helen memorized these behavioral steps, and started to think about where and when she would use them with Tom. As she rode to work on the bus that day, she "tried on" the steps, one at a time, trying really hard to imagine what she would actually say, and how Tom might react. She wanted to be sure that when she actually tried to instruct Tom on what she wanted him to do, she'd say it just right—tone of voice, not too soft, not yelling.

On Saturday, when Tom and the kids were out, she got out the little cassette recorder and spoke into it exactly what she thought she'd say, and then listened as openly as she could to her own words and voice. When her friend Lenore came over for coffee, Helen asked her if she'd mind being a sounding board. She described what she was trying to straighten out with Tom, and how she was going to do it. Lenore listened as carefully and objectively as she could to Helen's live rehearsal, and then told her straight out what she thought Tom's reaction might be. Overall, Lenore's feedback was very positive, and Helen felt ready for the real thing. She decided on instructions to him about some shopping that had to be done, instructions she would give him that same evening [behavioral step 1]. Right after dinner that night, in a moderate tone of voice, Helen looked straight at Tom and said, "Tom, there's just too much around here for me to do all by myself, and keep my job, and shop, and whatever. We've got to share chores more. I'd really like you to stop at the supermarket on the way home from work tomorrow and get the stuff on this list, and also pick up the package from the cleaning store [behavioral step 2]. You'd probably be best off going to the cleaner's first, and then on over to the Archway Supermarket. And see that last item on the list? Be sure to get skim, not regular [behavioral step 3] milk. Do you see any problems in handling this [behavioral step 4]?"

Tom's first reaction was a sort of surprise, even a bit of shock. But she could see he was thinking about it. The surprise faded and he said he'd do it. But he'd rather do it right then, and avoid the evening traffic tomorrow. Helen said that that would be fine [behavioral step 5]. She turned away to do the dishes, a small smile on her face, from the satisfaction of a new skill, well used. She went into the kitchen, dirty dishes in hand, starting to rehearse to herself how she'd instruct Tom about sharing this chore next.

Bibliography

Achenbach, T.M. The classification of children's psychiatric symptoms: A factor-analytic study. *Psychological monographs*, 1966, **80** (Whole No. 615).

Achenbach, T.M. & Edelbrock, C.S. The classification of child psychopathology: A review and analysis of empirical efforts. *Psychological Bulletin*, 1978, **85**, 1275–1301.

Adkins, W.R. Life skills: Structured counseling for the disadvantaged. *Personnel and Guidance Journal*, 1970, **49**, 108–116.

Adkins, W.R. Life coping skills: A fifth curriculum. *Teachers College Record*, 1974, **75**, 507–526.

Agras, W.S. Transfer during systematic desensitization therapy. *Behavior Research and Therapy*, 1967, **5**, 193–199.

Anderson, L. Role playing ability and young children: The prescriptive question. Unpublished masters thesis, Syracuse University, 1981.

Argyle, M., Trower, P., & Bryant, B. Explorations in the treatment of personality disorders and neuroses by social skill training. *British Journal of Medical Psychology*, 1974, **47**, 63–72.

Atthowe, J.M. & Krasner, L. A preliminary report on the application of contingent reinforcement procedures (token economy) on a "chronic" psychiatric ward. *Journal of Abnormal Psychology*, 1968, **73**, 37–43.

Atwater, S.K. Proactive inhibition and associate facilitation as affected by degree of prior learning. *Journal of Experimental Psychology*, 1953, **46**, 400–404.

Authier, J., Gustafson, K., Guerney, B.G., Jr., & Kasdorf, J.A. The psychological practitioner as teacher. *The Counseling Psychologist*, 1975, **5**, 1–21.

Axelrod, S., Hall, R.V., & Maxwell, A. Use of peer attention to increase study behavior. *Behavior Therapy*, 1972, **3**, 349–350.

Ayllon, T. & Azrin, N.H. *The token economy: A motivational system for therapy and rehabilitation.* New York: Appleton, 1968.

Bailey, J.S., Timbers, G.D., Phillips, E.L., & Wolf, W.W. Modification of articulation errors of pre-delinquents by their peers. *Journal of Applied Behavior Analysis*, 1971, **4**, 265–281.

Bailey, J.S., Wolf, W.W., & Phillips, E.L. Home-based reinforcement and the modification of pre-delinquents' classroom behavior. *Journal of Applied Behavior Analysis*, 1970, **3**, 223–233.

Baldwin, W.K. The educable mentally retarded child in the regular grades. *Exceptional Children*, 1958, **25**, 106–108.

Bandura, A. *Aggression: A social learning analysis.* Englewood Cliffs, N.J.: Prentice-Hall, 1973.

Bandura, A. Self-efficacy: Toward a unifying theory of behavioral change. *Psychological Review*, 1977, **84**, 191–215.

Bash, M.S. & Camp, B.W. Teacher training in the Think Aloud Classroom Program. In G. Cartledge & J.F. Milburn (Eds.), *Teaching social skills to children.* New York: Pergamon Press, 1980. Pp. 143–178.

Bassiouni, M.E. (Ed.) *International terrorism and political crimes.* Springfield, Ill.: Charles C. Thomas, 1975.

Beck, J.C., Kanto, D., & Gelineau, V.A. Follow-up study of chronic psychotic patients "treated" by college case-aide volunteers. *American Journal of Psychiatry*, 1963, **120**, 269–271.

Becker, W.C., Madsen, C.H., Jr., Arnold, C.R., & Thomas, D.R. The contingent use of teacher attention and praise in reducing classroom behavior problems. *Journal of Special Education*, 1967, **1**, 287–307.

Bellack, A.S. & Hersen, M. *Research and practice in social skills training.* New York: Plenum, 1979.

Berlin, R.J. Training of hospital staff in accurate affective perception of fear-anxiety from vocal cues in the context of varying facial cues. Unpublished masters thesis, Syracuse University, 1974.

Berlin, R. Teaching acting-out adolescents prosocial conflict resolution through structured learning training of empathy. Unpublished doctoral dissertation, Syracuse University, 1977.

Blanchard, E. The generalization of vicarious extinction effects. *Behavior Research and Therapy*, 1970, **8**, 323–330.

Bloom, B.L. & Arkoff, A. Role playing in acute and chronic schizophrenics. *Journal of Consulting Psychology*, 1961, **25**, 24–28.

Botwinick, J. *Aging and behavior.* New York: Springer, 1973.

Brady, R.C. Effects of success and failure on impulsivity and distractability of three types of educationally handicapped children. Unpublished doctoral dissertation, University of Southern California, 1970.

Broen, W. *Schizophrenia.* New York: Academic Press, 1968.

Brown, R.C., Helm, B., & Tedeschi, J.T. Attraction and verbal conditioning. *Journal of Social Psychology*, 1973, **91**, 81–85.

Bruch, M. Influence of mode characteristics on psychiatric inpatients' interview anxiety. *Journal of Abnormal Psychology*, 1975, **84**, 209–214.

Bruininks, R., Rynders, J., & Gross, J. Social acceptance of educable mentally retarded pupils in resource rooms and regular classes. *American Journal of Mental Deficiency*, 1974, **70**, 377–383.

Buckley, N.K. & Walker, H.M. *Modifying classroom behavior.* Champaign, Ill.: Research Press, 1972.

Buehler, R.E., Patterson, G.R., & Furniss, J.M. The reinforcement of behavior in institutional settings. *Behavior Research and Therapy*, 1966, **4**, 157–167.

Burka, J., Hubbell, R., Preble, M., Spinelli, R., & Winter, N. *Communication skills workshop manual.* Fort Collins, Colo.: University of Colorado Counseling Center, 1972.

Burnaska, R.F. The effects of behavioral modeling training upon managers' behaviors and employees' perceptions. Presented at American Psychological Association, Chicago, 1975.

Callantine, M.F. & Warren, L.M. Learning sets in human concept formation. *Psychological Reports*, 1955, **1**, 363–367.

Cameron, N. Experimental analysis of schizophrenic thinking. In J.S. Kasanin (Ed.), *Language and thought in schizophrenia.* Berkeley: University of California Press, 1944. Pp. 50–63.

Cantor, J.H. Amount of pretraining as a factor in stimulus pre-differentiation and performance set. *Journal of Experimental Psychology*, 1955, **50**, 180–184.

Carkhuff, R.R. *Helping and human relations.* New York: Holt, Rinehart & Winston, 1969.

Carkhuff, R.R. *Cry twice.* Amherst, Mass.: Human Resources Development Press, 1974.

Carkhuff, R.R. & Berenson, B.G. *Beyond counseling and psychotherapy.* New York: Holt, Rinehart & Winston, 1967.

Cartledge, G. & Milburn, J.F. (Eds.) *Teaching social skills to children.* New York: Pergamon Press, 1980.

Chan, K. & Keogh, B. Interpretation of task interruption and feelings of responsibility for failure. *Journal of Special Education*, 1974, **8**, 175–178.

Chandler, M. Egocentrism and antisocial behavior: The assessment and training of social perspective taking skills. *Developmental Psychology*, 1973, **9**, 326–332.

Chandler, M., Greenspan, S., & Barenboim, C. Assessment and training of role-taking and referential communication skills in institutionalized emotionally disturbed children. *Developmental Psychology*, 1974, **10**, 546–553.

Chandler, M. & Greenspan, S. Ersatz egocentrism: A reply to H. Borke. *Developmental Psychology*, 1972, **7**, 104–106.

Cicchetti, D., Taraldson, B., & Egeland, B. Perspectives in the treatment and understanding of child abuse. In A.P. Goldstein (Ed.), *Prescriptions for child mental health and education.* New York: Pergamon Press, 1978. Pp. 301–391.

Clutterbuck, R. *Living with terrorism.* New Rochelle, N.Y.: Arlington House, 1975.

Cohen, A.R. *Attitude change and social influence.* New York: Random House, 1966.

Cox, R.D. & Gunn, W.B. Interpersonal skills in the schools: Assessment and curriculum development. In D.P. Rathjen & J.P. Foreyt (Eds.), *Social competence: Interventions for children and adults.* New York: Pergamon Press, 1980. Pp. 113–132.

Craig, C.S., Sternthal, B., & Olshan, K. The effect of overlearning on retention. *Journal of General Psychology,* 1972, **87,** 85–94.

Curran, J.P. Skills training as an approach to the treatment of heterosexual-social anxiety: A review. *Psychological Bulletin,* 1977, **84,** 140–157.

Danish, S. & Hauer, A. *Helping skills: A basic training program.* New York: Behavioral Publications, 1973.

Debus, R. Effects of brief observation of model behavior on conceptual tempo of impulsive children. *Developmental Psychology,* 1970, **2,** 22–32.

Dreikurs, R., Schulman, B.H., & Mosak, H. Patient-therapist in multiple psychotherapy: Its advantages to the therapist. *Psychiatric Quarterly,* 1952, **26,** 219–227.

Duncan, C.P. Transfer after training with single versus multiple tasks. *Journal of Experimental Psychology,* 1958, **55,** 63–73.

Duncan, C.P. Recent research on human problem solving. *Psychological Bulletin,* 1959, **56,** 397–429.

Durlak, J.A. Comparative effectiveness of paraprofessional and professional helpers. *Psychological Bulletin,* 1979, **86,** 80–92.

D'Zurilla, T.J. & Goldfried, M.R. Problem solving and behavior modification. *Journal of Abnormal Psychology,* 1971, **78,** 107–126.

Edelman, E. Behavior of high versus low hostility-guilt structured learning trainers under standardized client conditions of expressed hostility. Unpublished masters thesis, Syracuse University, 1977.

Egan, G. *Interpersonal living.* Monterey, Calif.: Brooks/Cole, 1976.

Elardo, P. & Cooper, M. *AWARE: Activities for social development.* Reading, Mass.: Addison-Wesley, 1977.

Ellis, H. *The transfer of learning.* New York: Macmillan, 1965.

Emshoff, J.G., Redd, W.H., & Davidson, W.S. Generalization training and the transfer of prosocial behavior in delinquent adolescents. *Journal of Behavior Therapy and Experimental Psychiatry,* 1976, **7,** 141–144.

Erickson, R.C. & Scott, M.L. Clinical memory testing. *Psychological Bulletin,* 1977, **84,** 1130–1149.

Esty, G.W. The prevention of psychosocial disorders of youth: A challenge to mental health, public health, and education. *Journal of School Health,* 1967, **37,** 19–23.

Faris, R.E. & Dunham, H.W. *Mental disorders in urban areas: An ecological study of schizophrenia and other psychoses.* Chicago: University of Chicago Press, 1960.

Feffer, M.H. Developmental analysis of interpersonal behavior. *Psychological Review,* 1970, **77,** 197–214.

Flavell, J.H., Botkin, P.T., Fry, C.L., Wright, J.W., & Jarvis, P.E. *The development of role-taking and communication skills in children.* New York: Wiley, 1968.

Fleming, E.R. Training passive and aggressive educable mentally retarded children for assertive behaviors using three types of structured learning training, Unpublished doctoral dissertation, Syracuse University, 1976.

Fleming, J. Pupil tutors and tutees learn. *Today's Education,* 1969, **58,** 22–24.

Frank, J.D. The role of hope in psychotherapy. *International Journal of Psychiatry,* 1968, **5,** 383–395.

Frank, J.D. *Psychotherapy and the Human Predicament.* New York: Schocken Books, 1978.

Frank, R. Rotating leadership in a group therapy setting. *Psychotherapy: Theory, Research & Practice,* 1973, **10,** 337–338.

Freeman, D.S. Effects of utilizing children with problem behaviors as behavior modifiers for their peers. Unpublished doctoral dissertation, University of Tennessee, 1970.

Fremouw, W.J. & Harmatz, M.G. A helper model for behavioral treatment of speech anxiety. *Journal of Consulting and Clinical Psychology,* 1975, **43,** 652–660.

Gagne, R.M. & Foster, H. Transfer to a motor skill from practice on a pictured representation. *Journal of Experimental Psychology,* 1949, **39,** 342–354.

Galassi, M.D. & Galassi, J.P. *Assert yourself!* New York: Human Sciences Press, 1977.

Gardner, E.F. & Thompson, G.G. *Syracuse scales of social relations. Manual for elementary, junior high and senior high levels.* Yonkers, N.Y.: World Book, 1959.

Gartner, A., Kohler, M. & Riessman, F. *Children teach children: Learning by teaching.* New York: Harper & Row, 1971.

Gelles, R.J. Child abuse as psychopathology: A sociological critique and reformulation. *American Journal of Orthopsychiatry,* 1973, **43,** 1–21.

Gilstad, R. Acquisition and generalization of empathic response through self-administered and leader-directed structured learning training and the interaction between training method and conceptual level. Unpublished doctoral dissertation, Syracuse University, 1978.

Goldbeck, R.A., Bernstein, B.B., Hillix, W.A., & Marx, M.H. Application of the half split technique to problem solving tasks. *Journal of Experimental Psychology,* 1957, **53,** 330–338.

Goldfried, M.R. & Trier, C.A. Effectiveness of relaxation as an active coping skill. *Journal of Abnormal Psychology,* 1974, **83,** 348–355.

Goldstein, A.P. *Psychotherapeutic attraction.* New York: Pergamon Press, 1971.

Goldstein, A.P. *Structured learning therapy: Toward a psychotherapy for the poor.* New York: Academic Press, 1973.

Goldstein, A.P. (Ed.) *Prescriptions for child mental health and education.* New York: Pergamon Press, 1978.

Goldstein, A.P. & Dean, S.J. (Eds.) *The investigation of psychotherapy.* New York: Wiley, 1966.

Goldstein, A.P. & Goedhart, A. The use of structured learning for empathy enhancement in paraprofessional psychotherapist training. *Journal of Community Psychology,* 1973, **3,** 168–173.

Goldstein, A.P., Heller, K., & Sechrest, L.B. *Psychotherapy and the psychology of behavior change.* New York: Wiley, 1966.

Goldstein, A.P., Hoyer, W., & Monti, P. *Police and the elderly.* New York: Pergamon Press, 1979.

Goldstein, A.P. & Kanfer, F.H. (Eds.) *Maximizing treatment gains: Transfer enhancement in psychotherapy.* New York: Academic Press, 1979.

Goldstein, A.P., Monti, P.J., Sardino, T.J., & Green, D.J. *Police crisis intervention.* New York: Pergamon Press, 1977.

Goldstein, A.P. & Sorcher, M. Changing managerial behavior by applied learning techniques. *Training and Development Journal,* 1973, March, 36–39.

Goldstein, A.P. & Sorcher, M. *Changing supervisor behavior.* New York: Pergamon Press, 1974.

Goldstein, A.P., Sprafkin, R.P., & Gershaw, N.J. *Skill training for community living.* New York: Pergamon Press, 1976.

Goldstein, A.P., Sprafkin, R.P., & Gershaw, N.J. *I know what's wrong, but I don't know what to do about it.* Englewood Cliffs, N.J.: Spectrum, 1979.

Goldstein, A.P., Sprafkin, R.P., Gershaw, N.J., & Klein, P. *Skillstreaming the adolescent.* Champaign, Ill.: Research Press, 1980.

Goldstein, A.P. & Stein, N. *Prescriptive psychotherapies.* New York: Pergamon Press, 1976.

Gordon, T. *Parent effectiveness training.* New York: Van Rees Press, 1970.

Gottlieb, J. Attitudes toward mentally retarded children: Effects of labelling and academic performance. *Journal of Educational Psychology*, 1974, **29**, 268–273.

Gottlieb, J. & Budoff, J. Social acceptability of retarded children in nongraded schools differing in architecture. *American Journal of Mental Deficiency*, 1973, **78**, 15–19.

Gottlieb, J., Cohen, L., & Goldstein, L. Social contact and personal adjustment as variables relating to attitudes toward educable mentally retarded children. *Training School Bulletin*, 1974, **71**, 9–16.

Gottman, J., Motarius, C., Gonso, J., & Markham, H. *A couple's guide to communication.* Champaign, Ill.: Research Press, 1977.

Greenleaf, D.O. The use of structured learning therapy and transfer of training programming with disruptive adolescents in a school setting. Unpublished masters thesis, Syracuse University, 1978.

Group for the Advancement of Psychiatry. *Psychopathological disorders in childhood: Theoretical considerations and a proposed classification.* (GAP report no. 62.) Washington, D.C.: American Psychiatric Association, 1966.

Gruber, R.P. Behavior therapy: Problems in generalization. *Behavior Therapy*, 1971, **2**, 361–368.

Gruver, G.G. College students as therapeutic agents. *Psychological Bulletin*, 1971, **76**, 111–127.

Guerney, B.G., Jr. *Relationship enhancement.* San Francisco: Jossey-Bass, 1977.

Gutride, M.E., Goldstein, A.P, & Hunter, G.F. The use of modeling and role playing to increase social interaction among asocial psychiatric patients. *Journal of Consulting and Clinical Psychology*, 1973, **40**, 408–415.

Gutride, M.E., Goldstein, A.P., & Hunter, G.F. Structured learning therapy with transfer training for chronic inpatients. *Journal of Community Psychology*, 1974, **30**, 277–280.

Guzzetta, R.A. Acquisition and transfer of empathy by the parents of early adolescents through structured learning training. Unpublished doctoral dissertation, Syracuse University, 1974.

Haley, J. *Problem solving therapy.* San Francisco: Jossey-Bass, 1976.

Hanson, R.W. Assertion training program. Unpublished manuscript. Palo Alto, Calif.: Veterans Administration Hospital, 1971.

Hanson, R.W. Training program in basic communication skills. Unpublished manuscript. Palo Alto, Calif.: Veterans Administration Hospital, 1972.

Hare, M.A. Teaching conflict resolution simulations. Presented at Eastern Community Association, Philadelphia, March, 1976.

Hawley, R.C. & Hawley, I.L. *Developing human potential: A handbook of activities for personal and social growth.* Amherst, Mass.: Education Research Association, 1975.

Healy, J.A. Training of hospital staff in accurate affective perception of anger from vocal cues in the context of varying social cues. Unpublished doctoral dissertation, Syracuse University, 1975.

Heiman, H. Teaching interpersonal communications. *N. Dakota Speech & Theatre Association Bulletin*, 1973, **2**, 7–29.

Hendrickson, G. & Schroeder, W.H. Transfer of training in learning to hit a submerged target. *Journal of Educational Psychology*, 1941, **32**, 205–213.

Hersen, M. & Eisler, R.M. Social skills training. In W.E. Craighead, A.E. Kazdin, & M.J. Mahoney (Eds.), *Behavior modification: Principles, issues and applications.* Boston: Houghton Mifflin, 1976.

Hewitt, L.E. & Jenkins, R.L. *Fundamental patterns of maladjustment. The dynamics of their origin.* Springfield, Ill.: State of Illinois, 1946.

Hoehn-Saric, R., Frank, J.D., Imber, S.D., Nash, E.H., Stone, A.R., & Battle, C.C. Systematic preparation of patients for psychotherapy. I. Effects on therapy behavior and outcome. *Journal of Psychiatric Research*, 1964, **2**, 267–281.

Hollingshead, A.B. & Redlich, F.C. *Social class and mental illness.* New York: Wiley, 1958.

Holmes, D.S. Round robin therapy: A technique for implementing the effects of psychotherapy.

Journal of Consulting and Clinical Psychology, 1971, **37**, 324–331.

Holzberg, J.D., Knapp, R.H., & Turner, J.L. College students as companions to the mentally ill. In E.L. Cowen, E.A. Gardner, & M. Zax (Eds.), *Emergent approaches to mental health problems*. New York: Appleton, 1967. Pp. 91–109.

Hoyer, W.J., Lopez, M.A., & Goldstein, A.P. Correlates of social skill acquisition and transfer by elderly patients. Unpublished manuscript, Syracuse University, 1981.

Hulicka, I.M. & Weiss, R.L. Age differences in retention as a function of learning. *Journal of Consulting Psychology*, 1965, **29**, 125–129.

Hummel, J.W. Teaching pre-adolescents alternatives to aggression using structured learning training under different stimulus conditions. Unpublished doctoral dissertation, Syracuse University, 1980.

Hunt, D.E. Adaptability in interpersonal communication among training agents. *Merrill Palmer Quarterly*, 1970, **16**, 325–344.

Hunt, D.E. *Matching models in education: The coordination of teaching methods with student characteristics*. Toronto: Ontario Institute for Studies in Education, 1971.

Hunt, D.E. & Sullivan, E.V. *Between psychology and education*. Hinsdale, Ill.: Dryden, 1974.

Inglis, J.A. A paired-associate learning test for use with elderly psychiatric patients. *Journal of Mental Science*, 1959, **105**, 440–443.

Irving, S.G. Parental empathy and adolescent adjustment. *Dissertation Abstracts*, 1966, 27, 967–968.

Ivey, A.E. & Authier, J. *Microcounseling*. Springfield, Ill.: Charles C. Thomas, 1978.

Johnson, D.L. The effect of confrontation in counseling. Unpublished doctoral dissertation, University of Minnesota, 1970.

Johnson, D.W. The use of role reversal in intergroup competition. *Journal of Personality and Social Psychology*, 1967, **7**, 135–141.

Johnson, D.W. *Human relations and your career: A guide to interpersonal skills*. Englewood Cliffs, N.J.: Prentice-Hall, 1978.

Johnson, D.W. Role reversal: A summary and review of the research. *International Journal of Group Tensions*, 1971, **1**, 318–334.

Johnson, G.O. A study of social position of mentally handicapped children in the regular grades. *American Journal of Mental Deficiency*, 1950, **55**, 60–89.

Judd, C.H. The relation of special training to general intelligence. *Educational Review*, 1902, **36**, 28–42.

Justice, B. & Justice, R. *The abusing parent*. New York: Human Sciences Press, 1976.

Kagan, N. *Influencing human interaction*. Washington, D.C.: American Personnel and Guidance Association, 1975.

Kahn, R., Goldfarb, A., Pollack, M., & Peck, A. Brief objective measures for the determination of mental status in the aged. *American Journal of Psychiatry*, 1980, **117**, 326–328.

Karlins, M. & Abelson, H.I. *Persuasion*. New York: Springer, 1970.

Karoly, P. & Steffen, J.J. (Eds.) *Improving the long-term effects of psychotherapy*. New York: Gardner Press, 1980.

Kasius, R.V. The social breakdown syndrome in a cohort of long-stay patients in the Dutchess County Unit, 1960–1963. In E.M. Gruenberg (Ed.), *Evaluating the effectiveness of community mental health services*. New York: Milbank, 1966.

Kazdin, A.E., *Behavior modification in applied settings*. Homewood, Ill.: Dorsey Press, 1975.

Kazdin, A. & Wilcoxon, L.A. Systematic desensitization and non-specific treatment effects: A methodological evaluation. Psychological Bulletin, 1976, **83**, 729–758.

Kelly, G.A. *The psychology of personal constructs*. New York: Norton, 1955.

Kendall, P.C. & Finch, A.J., Jr. Case study: A cognitive behavioral treatment for impulse control. *Journal of Consulting and Clinical Psychology*, 1976, **44**, 852–862.

Kiesler, D.J. Some myths of psychotherapy research and the search for a paradigm. *Psychological Bulletin*, 1966, **65**, 110–136.

Kiesler, D.J. A grid model for theory and research. In L.D. Eron & R. Callahan (Eds.), *The relation of theory to practice in psychotherapy.* Chicago: Aldine, 1969.

Kirk, R.E. *Experimental design: Procedures for the behavioral sciences.* Belmont, Calif.: Brooks Cole, 1968.

Klett, C.J. & Mosley, E.C. The right drug for the right patient. Cooperative studies in psychiatry, Veterans Administration, Report No. 54, November, 1963.

Kornhaber, R. & Schroeder, J. Importance of model similarity on extinction of avoidance behavior in children. *Journal of Consulting and Clinical Psychology,* 1975, **43,** 601–607.

L'Abate, L. Toward a theory and technology for social skills training. *Academic Psychology Bulletin,* 1980, **2,** 207–228.

Lack, D.Z. The effects of problem solving, structured learning and contingency management in training paraprofessional mental health personnel. Unpublished doctoral dissertation, Syracuse University, 1975.

Landrum, J.W. & Martin, M.D. When students teach others. *Educational Leadership,* 1970, **27,** 446–448.

Lang, P. Fear reduction and fear behavior problems in treating a construct. In J.M. Shlien (Ed.), *Research in psychotherapy,* Vol. 3, Washington, D.C.: American Psychological Association, 1968. Pp. 90–102.

Latham, G.P. & Saari, L.M. Application of social learning theory to training supervisors through behavioral modeling. *Journal of Applied Psychology,* 1979, **64,** 239–246.

Lawrence, E. & Winschel, J. Locus of control: Implications for special education. *Exceptional Children,* 1975, **41,** 483–491.

Lawton, M.P. The Philadelphia Geriatric Center Morale Scale: A revision. *Journal of Gerontology,* 1975, **30,** 85–89.

Lazarus, A.A. Toward a flexible, or personalistic system of psychotherapy. In A.A. Lazarus, *Behavior therapy and beyond.* New York: McGraw-Hill, 1971. Pp. 31–47.

Lerner, B. *Therapy in the ghetto.* Baltimore: Johns Hopkins University Press, 1972.

Liberman, B.L. The role of mastery in psychotherapy. In J.D. Frank, R. Hoehn-Saric, S.D. Imber, B.L. Liberman, & A.R. Stone, The effective ingredients of successful psychotherapy. New York: Brunner Mazel, 1977.

Liberman, R.P., King, L.W., DeRisi, W.J., & McCann, M. *Personal effectiveness.* Champaign, Ill.: Research Press, 1975.

Litwack, S.E. The helper therapy principle as a therapeutic tool: Structured learning therapy with adolescents. Unpublished doctoral dissertation, Syracuse University, 1976.

Lopez, M.A. The influence of vocal and facial cue training on the identification of affect communicated via paralinguistic cues. Unpublished masters thesis, Syracuse University, 1977.

Lopez, M.A. Social skills training with institutionalized elderly: Effects of precounseling structuring and overlearning on skill acquisition and transfer. *Journal of Counseling Psychology,* 1980, **27,** 286–293.

Lorian, R.P., Cowen, E.L., & Caldwell, R.A. Normative and parametric analyses of school maladjustment. *American Journal of Community Psychology,* 1975, **3,** 291–301.

Lorr, J.A. The application of reinforcement principles in the elementary classroom. Unpublished doctoral dissertation, University of Maryland, 1970.

Lorr, M. & Vestre, N.D. *Psychotic inpatient profile, test and manual.* Los Angeles: Western Psychological Services, 1968.

Loveless, A. & Brody, C. The cognitive base of psychotherapy. *Psychotherapy: Theory, Research and Practice,* 1974, **11,** 133–137.

MacGregor, R., Ritchie, A.M., Serrano, A.C., & Schuster, F.P. *Multiple impact therapy with families.* New York: McGraw-Hill, 1964.

Madsen, C.H., Jr., Becker, W.C., & Thomas, D.R. Rules, praise and ignoring: Elements of elementary classroom control. *Journal of Applied Behavior Analysis,* 1968, **1,** 139–150.

Madsen, M. & Connor, C. Cooperative and competitive behavior of retarded and non-retarded children at two ages. *Child Development*, 1973, **44**, 175–178.

Magaro, P.A. A prescriptive treatment model based on social class and premorbid adjustment. *Psychotherapy: Theory, Research and Practice*, 1969, **6**, 57–70.

Magaro, P.A., Gripp, R., & McDowell, D.J. *The mental health industry*. New York: Wiley, 1978.

Magaro, P.A. & West, A.N. The effects of structured learning therapy with chronic patients and level of pathology. Unpublished manuscript, University of Maine, 1981.

Mainord, W.A., Burk, H.W., & Collins, G.L. Confrontation vs. diversion in group therapy with chronic schizophrenics as measured by a "positive incident criterion." *Journal of Clinical Psychology*, 1965, **21**, 222–225.

Mandler, G. Transfer of training as a function of degree of response overlearning. *Journal of Experimental Psychology*, 1954, **47**, 411–417.

Mandler, G. & Heinemann, S. H. Effects of overlearning of a verbal response on transfer of training. *Journal of Experimental Psychology*, 1956, **52**, 39–46.

Manster, G.J. *Adolescent development and the life tasks*. Boston: Allyn & Bacon, 1977.

Marholin, D. & Touchette, P. E. The role of stimulus control and response consequences. In A.P. Goldstein & F.H. Kanfer (Eds.), *Maximizing treatment gains: Transfer enhancement in psychotherapy*. New York; Academic Press, 1979.

McFall, R.M. *Behavioral training: A skill acquisition approach to clinical problems*. Chicago: General Learning Press, 1976.

McFall, R.M. & Twentyman, C.T. Four experiments on the relative contributions of rehearsal, modeling and coaching to assertion training. *Journal of Abnormal Psychology*, 1973, **81**, 199–218.

McGhee, W. & Tullar, W.L. A note on evaluating behavior modification and behavior modeling as industrial training techniques. *Personal Psychology*, 1978, **31**, 477–484.

Meichenbaum, D. Examination of model characteristics in reducing avoidance behavior. *Journal of Personality and Social Psychology*, 1971, **17**, 298–307.

Meichenbaum, D. Self-instructional methods. In F. Kanfer & A.P. Goldstein (Eds.), *Helping people change: A textbook of methods*. New York: Pergamon Press, 1975.

Meichenbaum, D.H., Bowers, K., & Ross, R.R. Modification of classroom behavior of institutionalized female adolescent offenders. *Behavior Research and Therapy*, 1968, **6**, 343–353.

Meyer, R. Structured learning manual for blind trainees. Unpublished (braille) manuscript, Syracuse, N.Y., 1978.

Meyers, J.M. & Bean, L.L. *A decade later: A follow-up of social class and mental illness*. New York: Wiley, 1965.

Miller, G.A., Heise, G.A., & Lichten, W. The intelligibility of speech as a function of test materials. *Journals of Experimental Psychology*, 1951, **41**, 329–335.

Miller, G.A., Pribram, K.H., & Galanter, E. *Plans and the structure of behavior*. New York: Holt, Rinehart & Winston, 1960.

Miller, S., Nunnally, E.W., & Wachman, D.B. *Alive and aware: Improving communication in relationships*. Minneapolis: Interpersonal Communication Programs, 1975.

Miron, M. & Goldstein, A.P. *Hostage*. New York: Pergamon Press, 1979.

Mitchell, K.M., Bozarth, J.D., & Krauft, C.C. A reappraisal of the therapeutic effectiveness of accurate empathy, nonpossessive warmth, and genuineness. In A.S. Gurman & A.M. Razin (Eds.), *Effective psychotherapy: A handbook of research*. New York: Pergamon Press, 1977. Pp. 482–502.

Moos, R.H. *Ward atmosphere scale, test and manual*. Stanford: Stanford University School of Medicine, 1969.

Moses, J.L. & Ritchie, R.J. Supervisory relationships training: A behavioral evaluation of a behavior modeling program. Presented at American Psychological Association, Chicago, 1975.

Mudd, S. *Teacher-student relationships, Training manual*. Gettysburg, Pa.: Gettysburg College, 1979.

Myers, J.K., Bean, L.L., & Pepper, M.P. Social class and psychiatric disorders. A ten-year follow up. *Journal of Health and Human Behavior*, 1965, **6**, 74–79.

Nay, W.R. Parents as real life reinforcers: The enhancement of parent-training effects across conditions other than training. In A.P. Goldstein & F.H. Kanfer (Eds.), *Maximizing treatment gains: transfer enhancement in psychotherapy*. New York: Academic Press, 1979. Pp. 249–302.

Neale, J.M. Egocentrism in institutionalized and non-institutionalized children. *Child Development*, 1966, **37**, 97–101.

Nelson, C.M., Worell, J., & Polsgrove, L. Behaviorally disordered peers as contingency managers. *Behavior Therapy*, 1973, **4**, 270–276.

Nietzel, M.T., Winett, R.A., McDonald, M.L., & Davidson, W.S. *Behavioral approaches to community psychology*. New York: Pergamon Press, 1977.

Nisbett, R.E. & Schachter, S. The cognitive manipulation of pain. *Journal of Experimental Social Psychology*, 1966, **2**, 227–236.

Noonan, J.R. & Thibeault, R. Primary prevention in Appalachian Kentucky: Peer reinforcement of classroom attendance. *Journal of Community Psychology*, 1974, **2**, 260–264.

Novaco, R.W. *Anger control*. Lexington, Mass.: Lexington Books, 1976.

O'Brien, D. Control and affection in structured learning therapy trainers. Unpublished masters thesis, Syracuse University, 1977.

O'Brien, D. Effects of cognitive therapy, using a structured learning therapy format, and a mastery manipulation on depression. Unpublished doctoral dissertation, Syracuse University, 1981.

Offer, D. *The psychological world of the teen-ager*. New York: Basic Books, 1969.

O'Leary, D. & O'Leary, S.G. *Classroom management: The successful use of behavior modification*. New York: Pergamon Press, 1972.

Osgood, C.E. *Method and theory in experimental psychology*. New York: Oxford University Press, 1953.

Palmer, T. Juvenile delinquency. In A.P. Goldstein (Ed.), *Prescriptions for child mental health and education*. New York: Pergamon Press, 1978. Pp. 272–300.

Parke, R. & Collmer, C. Child abuse: An interdisciplinary analysis. In E.M. Hetherington (Ed.), *Review of child development research*. Vol. 5. Chicago: University of Chicago Press, 1975.

Parry, A. *Terrorism, from Robespierre to Arafat*. New York: Vanguard Press, 1976.

Patterson, G.R. Intervention for boys with conduct problems: Multiple settings, treatment and criteria. *Journal of Consulting and Clinical Psychology*, 1974, **42**, 471–481.

Patterson, G.R. & Anderson, D. Peers as social reinforcers. *Child Development*, 1964, **35**, 956–960.

Patterson, G.R., Hops, H., & Weiss, R.L. Interpersonal skills training for couples in early stages of conflict. *Journal of Marriage and Family*, 1975, **37**, 295–301.

Paul, G.L. Chronic mental patients: Current status—future directions. *Psychological Bulletin*, 1969, **71**, 81–94.

Peterson, D.R., Quay, H.C., & Tiffany, T.L. Personality factors related to juvenile delinquency. *Child Development*, 1961, **32**, 355–372.

Phillips, E.L. *Psychotherapy: A modern theory and practice*. Engelwood Cliffs, N.J.: Prentice-Hall, 1956.

Piaget, J. & Inhelder, B. *The child's conception of space*. London: Routledge & Kegan Paul, 1956.

Plutchik, R., Conte, H., Lieberman, M., Bakus, M., Grossman, J., & Lehrman, N. Reliability and validity of a scale for assessing the functioning of geriatric patients. *Journal of the American Geriatric Society*, 1970, **18**, 491–500.

Quay, H.C. Dimensions of personality in delinquent boys as inferred from the factor analysis of case history data. *Child Development*, 1964, **35**, 479–484.

Quay, H.C. Personality patterns in pre-adolescent delinquent boys. *Educational Psychological Measurement*, 1966, **26**, 99–110.

Rathjen, D.P. & Foreyt, J.P. *Social competence: Interventions for children and adults.* New York: Pergamon Press, 1980.

Reif, T.F. & Stollak, G.E. *Sensitivity to young children: Training and its effects.* East Lansing: Michigan State University Press, 1972.

Rhode, N., Rasmussen, D., & Heaps, R.A. *Let's communicate: A program designed for effective communication.* Presented at American Personnel and Guidance Association, April, 1971.

Riessman, F. The helper therapy principle. *Social Work*, 1965, **10**, 27–32.

Robertson, B. The effects of structured learning trainers' need to control on their group leadership behavior with aggressive and withdrawn trainees. Unpublished masters thesis, Syracuse University, 1977.

Robin, A. Parent-adolescent conflict: A skill-training approach. In D.P. Rathjen & J.P. Foreyt (Eds.), *Social competence: Interventions for children and adults.* New York: Pergamon Press, 1980. Pp. 147–211.

Rosenbaum, P.S. *Peer-mediated instruction.* New York: Teachers College Press, 1973.

Rosenthal, N.R. Matching trainee's conceptual level and training approaches: A study in the acquisition and enhancement of confrontation skills. Unpublished doctoral dissertation, Syracuse University, 1975.

Ross, A.O., Lacey, H.M., & Parton, D.A. The development of a behavior checklist for boys. *Child Development*, 1965, **36**, 1013–1027.

Ross, D. & Ross, S. Cognitive training for the EMR child: Situational problem solving and planning. *American Journal of Mental Deficiency*, 1973, **78**, 20–26.

Ross, D., Ross, S., & Evans, T. The modification of extreme social withdrawal by modeling with guided participation. *Journal of Behavior Therapy and Experimental Psychiatry*, 1971, **2**, 273–279.

Rotheram, M.J. Social skills training programs in elementary and high school classrooms. In D.P. Rathjen & J.P. Foreyt (Eds.), *Social competence: Interventions for children and adults.* New York: Pergamon Press, 1980.

Rubin, J.Z. & Brown, B.R. *The social psychology of bargaining and negotiation.* New York: Academic Press, 1975.

Sadler, O. & Seyden, T. Groups for parents: A guide for teaching child management to parents. *Journal of Community Psychology*, 1976, **4**, 3–63.

Sanders, R., Smith, R.S., & Weinman, B.S. *Chronic psychoses and recovery*, San Francisco: Jossey-Bass, 1967.

Sapon-Shevin, M. teaching cooperation in early childhood settings. In G. Cartledge & J.R. Milburn (Eds.), *Teaching social skills to children.* New York: Pergamon Press, 1980. Pp. 229–248.

Schlossberg, H. *Psychologist with a gun.* New York: Coward, McCann & Geoghegan, 1974.

Schneiman, R.S. An evaluation of structured learning and didactic learning as methods of training behavior modification skills to low and middle socioeconomic level teacher-aides. Unpublished doctoral dissertation, Syracuse University, 1972.

Schofield, W. *Psychotherapy, the purchase of friendship.* Englewood Cliffs, N.J.: Prentice-Hall, 1964.

Schutz, W.C. *The FIRO scales, test and manual.* Palo Alto, Calif.: Consulting Psychologists Press, 1957.

Shore, E. & Sechrest, L. Concept attainment as a function of number of positive instances presented. *Journal of Educational Psychology*, 1961, **52**, 303–307.

Siegel, J.M. & Spivack, G. Problem-solving therapy: A new program for chronic schizophrenic patients. Research & Evaluation Report No. 23. Hahnemann Medical College and Hospital, Philadelphia. 1973.

Simeonson, R.J. Egocentric responses of normal and emotionally disturbed children in different treatment settings. *Child Psychiatry and Human Development*, 1973, **3**, 179–186.

Skovholt, T.M. The client as helper: A means to promote psychological growth. *The Counseling Psychologist*, 1974, **4**, 58–64.

Slack, C.W. Experimenter-subject psychotherapy: A new method of introducing intensive office treatment for unreachable cases. *Mental Hygiene*, 1960, **44**, 238–256.

Slavin, D.R. Response transfer of conditional affective responses as a function of an experimental analog of psychotherapy. Unpublished doctoral dissertation, Northwestern University, 1967.

Smith, P.E. Management modeling training to improve morale and customer satisfaction. Presented at American Psychological Association, Chicago, 1975.

Solomon, E.J. Structured learning therapy with abusive parents: Training in self-control. Unpublished doctoral dissertation, Syracuse University, 1978.

Solomon, R.W. & Wahler, R.G. Peer reinforcement control of classroom problem behavior. *Journal of Applied Behavior Analysis*, 1973, **6**, 49–56.

Sorcher, M. & Goldstein, A.P. A behavior modeling approach to manager and supervisor training. *Personnel Administration*, 1972, **35**, 35–41.

Spielberger, C.D., Gorsuch, R.L., & Lushene, R.E. *Manual for the State-Trait Anxiety Inventory*. Palo Alto, Calif.: Consulting Psychologists Press, 1970.

Spivack, G., Platt, J.J., & Shure, M.B. *The problem-solving approach to adjustment*. San Francisco: Jossey-Bass, 1976.

Stephens, T.M. *Directive teaching of children with learning and behavioral handicaps*. Columbus: Charles E. Merrill, 1976.

Stephens, T.M. *Social skills in the classroom*. Columbus: Cedars Press, 1978.

Sturm, D. Therapist aggression tolerance and dependency tolerance under standardized client conditions of hostility and dependency. Unpublished masters thesis, Syracuse University, 1979.

Terkelson, C. Making contact: Parent-child communication skill program. *Elementary School Guidance and Counseling*, 1976, **11**, 89–99.

Tharp, R.G. & Wetzel, R.J. *Behavior modification in the natural environment*. New York: Academic Press, 1969.

Thelen, H.A. *Learning by teaching*. Chicago: University of Chicago, 1969.

Thiel, S.A. (Ed.) *Inventory of habilitation programs for mentally handicapped adults*. Portland: Portland Rehabilitation Center, 1977.

Thorndike, E.L. & Woodworth, R.S. The influence of improvement in one mental function upon the efficiency of other functions. *Psychological Review*, 1901, **8**, 247–261.

Tracy, J.J., Ballard, C.M., & Clark, C.H. Child abuse project: A follow-up. *Social Work*, 1975, **20**, 398–399.

Trief, P.M. The reduction of egocentrism in emotionally disturbed adolescents: Practical and theoretical aspects. Unpublished doctoral dissertation, Syracuse University, 1977.

Trower, P., Bryant, B., & Argyle, M. *Social skills and mental health*. Pittsburgh: University of Pittsburgh Press, 1978.

Truax, C.B. & Carkhuff, R. R. *Toward effective counseling and psychotherapy*. Chicago: Aldine, 1967.

Twentyman, C.T. & Zimering, R.J. Behavioral training of social skills: A critical review. In M. Hersen, R.M. Eisler, & P.M. Miller (Eds.), *Progress in Behavior Modification*, Vol. 7. New York: Academic Press, 1979.

Ulmer, G. Teaching geometry to cultivate reflective thinking: An experimental study with 1239 high school pupils. *Journal of Experimental Education*, 1939, **8**, 18–25.

Umbarger, C.C., Dalsimer, J.S., Morrison, A.P., & Breggin, P.R. *College students in a mental hospital*. New York: Grune & Stratton, 1962.

Underwood, B.J. & Schultz, R.W. *Meaningfulness and verbal behavior*. New York: Lippincott, 1960.

Valins, S. & Ray, A. Effects of cognitive desensitization on avoidant behavior. *Journal of Personality and Social Psychology*, 1967, **7**, 345–350.

Vorrath, H.H. & Brendtro, L.K. *Positive peer culture*. Chicago: Aldine Publishing Co., 1974.

Walker, H.M. & Buckley, N.K. Programming generalization and maintenance of treatment effects across time and across settings. *Journal of Applied Behavior Analysis*, 1972, **5**, 209–224.

Watkins, B.R. The development and evolution of a transductive learning technique for the treatment of social incompetence. *Dissertation Abstracts International*, 1972, **33**, 2361.

Weschler, D. *The measurement and appraisal of adult intelligence*, 4th ed. Baltimore: Williams & Wilkins, 1958.

Wehman, P. & Schleien, S. Social skills development through leisure skills programming. In G. Cartledge & J.F. Milburn (Eds.), *Teaching social skills to children*. New York: Pergamon Press, 1980. Pp. 203–228.

Weiss, D.M. Effects of structured learning therapy on social skill functioning of behavior disordered convicted felons. Unpublished masters thesis, Syracuse University, 1979.

Willey, N. & McCandless, B. Social stereotypes for normal educable retarded and orthopedically handicapped children. *Journal of Special Education*, 1973, **7**, 283–288.

Winer, B.J. *Statistical principles in experimental design*. New York: McGraw-Hill, 1962.

Wood, M.A. Acquisition and transfer of assertiveness in passive and aggressive adolescents through the use of structured learning therapy. Unpublished doctoral dissertation, Syracuse University, 1977.

Woodrow, H. The effect of type of training upon transference. *Journal of Educational Psychology*, 1927, **18**, 159–172.

Zung, W.W. A self-rating depression scale. *Archives of General Psychiatry*, 1965, **12**, 63–70.

Zusman, J. Development of the social breakdown syndrome concept. Some explanations of the changing appearance of psychotic patients: Antecedents of the social breakdown concept. *Milbank Memorial Fund Quarterly*, 1966, **44**, 363–394.

Author Index

Subject Index

About the Author

Arnold P. Goldstein is Professor of Psychology at Syracuse University. He received his doctorate in 1959 from Pennsylvania State University, and worked at the University of Pittsburgh and the Veteran's Administration Outpatient Research Laboratory (Washington, D.C.) before coming to Syracuse in 1963. He is also the Director of the Syracuse University Counseling and Psychotherapy Center and the Center for Research on Aggression. His career-long interests have been in studying the effectiveness of psychotherapy and related small group intervention procedures, particularly with resistive or aggressive individuals. His publications include *Structured Learning Therapy: Toward a Psychotherapy for the Poor, Skill Training for Community Living, Skillstreaming the Adolescent, Aggression in Global Perspectives, Agress-Less, Hostage,* and *Police Crisis Intervention.*

Pergamon General Psychology Series

Editors: Arnold P. Goldstein, Syracuse University
Leonard Krasner, SUNY, Stony Brook